GORDON BORRIE
AND AUBREY L. DIAMOND

THE CONSUMER, SOCIETY
AND THE LAW

THIRD EDITION

PENGUIN BOOKS

Penguin Books Ltd, Harmondsworth, Middlesex, England
Penguin Books Inc., 7110 Ambassador Road, Baltimore, Maryland 21207, U.S.A.
Penguin Books Australia Ltd, Ringwood, Victoria, Australia
Penguin Books Canada Ltd, 41 Steelcase Road West, Markham, Ontario, Canada

—

First published in Penguin Books 1964
Revised edition published by MacGibbon & Kee Ltd 1966
Second edition 1968
Third edition 1973
Reprinted 1974

—

Copyright © Gordon Borrie and Aubrey L. Diamond 1964, 1968, 1973

—

Made and printed in Great Britain
by Hazell Watson & Viney Ltd
Aylesbury, Bucks
Set in Linotype Baskerville

CONTENTS

PREFACE TO
THE THIRD EDITION

THE law never stands still. Hardly a month passes without some significant development – new Acts of Parliament, decisions of the courts, governmental regulations, reports by official or unofficial bodies – which must be considered by anyone trying to convey a picture of the law as it affects the citizen. Since this book was first published much we have criticized has changed for the better, though some changes have been for the worse. This third edition includes references to recent court cases, to Acts of Parliament such as the Trade Descriptions Act 1968, the Unsolicited Goods and Services Act 1971 and the Criminal Justice Act 1972, to regulations such as the Labelling of Food Regulations 1970 (amended in 1972) and to reports such as that of the Crowther Committee on Consumer Credit published in 1971. We have been able to include details of the Bills that will become the Supply of Goods (Implied Terms) Act 1973 and the Fair Trading Act 1973.

We would like to record our thanks for the valuable help and advice in writing this book which was generously given to us by our good friend Master I. H. Jacob, a Master of the Supreme Court, Queen's Bench Division. For the third edition Mrs Valentine Korah, Reader in English Law at University College, London, has helped us to re-write chapters 11 and 12 which have been re-arranged on her advice: we are most grateful to her for her willing assistance. Finally, Aubrey Diamond, who now holds an official appointment, stresses that the personal views expressed in this book are those of the authors alone.

January 1973.

G.B.
A.L.D.

INTRODUCTION

Is there any real need for consumer protection? In the simple transactions of the market place, no doubt the consumer is his own best guide. When he buys a pound of tomatoes, he has only himself to blame if they are unripe. Yet, even in medieval times, the law stepped in to protect the buyer of adulterated wine or mouldy bread. Now, with an enormous variety of goods available for purchase, many of them pre-packed or mechanical or of intricate workmanship, so that any deficiencies are inevitably hidden, far greater consumer protection is called for. In the complex field of consumer services too – repairers, dry cleaners, garages, insurance companies – legal rules are required to redress the natural imbalance between the individual consumer and 'Them'.

Until the establishment in 1965 of the Law Commission there was no government agency charged with the general responsibility of seeing that the existing law was adequate for the needs of the day or of initiating proposals to reform it. Among the public, however, there has for some time been a growing realization that the law as it stands does not give sufficient protection to the consumer.

Retailers, manufacturers, and those who provide the manifold consumer services have long joined together in trade organizations and associations to promote their respective interests. It is only within the last twenty years that consumers too have recognized the need for organization, and the growth of the consumer movement has been a major phenomenon of recent years. As recently as 1955, consumers had no collective voice. Today some 600,000 people subscribe to *Which?*, published by the Consumers'

Association; there are over eighty Consumer Groups throughout the country, with about twenty thousand members; and the Advisory Centre for Education publishes independent information and comment on schools, Universities, and teaching methods in *Where?* These developments are, of course, paralleled in other countries, not only in Europe and America.

For the first time, ordinary people, as buyers of goods and users of services, have their own pressure groups. Consumer organization already seems to have made a considerable impact on manufacturers and retailers, and in 1959 the Government appointed a Committee, under the chairmanship of Sir Joseph Molony QC, to report on what changes in the law were desirable 'for the further protection of the consuming public'. The Committee's lengthy report was published in July 1962. It dealt with a large number of topics vital to the consumer, from safety standards to hire purchase, from advertising to manufacturers' 'guarantees', though not, regrettably, with consumer services. The Committee made 214 separate recommendations. We shall have some criticisms to make of a number of points in the Report but no one can deny its significance. It is bound to stand out as a landmark, and changes in the law, designed to provide greater consumer protection, have now been made – notably by the Hire-Purchase Act of 1964 and the Trade Descriptions Act of 1968.

The Press and the political parties have been taking a much more lively interest in consumer matters. This is to be welcomed although, naturally, there are differences of approach in the policy statements put forward by the different political groups. Following the suggestions of the Molony Committee, a Conservative Government appointed a national Consumer Council in June 1963. It was envisaged as 'the authoritative and considered voice of the consumer', exerting its influence both on trade and on government. Unfortunately it survived for less than eight years: early in 1971 it was wound up, a new Conservative Government saying that its functions could be carried out by private enterprise. The Consumer Council sponsored valuable research, it engaged in important educational activities, and it certainly made the consumer's voice heard and noticed. The saving of money which prompted its demise soon proved to be an ill-considered economy: in November 1972 the Government recognized its earlier error and appointed for the first time a Cabinet Minister with special responsibility for consumer affairs who soon afterwards introduced what is to become the Fair Trading Act 1973 (see p. 152 below).

The militant march of the consumer has resulted in the publication of a number of books which attempt to guide the consumer in the many transactions into which he enters, to tell him what his legal rights are, and to advise him how to exercise them. This book is not another. There is, it must be admitted, a considerable amount of practical law in this book, and the consumer may find here guidance on particular problems. But our main purpose was not to write a legal textbook or a handbook of do's and don'ts for consumers. It was to describe how the law has evolved: how it became what it is today and how it might evolve in the future; and to try to evaluate how far it serves the ends of society, and in particular the consumer, in the second half of the twentieth century.

Consumer transactions cover such a wide field that we are conscious of the staccato effect of the ensuing chapters. After tracing the growth of modern law from its early beginnings, we seek to show how Victorian ideas of freedom and sanctity of contract, embodied in court decisions, stand in the way of much needed reform. Too often, to borrow the words of a former Master of the Rolls, 'the dead hand of the past fastens on the living present'. Lawyers will recognize that the early chapters are largely concerned with the law of contract and with various aspects of the law of sale of goods, while hire purchase (considered in the sixth chapter) is closely related. Then we range from consumer services and bailments to banking, insurance, and travel. Two chapters are devoted to the post-war legislation on monopolies and restrictive practices, including resale price maintenance. In the final chapter, an attempt is made to draw the threads together.

Convinced as we are of the need and value of legislating for improvements in the law, we have to admit that 'you cannot legislate for fools'. No legislation is going to change us overnight into a nation of knowledgeable, prudent, and discriminating shoppers. Law reform has to be accompanied by consumer education. We would like to see the work of the consumer organizations in this field supplemented not only by greater Press and Television coverage but also by the schools giving consumer matters a prominent place in their curricula.

Our concern throughout will be with English law, though we have, where necessary, drawn parallels and ideas from American and Commonwealth sources. Scottish law, although similar in many matters of detail, is fundamentally part of a different legal tradition, and nothing in this book can be regarded as authoritative north of the Tweed.

To lawyers, we ought to explain a perhaps unconventional matter of referring to judges. We take it that the lay reader is more concerned with the personal identity of the individual judge than with his judicial office, so that where a judge has been raised to the peerage we consistently refer to him by his ultimate title. Thus, the reader, familiar with the name of Lord Denning, will find him so described irrespective of his judicial status at the date his quoted words were spoken or written.

'Who knows when he openeth the stopple, what
may be in the bottle? Hath not a snail,
a spider, yea, a newt been found there?'

BEN JONSON: *Bartholomew Fair*

CHAPTER 1

THE LAW TAKES SHAPE

LAWYERS often pretend that The Law is an impersonal entity, an independent creature which has developed, and now exists, untouched by human hand. 'But that is the law,' they will say, shrugging their shoulders or throwing up their hands to indicate how helpless mere man is in dealing with this living being which dictates the rules governing our relationship with each other.

Nothing is further from the truth, of course. The law is a body of rules made by men which can be changed by men if they see the need for change. The law which affects the ordinary person as a buyer and user of goods and services supplied by others – economic man, he might be called, or the consumer in the modern phrase – is a typical example of a body of legal rules. Many of the rules were developed by judges in the course of deciding specific disputes which came before them – a process which, for our purposes, had its origins in the early Middle Ages and which, as we shall see, is still continuing. Other rules were laid down, not in relation to the facts of a quarrel between living men, but as more or less abstract rules, intended to be of general application, embodied in an Act of Parliament. Both types of rules inevitably reflect the outlook and philosophy of life of the men instrumental in making them.

In this field of law, perhaps as much as in any other, we can see the special reasons which guided these men, the sense of the purpose in society which they felt that law must achieve. Look, for example, at the rules laid down as to the duties of innkeepers. In an age of rugged individualism, when judges shrank from imposing obligations on men other than for deliberate acts, when there was not yet the concept of the sanctity of agreements, when damage caused by negligence rarely led to legal liability, innkeepers were held liable for the loss of goods belonging to their guests. They were responsible even if, for example, the goods were stolen despite every precaution on their part. The judges were explicit as to the reason for this unusually strict obligation. Innkeepers had greater opportunity for theft than most other people. They were, indeed, considered to be likely associates of thieves and cutpurses and it was, no doubt, a profitable hobby for them to be in league with highwaymen. When travel was a difficult and hazardous undertaking, travellers were at the mercy of dishonest innkeepers. There were, therefore, good reasons for imposing this strict liability, which we can find in the cases as early as 1368, and the judges willingly enforced 'the common custom of the realm', holding that responsibility for the loss of a guest's goods could be avoided only if the loss was shown to be caused by a natural disaster (an 'Act of God'), or by large-scale fighting ('the King's enemies'), or by the guest's own fault. Even today the relevance of social conditions to judicial decisions is seldom as apparent as in this early example.

CAVEAT EMPTOR

This clear illustration of consumer protection did not, however, reflect the general judicial attitude. It may be a cherished adage of the consuming public that the customer is always right, but in the eyes of the law this saying has never been significant. Far greater emphasis has been placed by the courts on the maxim *caveat emptor* – let the buyer beware – and no one should be surprised that nineteenth-century advocates of *laissez faire* individualist principles took to it with natural enthusiasm. They considered it an irrefutable proposition that every man must look out for himself. But eminently suited though it was to the prevailing ideas of the 1800s, *caveat emptor* had its origins deep in the Middle Ages.

In those far-off days, transactions of sale and even of barter between strangers were few and rare. When trading did take place, it was in markets and fairs where the goods were openly displayed. The cloths could be examined, the farm produce picked over. Because it was taken for granted in these dealings that the buyer relied on his own judgement – only a fool would rely on the word of a stranger he might never see again – the idea of *caveat emptor* merely reflected the actual practice.

This did not mean that a buyer never had a remedy if he was the victim of unprincipled salesmanship, but it was not enough to show that the seller boasted that the goods were sound or genuine. The buyer had to take the risk that they were faulty or worthless unless the seller had broken a positive promise – a 'warranty' – or was guilty of fraud. Fraud has never been easy to prove, for the burden of showing that the seller knew that what he said was false was a heavy one.

In the absence of fraud the buyer had to show that he had relied, not on the seller's statement, but on a warranty or promise. Writing in the sixteenth century, Mr Justice Fitzherbert, author of one of the earliest legal textbooks in this country, summed up the law in these words:

If a man sell unto another man a horse, and warrant him to be sound and good, if the horse be lame or diseased, that he cannot work, he shall have an action against him. ... But note: it behoveth that he warrant the horse to be sound, otherwise the action will not lie. For if he sell the horse without such warranty, it is at the other's peril, and his eyes ought to be his judges in that case.

And even an express promise by the seller would be of no

avail to the buyer if it related to something the buyer
could discover readily enough for himself. As the judge in
a fifteenth-century case said: 'if a man sells me a horse
and warrants that it has two eyes, and it has not, I shall
not have an action for I can know this for myself from
the beginning.'

How could the buyer show a warranty or promise? At
first it seems that he had to show that the seller used
words such as 'I warrant' or 'I promise'; nothing less
would convince the judges that it would be right to hold
the seller responsible for innocent statements. Thus the
case of *Chandelor* v. *Lopus*, in the early seventeenth century, was brought by the disappointed purchaser of a
bezoar stone – a 'stone' taken from the stomach of the
wild goat of Persia and much prized as a sovereign remedy
against 'the Venom' and other ills. The jeweller had described the stone as a bezoar and had charged £100 for it,
but the purchaser subsequently discovered that it was
nothing of the kind (the reports are tantalizingly silent as
to how the purchaser found out; perhaps its failure to
cure revealed the falsity of the jeweller's claim). The case
came before the courts on a number of occasions between
1603 and 1606. At first the buyer's claim was dismissed, for
he could point to no formal and deliberate promise by
the jeweller. 'This case,' said Sir John Popham, Chief Justice of the Court of King's Bench, 'is a dangerous case and
may be the cause of a multitude of actions, if it be
thought that the bare affirmation of the vendor causes the
action.' But later the buyer was able to satisfy the judges
that the jeweller had known all the time that his description was false, and on this ground – the seller's fraud – he
succeeded.

The first inroad on this insistence by the courts on express promises came some eighty years later, in 1688. In
Crosse v. *Gardner* the buyer bought two oxen; they were
in the seller's possession, and the seller stated that they

were his own. But they belonged to another, and were later taken away from the buyer. The buyer could not show that the seller *knew* they were not his property, nor could he point to any express warranty, but Sir John Holt, Chief Justice of the King's Bench at that time, held that the mere affirmation amounted to a warranty. In the earlier case the buyer could have examined the stone before the sale to see if it was truly a bezoar stone. Here, no amount of examination of the oxen would reveal their true owner, and 'credit given on the affirmation makes the action lie.'

Then, in *Pasley* v. *Freeman*, a hundred years further on, Mr Justice Buller, a great common lawyer who became a King's Bench judge at the age of thirty-two, some six years after his call to the bar, adopted a more sophisticated guide which still represents the law. There was no distinction, he said in 1789, between the words 'warranty' and 'affirmation'. The true test adopted by Chief Justice Holt, he said, was 'that an affirmation at the time of a sale is a warranty, provided it appears on the evidence to have been so intended'. Thus the courts must look, not at the words used, but at the intention of the parties to discover whether the affirmation is to be treated as a promise. Whether the buyer is in as good a position as the seller to judge the truth, or whether he can only rely on statements made by the seller, are facts which help the court to decide what the parties intended. (A modern echo, in the distinction between a representation or affirmation and a term of the contract or promise, can be found in the case of *Oscar Chess Ltd.* v. *Williams*, described on p. 69 below.)

NINETEENTH-CENTURY DEVELOPMENTS

In this way, by the beginning of the nineteenth century, the courts had moved away from their original insistence on words of promise. They would construe words not in the form of a warranty as a promise if the parties so intended. The next stage was more difficult and more important: would the courts infer a promise from the mere fact of sale, even though nothing was said? There is a lack of consistency in the judgements of the nineteenth century reflecting, no doubt, the conflict between the *laissez faire* outlook which characterized the convictions of most influential men in that age and the desire of judges to do justice in the individual case. The view was gaining ground that, though it was still for the buyer to look out for himself, there were situations where *caveat emptor* could no longer represent the practice of even the most prudent buyer – situations, becoming more common in an era of increasing trade, where the buyer had no opportunity to examine the goods before the sale. In a case heard in 1815, *Gardiner* v. *Gray*, the purchaser had agreed to buy twelve bags of 'waste silk' which turned out to be unmerchantable. The decision was given by Lord Ellenborough, a forceful Chief Justice who had a reputation for vigorous expression as well as for considerable intellectual powers. In the course of his judgement, the Chief Justice said that where there is no opportunity to inspect a commodity, the maxim *caveat emptor* cannot apply. 'The goods must be saleable,' he said, 'under the denomination mentioned in the contract between them. The purchaser cannot be supposed to buy goods to lay them on a dunghill.'

Some years later, in *Jones* v. *Bright* (1829), a man bought some copper from a manufacturer for the stated purpose of sheathing a ship. Instead of lasting the four years which was normal, the copper lasted for only four months. The Court of Common Pleas held that if a man sells goods for a particular purpose, it is impliedly understood that they are fit for that purpose so that, if they turn out not to be fit, the buyer must have a remedy.

In both of these cases, the court was imposing obligations on the seller deliberately. Sir William Best, Chief Justice of the Court of Common Pleas, put it in these words in *Jones* v. *Bright* itself:

It is the duty of the court in administering the law to lay down rules calculated to prevent fraud, to protect persons who are necessarily ignorant of the qualities of a commodity they purchase, and to make it the interest of manufacturers and those who sell to furnish the best article that can be supplied. ... I wish to put the case on a broad principle. If a man sells an article he thereby warrants that it is merchantable – that is, fit for some purpose. If he sells it for a particular purpose he thereby warrants it fit for that purpose.

Yet the policy forthrightly expressed in these words was not universally accepted by the judges, and in the succeeding years there were still cases where disappointed buyers found themselves without any remedy in the courts. The view of the legal profession was, broadly, that the principle of *caveat emptor* prevailed but that it was subject to a number of important exceptions. Many cases fell within these exceptions, and buyers could then succeed. But there were still cases subject to the basic principle itself.

THE SALE OF GOODS ACT 1893

The fourth quarter of the nineteenth century has been termed 'the era of commercial codification'. This was a time of keen and radical law reform, though the reforms related more to the machinery of the law than to its substance. There was considerable criticism, notably by businessmen, of the cumbersome and technical shape of the law – of the many volumes of law reports, of varying quality and poorly indexed, in which the law was contained, accessible in fact if not in theory only to the trained lawyer. To meet this objection, attempts were made to codify English law – not as a whole, but topic by topic. A start was made with some fields of the criminal law and then attention was turned to some branches of the law relating to commerce. In 1889 a Bill was introduced into the House of Lords to codify the law relating to the sale of goods. The Bill was drafted by Sir Mackenzie Chalmers, the judge of Birmingham County Court, and in his own words 'it endeavoured to reproduce as exactly as possible the existing law.' It eventually became law in a slightly amended form, and the Sale of Goods Act of 1893 still governs many consumer transactions.

Quite apart from its modern importance in the law, the Act is of historical interest. It is a carefully drafted statement of the law as it had developed by the end of the nineteenth century and records the almost complete erosion of the principle of *caveat emptor* by that time. Thus Chalmers, in his original draft, summed up the law as being that 'where there is a contract for the sale of goods by description, the goods must correspond with the description'. The law laid down in *Crosse* v. *Gardner* in 1688, the case of the two oxen, had by 1889 become a general principle that 'by a contract of sale the seller impliedly warrants his right to sell the goods', unless the circumstances showed that this could not be so. On the doctrine laid down by Chief Justice Best in *Jones* v. *Bright* in 1829, Chalmers was more cautious. He incorporated the idea of 'let the buyer beware' in express terms: 'there is no implied warranty of the quality, fitness, or condition of goods supplied under a contract of sale' – but went on to set out implied warranties of merchantable quality and fitness for purpose as exceptions to this general principle where the seller is a dealer in the goods sold and certain other requirements are met.

Thus the Act, which followed Chalmers' draft on these points in substance if not in words, cleared up the doubts which the courts had had and put into statutory form the principles which the judges had tentatively been establishing. This Act is of first importance in considering the extent to which the consumer today is protected by the law, and some of its provisions will be investigated in more detail when we come to Chapter 3 of this book.

COMMON CALLINGS

The idea that a special liability should attach to the seller of goods if he was selling in the course of his business – the implied terms of merchantable quality and fitness for purpose now to be found in section 14 of the Sale of Goods Act – was not a revolutionary idea of the nineteenth century. From its earliest days the common law had differentiated between the obligations of the ordinary man and the duties of those who professed a particular calling whose goods or services were available to all. The followers of these 'common callings' were subjected to liabilities that arose, not out of agreement, but rather from their status and from the idea that it was in the interests of the community that people who offered their services to the public at large should show care, skill, and honesty in their dealings.

We have already seen how innkeepers – the outstanding example of a 'common calling' – were under the strictest liability for losses; thus in 1368 a pilgrim whose belongings were missed from his room at an inn in Canterbury was able to recover compensation from the innkeeper. In 1348 the Humber ferryman was compelled to compensate the owner of cattle which had died because the boat had been overloaded. 'Common carriers' – carriers of goods who were willing to carry for anyone, and who did not pick and choose their customers – were under a liability similar to that of innkeepers, and for the same reasons. A veterinary surgeon who had undertaken to cure a horse but had negligently killed him was held liable. So were farriers, and barber-surgeons who performed similar functions for human beings.

Even some sellers were held liable on what later came to be known as 'implied warranties'. The exceptional commodity was food, and a judgement given in the fifteenth century shows that a seller of unwholesome food was held liable to compensate his buyer because it was his business to sell food, even though he had made no express promise as to the quality of his wares.

Thus the more general obligations imposed on sellers in the nineteenth century can be regarded as a logical extension of the duties imposed much earlier on the suppliers of food and of services. There was however a weak link in the chain which held this protection available for the consumer: the notion that the consumer could, if he wished, accept a lower standard than that made available to him by the general law.

AVOIDING LIABILITY

For centuries carriers of goods had made 'special contracts' with their customers whereby their ordinary liability for the safety of goods carried was excluded by words set out in consignment notes signed by the customer, or by tickets handed to the consignor, or by notices at their premises. Once the courts imposed obligations on the seller of goods not arising from his express promise he too sought a way of lessening his liability. Sir Mackenzie Chalmers, presenting his code on the Sale of Goods to the public, recognized that its chief function was to make it clear what rules the law would apply if nothing was said. 'If the parties know beforehand what their legal position is,' he wrote, 'they can provide for their particular wants by express stipulation ... The Act does not seek to prevent the parties from making any bargain they please.' To this end section 55 of the Sale of Goods Act made it possible to exclude all the obligations imposed on sellers under the earlier sections: 'Where any right, duty or liability would arise under a contract of sale by implication of law, it may be negatived or varied by express agreement. ...'

This was, of course, the result of two related ideas, freedom of contract and sanctity of contract, both of which became dominant in the nineteenth century. The Master of the Rolls, Sir George Jessel, spoke for his age when he proclaimed in clear terms in 1875:

> If there is one thing which more than another public policy requires it is that men of full age and competent understanding shall have the utmost liberty of contracting, and that their contracts when entered into freely and voluntarily shall be held sacred and shall be enforced by courts of justice.

Innkeepers alone were in a special position. For them, the public policy which for so long demanded their strict liability could not permit them to escape liability by any form of express contract, or by warning their guests to take their own precautions. Their responsibility for the safety of goods was, indeed, based on ancient custom rather than on their contract with the guest, and it needed an Act of Parliament, passed in 1863, to relieve them of some small part of their liability. But other suppliers of goods and services found it easier to evade their obligations.

CONDITIONS ON TICKETS AND RECEIPTS

All that was necessary was that they should be able to prove the terms of a contract between themselves and their customer. A signed document was the clearest way to show that the customer had agreed to the terms. Printed particulars and conditions at an auction sale served a similar purpose. Moreover, judgements in the last quarter of the nineteenth century showed that if the customer was handed a ticket or other document that contained terms and conditions, he might be bound by them to the same extent as if he had signed an agreement. In a case heard in 1883, *Watkins* v. *Rymill*, a man took his wagonnette to a repository for the sale of horses and carriages in the Barbican. He was handed a receipt on a printed form which read 'Received from —, subject to the conditions as exhibited on the premises.' The conditions referred to were exhibited in conspicuous positions in many parts of the premises, and among the conditions was one whereby the proprietor of the repository was free to sell any property sent to it which remained over one month, unless all expenses were previously paid. The wagonnette owner did not read the receipt but simply put it in his pocket. The proprietor of the repository sold the wagonnette when one month had gone by, and the court held that the proprietor had acted legally under the conditions referred to in the printed form. These conditions were binding on the wagonnette owner because he had accepted the form without raising any objection. The question turns on a principle easy to state, but not always easy to apply: the conditions on a ticket are binding if reasonable notice of them was given. As often no notice is given beyond printing them on the ticket, the ultimate judgement usually hinges on this question: would a reasonable man in the customer's position have read them?

The habits of the reasonable man are not easy to predict. It is well established that he reads receipts obtained at a railway cloakroom, railway tickets (certainly excursion tickets obtained at a reduced rate, and possibly others), and steamship tickets, but he is not expected to read deckchair tickets nor, probably, bus tickets. But even if he is bound by these conditions, they may not always affect him adversely. To this question we shall return in the next chapter. For the moment we must return to the supplier of goods, and the limitations of the law.

LIABILITY BOUNDED BY CONTRACT

The liability imposed by the law on the seller was essentially founded on the contract of sale – it notionally formed part of the agreement between seller and buyer. The duties created by this contract were owed by the seller to the buyer alone. If a man bought faulty goods, he might have the right to sue the seller for breach of an express or implied provision in the contract. But what if the defect in the goods resulted in injury to the man's wife, or son, or for that matter anyone else? Since none of these people would be parties to the contract of purchase, none of them could have any contractual remedy against the seller, that is, any remedy based on the seller's breach of an express or implied term of the contract. Then again, while a buyer of faulty goods might have a contractual remedy against the seller, he normally had no such remedy against the manufacturer of the goods, even though the defect might be clearly attributable to the fault of the manufacturer, because he had made no contract with the manufacturer. The manufacturer's liability was bounded by his contract with the wholesaler or dealer, and he could not be made liable to anyone else. This gap in the law might be serious to a consumer who suffered personal injuries as a result of faulty goods if the seller was not worth suing.

THE MANUFACTURER'S LIABILITY

In the early nineteenth century there were only two possible instances where a seller of goods could be made liable for defects to someone other than the purchaser. One was where the seller made fraudulent representations about the goods which were meant to be relied on by others. The second was where the goods sold were by their nature dangerous. In *Langridge* v. *Levy*, a case heard in 1837, a man bought a gun for £24 at a gunmaker's shop in Bristol, for the use of himself and his sons. One of his sons was injured when the gun exploded and his right hand had to be amputated. The seller was held liable to pay the son damages although he had not sold the gun to him and there was no contract with him: the seller knew the gun would be used by the purchaser's sons, and had fraudulently represented that the gun was safe when he knew it was not, and the son was taken to have relied on the representation. In more than one case, the courts recognized that a supplier of inherently dangerous goods, like a loaded gun or explosives, should be made liable to anyone who might be injured by them.

Beyond these two instances, however, the courts were not prepared to go. In a case decided in 1842, *Winterbottom* v. *Wright*, the driver of a mail-coach which plied between Hartford, in Cheshire, and Holyhead was lamed for life in an accident caused by the defective construction of the coach. He was unable to recover compensation from the maker of the coach. The maker's contract was not with the driver, or indeed with the driver's employers, but with the Postmaster-General. Judicial fear of a flood of litigation if actions like this were permitted seems to have been the prime reason for the dismissal of the action. Lord Abinger was concerned about 'letting in upon us an infinity of actions'. Baron Alderson said that if the court were to hold that the plaintiff could sue in such a case, there would be no point at which such actions would stop. 'The only safe rule,' he said, 'is to confine the right to recover to those who enter the contract; if we go one step beyond that, there is no reason why we should not go fifty.' These apprehensions followed exactly those expressed by Chief Justice Popham in 1606 and, in spite of the admitted hardship that resulted, deprived the driver of a remedy.

Judicial conservatism prevailed also in the case of *Longmeid* v. *Holliday*, heard by Lord Wensleydale, a judge renowned for his gift of lucid expression, in the year of the Great Exhibition, 1851. A seller of lamps sold one to a man to be used by both him and his wife. The lamp had been defectively constructed and, when the wife attempted to use it, it exploded and injured her. Obviously the lamp was not an article dangerous in its nature; moreover, there was no evidence that the seller was guilty of any fraudulent representation about the lamp. In a clear exposition of the existing law, the judge concluded that the wife, not being in contractual relationship with the seller of the lamp, had no possible remedy in respect of her injuries against the seller. It made no difference whether or not the defect could have been discovered by the exercise of reasonable care on the part of the seller.

The first sign of a break in this judicial attitude, which regarded the duties of a supplier of goods as being bounded by contract, came in 1869. In *George* v. *Skivington*, a man bought from a retail chemist a bottle containing a chemical compound made up by the chemist as a hairwash. To the chemist's knowledge, the man bought it for use by his wife in washing her hair. As a result of using this compound, the wife's health was injured. There was no suggestion that the chemist knew the compound was unsuitable but the Court of Exchequer nevertheless held the chemist liable in damages to the purchaser's wife. This decision went well beyond the existing law because it was based on the view that a seller of goods could be liable for negligence as well as for fraud to someone other than the purchaser who used the goods. But the case stands in splendid and solitary isolation in the law reports of the last century, and courts in later cases refused to follow it. It was a decision very much in advance of its age, but though it was criticized, ignored, or rejected, as the years went by, it was destined eventually to be revived and restored by the House of Lords in the celebrated case of *Donoghue* v. *Stevenson*, in 1932. Though, as Lord Buckmaster put it in that case, 'few cases can have lived so dangerously and lived so long,' in the words of another Law Lord, Lord Asquith of Bishopstone, some twenty years later, the decision 'after a long and rough crossing has limped into port.'

DONOGHUE *v.* STEVENSON

Only in 1932 was it firmly established by a House of Lords decision (and even then only by a three-to-two majority) that manufacturers owed a duty to the ultimate consumer to take care in making their goods where there is no likelihood of their being examined before they reach the ultimate consumer. The old fear of the far-reaching consequences of burdening manufacturers with such a duty – 'it is difficult to see how, if that were the law, trade could be carried on' – was voiced by the dissenting Law Lords, Lords Buckmaster and Tomlin. The majority, however, believed that social convenience and policy demanded that a consumer injured as a result of defective goods should have a remedy against the manufacturer if the defects were attributable to his negligence. In a later case, Lord Denning contrasted the 'timorous souls who were fearful of allowing a new cause of action', and 'the bold spirits who were ready to allow it if justice so required'. The former had held the field long enough and time was to show their fears to be groundless, as so often has been the case.

The facts of *Donoghue* v. *Stevenson* were that a shop

assistant, Mrs Donoghue, went with a lady friend to a café in Paisley, run by one Minchella. The friend bought for Mrs Donoghue a bottle of ginger-beer and some ice-cream. The bottle was made of dark opaque glass and Mrs Donoghue had no reason to suspect that it contained anything but pure ginger-beer. Minchella poured some of the ginger-beer over the ice-cream which was contained in a tumbler, and Mrs Donoghue drank a little of it. Her friend then proceeded to pour the remainder of the contents of the bottle into the tumbler when a snail, in a state of decomposition, floated out of the bottle. As a result of what Mrs Donoghue described as the 'nauseating sight of the snail', and the impurities of the ginger-beer already consumed, Mrs Donoghue suffered from shock and gastro-enteritis. She brought an action against Stevenson, the manufacturer of the ginger-beer and the person responsible for the bottling of it. The House of Lords held, by a majority, that these facts did disclose a good cause of action against Stevenson. There was of course no contract between Mrs Donoghue and Stevenson, and the effect of the decision is that a manufacturer owes a general duty to take care to the ultimate consumer. This is how Lord Atkin explained the principle:

... a manufacturer of products, which he sells in such a form as to show that he intends them to reach the ultimate consumer in the form in which they left him with no reasonable possibility of intermediate examination, and with the knowledge that the absence of reasonable care in the preparation or putting up of the products will result in an injury to the consumer's life or property, owes a duty to the consumer to take that reasonable care.

The justification for this striking development in the law, of great importance in the extension of legal protection for the consumer, was that only by imposing such an obligation on a manufacturer could legal liability be laid at the door of the person responsible. As Lord Atkin pointed out, if someone is injured by consuming bottled beer or chocolates, poisoned because of the negligence of the manufacturer, or by using what should be harmless proprietory medicines, soap, or cleansing powders, surely the manufacturer should be under a legal liability to compensate for the harm done. They are all examples of things intended to reach the consumer in the condition in which they leave the manufacturer, and, particularly since the growth of brand names and direct advertising by the manufacturer, it is to the manufacturer (and not to the retailer) that the consumer looks for reliability and quality. Indeed, for persons other than the actual purchaser – members of his family or his guests, for example – injured by defectively manufactured articles, a remedy against the negligent manufacturer was the only possible way of relieving their hardship, since they would have no contractual relationship with the retailer. Lord Atkin said he did not think so ill of our jurisprudence to suppose that its principles were so remote from the ordinary needs of civilized society and the ordinary claims it makes upon its members as to deny a legal remedy where there is obviously a social wrong.

Since 1932, the principle of *Donoghue* v. *Stevenson* has been applied in many cases – in claims against manufacturers of underwear, hair dye, and cars, and in claims against repairers and local authorities responsible for the water supply as well as against manufacturers. The late Professor W. Friedmann of Columbia University said in his book *Law in a Changing Society* that it was almost certain that the common law would no longer exist if great judges had not from time to time accepted the challenge and boldly laid down new principles to meet new social problems. Sociologically, the case of *Donoghue* v. *Stevenson* was a recognition on the part of the judiciary of the age of mass manufacture and standardized products, an age in which the economic position of the retailer was vitally changed. Only too often judges speak and act on the basis that their task is not to make law, which they regard as a matter for the legislature, but merely to apply the law as it exists in statutes and in earlier judgements. They are deterred by the argument of the novelty of the action from remedying gaps or defects in the law. Fortunately, some judges at some stages in our legal history have been prepared to take on a more creative role in adapting law to changing social conditions. It is to judges of this spirit that we owe the existence for consumers of legal remedies against the manufacturers of faulty goods.

THE CONSUMER MOVEMENT

There have been several important developments in the law since *Donoghue v. Stevenson*, many of which will be described in the following pages. But perhaps the most significant development since the Second World War has taken place outside the field of law itself.

Consumers have always, almost inevitably, been unorganized and relatively inarticulate. Manufacturers and suppliers, entering into many similar transactions each week, can afford to take expert advice, both technical and legal. Often they are themselves experts in their own province of business. Each deal by a consumer, on the other hand, is in the nature of an isolated transaction. Strangely enough, only recently has there been any attempt by consumers to band together, to pool resources and experience.

In 1955 the British Standards Institution set up its Consumer Advisory Council (which disbanded when the Government set up the Consumer Council) to ensure that the consumer had a say in matters which had hitherto been regarded as the exclusive concern of traders and manufacturers. Early in 1957, following American precedents, it published the first issue of *Shopper's Guide* which, for the first time in this country, gave its readers critical accounts of different consumer goods, comparing one make with another on the basis of strictly-controlled tests. Later in 1957 came *Which?*, published by the Consumers' Association. This magazine, although available only to subscribers, has had an outstanding success and now goes monthly to some 600,000 members. From 1957 to 1962 *Shopper's Guide*, which ceased publication in 1963, also offered its readers a 'complaints service' to obtain redress.

In their new organizations consumers have become a force for manufacturers and retailers to reckon with, and many manufacturers have heeded criticisms in these magazines and modified their products. An even more recent development has been the formation of local consumer groups in many different parts of the country, testing and reporting on local shops and services.

The greatest success of the consumer movement so far has been its impact on public opinion. All three political parties are now committed to policies of law reform to benefit consumers, and in recent years both Conservative and Labour Governments have introduced measures of reform, culminating in 1972 in the appointment of the Minister for Trade and Consumer Affairs with a seat in the Cabinet and the introduction of the Fair Trading Bill (see p. 152 below).

THE LAW OF CONTRACT

If, having surveyed the development of English law over the ages, one had to pick out the two supremely important concepts in the present-day law, there can be little doubt what they would be: the idea of 'negligence', with its duty to take care; and the law of contract, which still governs the duties of sellers of goods and suppliers of services. Both of these concepts are creations of the common law – that is to say, they have been created by judges in the course of deciding cases in the courts. It is at the common law theory of contract that we must now look in more detail.

CHAPTER 2

FREEDOM OF CONTRACT

LIABILITY to pay damages for breach of contract can be expensive, but avoiding that liability can also cost money. Careful inspection, frequent testing, and constant supervision of workers all increase costs, so it is not surprising that suppliers of goods and services sought cheaper ways of avoiding liability.

Since the duties were notionally imposed as clauses in the contract the way out was clear. If the parties had agreed expressly that the seller or supplier was not to be liable, there would be no room for the courts to infer a clause imposing liability. It was one thing for the courts to create a fictitious intention; it was another for them to disregard a stated intention.

There are abundant examples of express agreements designed for this purpose. Thus, a notice at a garage: 'All work done at owner's risk.' A dry-cleaner's receipt: 'No liability can be accepted for loss or damage to goods.' A guarantee for an electric toaster: 'We will not in any case be liable to pay compensation for any loss or damage whatsoever sustained by the purchaser.' A hire-purchase agreement: 'All conditions and warranties are hereby excluded.' A cloakroom ticket: 'The company will not be responsible for any package exceeding £10.'

'FREELY NEGOTIATED'

It is obvious from the examples just cited that in reality there has been no express agreement between the parties. If the 'implied terms' imposing liability were a legal fiction, so too were the 'express terms' excluding liability.

For these express terms were contained in written documents drawn up by one party and never freely accepted by the other.

How, for example, are the 'express terms' in railway tickets agreed between the railway authority and the passenger? The case of *Thompson* v. *London, Midland and Scottish Railway Co.*, decided in 1930, is a typical example. On a January day in 1928 Mrs Thompson bought a half-day excursion ticket from Darwen to Manchester and return for 2s. 7d. If she had looked at the ticket she would have seen, on its face, the words 'For conditions see back'. If she had then turned over the ticket, she would have seen the words 'Issued subject to the conditions and regulations in the company's timetables and notices and excursion and other bills'. If she had then looked at the posters exhibited at the station she would have seen on the excursion bill the words 'Excursion tickets are issued subject to the notices and conditions shown in the company's current timetables'. There was only one copy of the company's timetable in the booking office at Darwen station, and it cost 6d. If Mrs Thompson had bought it and read it, she would eventually have come to page 552. There she would have found, among a host of other conditions, the following crucial words: 'Excursion tickets . . . are issued subject to . . . the condition that neither the holders nor any other person shall have any right of action against the company . . . in respect of . . injury (fatal or otherwise), loss, damage or delay, however caused.' (Such a clause cannot now be used by British Rail, as we shall see in Chapter 10.)

At 10 p.m. on the same January day the returning excursion train pulled into Darwen station. Mrs Thompson's carriage stopped alongside the ramp at the end of the platform and, as a result of the negligence of the employees of the railway company, she slipped when getting out of the carriage in the dark and was injured. The

Court of Appeal dismissed her claim to damages on the ground that she had agreed to the condition on page 552 of the timetable and had therefore voluntarily given up her ordinary rights. She had not read the ticket or the timetable, but she had 'agreed' to the condition by accepting the ticket which drew her attention to it, devious though the treasure hunt was.

There has been a welcome appreciation by some judges of the unreality of the situation in this type of case. In *Thornton* v. *Shoe Lane Parking Ltd* (1971) a motorist drove up to the entrance to an automatic car park. As he approached a ticket came out of a machine: he took it, and the automatic barrier rose and permitted him to drive in. When he came back to his car some hours later he was severely injured in an accident caused in part by the negligence of the car park owners. When he sued they relied on a condition exempting them from liability for injury to their customers. The ticket which came out of the machine carried words saying that it was issued subject to the conditions displayed on the premises. Exhibited at several places were printed conditions.

The Court of Appeal held that the company had not taken reasonable steps to draw Mr Thornton's attention to the condition, and he was not bound by it. As Lord Justice Megaw pointed out, 'It does not take much imagination to picture the indignation of the defendants if their potential customers, having taken their tickets and observed the reference therein to contractual conditions which, they said, could be seen in notices on the premises, were one after the other to get out of their cars, leaving the cars blocking the entrances to the garage, in order to search for, find and peruse the notices! Yet, unless the defendants genuinely intended the potential customers to do just that, it would be fiction, if not farce, to treat those customers as persons who have been given a fair opportunity, before the contracts are made, of discovering the conditions by which they are to be bound.'

Where there is a written document signed by both parties, there is at least a semblance of agreement. In the case of *L'Estrange* v. *F. Graucob Ltd*, in 1934, a company engaged in selling automatic machines employed canvassers to go round the country seeking sales. Miss L'Estrange, who owned a café in Llandudno, was persuaded to buy a cigarette slot-machine. The canvasser produced for her signature a 'Sales Agreement' which included a number of clauses in small print, one of which said that 'any express or implied condition, statement or warranty, statutory or otherwise, is hereby excluded'. Miss L'Estrange signed this agreement. She gave evidence that she had never read the document, which she thought was an order form, and that she had no clear idea of what she was signing; and the court found as a fact that she had no knowledge of the detailed contents of the document. Nevertheless the judges felt bound to give effect to the words in the contract, so that when the machine soon jammed and became unworkable Miss L'Estrange found that she had no rights. 'When a document containing contractual terms is signed,' said Lord Justice Scrutton, 'then, in the absence of fraud, or ... misrepresentation, the party signing it is bound, and it is wholly immaterial whether he has read the document or not.' Lord Maugham agreed, saying: 'I regret the decision to which I have come, but I am bound by legal rules and cannot decide the case on other considerations.'

Yet even here it can be said that to talk of 'agreement' is a misuse of language. The contract signed by Miss L'Estrange was drawn up by a lawyer, for as Lord Justice Scrutton pointed out the framer of the document had had in mind the relevant court decisions and had sought to avoid them. Miss L'Estrange, on the other hand, even if she had read the conditions, would not have understood them without legal advice.

That is not all. The courts have treated this kind of contract with as much respect as if it was the outcome of mutual agreement between equals. The concept of 'contract' in the minds of the judges was that of bargains freely negotiated and freely entered into. If the form of contract proposed by the supplier is unfair to the consumer, the consumer's proper course is to put forward amendments to make the contract more equitable. And if the amendments are not accepted, the consumer still has his freedom: he can refuse to enter into the contract at all. If he does not like the conditions set out in British Rail's by-laws and timetables, he can refuse to travel by train. If he does not like the conditions set out in the Electricity Board's form of agreement, he can refuse to have electricity. And if he chooses to accept the goods or services on the terms offered, rather than do without, he has no one to blame but himself. This has indeed been the attitude of many judges. For example, in 1938 Lord Justice MacKinnon had before him a hire-purchase agreement, the terms of which were much the same as those of most other hire-purchase agreements; 'if anybody is so foolish as to enter into an agreement such as this,' said the judge, 'I do not know that his case can be considered harsh.'

The doctrine that all agreements are sacred – the principle of sanctity of contract – is blind to the lack of bargaining equality. Judges may be increasingly aware that it is unreal to talk of freely negotiated bargains when a man takes out a policy of fire insurance, arranges for the supply of gas to his house, or takes a car on hire purchase. Yet even today, though some inroads on the doctrine have been made both by court decisions and by legislation, the fiction of 'freedom of contract' prevails over reality.

Take, for example, the attitude of Lord Devlin, an outstanding judge who was appointed to the Bench in 1948 at the early age of forty-two and retired in 1964 to become

for a time chairman of the Press Council. In a lecture
delivered in 1956 Lord Devlin referred to nineteenth-
century thinkers who talked of political freedom and freedom under the law and ignored economic freedom. 'They
failed to see,' he commented, 'that it was no use leaving a
man free to make what bargain he liked if he had no
bargaining power.' Even in the nineteenth century, he
pointed out, Parliament appreciated that a working man's
bargaining power was unequal to his employer's, and
deliberately interfered with freedom of contract by passing the Truck Acts, the Employers' Liability Acts, and
the Workmen's Compensation Acts. But men much higher
in the economic scale, continued Lord Devlin, could find
themselves in a position in which it was difficult to bargain, and were faced with the take-it-or-leave-it attitude
that stares you in the face from a railway ticket. 'In this
type of case,' said Lord Devlin, 'the courts did their best
to relieve hardship *but they had to keep within the
bounds of freedom of contract.*' (Our italics.) In other
words, though in various ways the courts have been willing and able to do battle on behalf of the consumer
against the supplier of goods or services, they have made
it more difficult for themselves to wage this battle effectively by their reluctance to overthrow the fiction of
freedom of contract. The efforts of the courts have been
enfeebled because they have in the twentieth century
perpetuated nineteenth-century notions of unbridled
laissez-faire.

THE COURTS STRIKE BACK

How, then, could the courts relieve hardship while stay-
ing within the bounds of freedom of contract? A number
of techniques have been evolved by the courts to deal with
contracts which attempt to evade obligations imposed by
the law. The pattern of legal development has been uni-

form: first, an attempt to exclude the law's requirements – an exemption or exclusion clause; next, a decision which overrides the exemption clause; then, an attempt to outflank the decision by a fresh form of words; and finally, either an admission of defeat by the courts, or a further blow at the exemption clause which sets the whole cycle in motion again.

An early technique adopted by the courts had been a rigid and formalistic approach to the words used in exemption clauses. If the words formed part of the contract, they had to be applied. But what did the words mean? This was for the courts to say. And they could construe the words as narrowly and strictly as they wished.

A leading illustration is a case decided by the Court of Appeal in 1933: *Andrews Brothers (Bournemouth) Ltd* v. *Singer and Co. Ltd.* A firm of car dealers in Bournemouth entered into a contract appointing them sole dealers in new Singer cars. They ordered a 'new 18 h.p. saloon car' from Singers under the contract, which contained the following clause: 'All conditions, warranties and liabilities implied by statute, common law or otherwise are excluded.' The car delivered was not new, and the car dealers argued that Singers had broken their contract by failing to deliver a new car.

The Court held that Singers were not protected by the exemption clause. The wording only mentioned *implied* terms, and the sellers' promise to deliver a new car was not implied by law, but was an *express* term of the contract. The clause might have been effective, for example, to relieve the sellers from liability for breach of the condition implied by the Sale of Goods Act that the car should be of merchantable quality, but the Court was able to say that it did not relieve the sellers from liability for failing to do what they had expressly agreed. The sellers had therefore to pay damages.

Although the buyers were protected in this case, this

kind of technical juggling with words contains within it the seeds of its own destruction. Each decision of this nature is an invitation to lawyers to produce a new exemption clause to close the loophole found by the courts. The clause in *Andrews* v. *Singer* itself was an attempt to close the gap in earlier decisions, and the courts entered into the spirit of this game of verbal chess. Lord Justice Scrutton, giving judgement in *Andrews* v. *Singer*, actually said: 'If a vendor desires to protect himself from liability in such a case he must do so by much clearer language than this.'

This remark, and the very reasoning of the judgement, led people to think that the decision could easily be evaded. Indeed, only a few months later the contract in the cigarette slot-machine case, *L'Estrange* v. *Graucob*, came before Lord Justice Scrutton himself. The exemption clause in the 'Sales Agreement' in that case, it will be recalled, purported to exclude 'any *express* or implied condition, statement or warranty' and, overlooking the fact that the contract was signed before the decision in *Andrews* v. *Singer*, the Lord Justice suggested that this clause was intended to circumvent his earlier decision. *L'Estrange* v. *Graucob*, in fact became known as the 'canvassers' charter'. But the King's Bench Divisional Court did not have to pronounce on the legal effect of the exemption clause for Miss L'Estrange's lawyers did not argue the point, and in more recent years authoritative doubts have been expressed on the efficacy of such a clause.

After all, what does a contract containing such a clause amount to? Reduced to its bare essentials, it looks something like this:

first, an express promise: 'We will sell you a new Singer car';
then, an exemption clause: 'All express promises are hereby excluded.'

The effect of the exemption clause then, if it is to be taken literally, is to wipe out the express promise itself. Thus nothing is left of the contract: the ultimate in exclusion clauses is reached, and the whole transaction is itself excluded.

Such a nonsensical result cannot represent the law, and in recent years the courts have evolved a fresh approach to exemption clauses which makes it plain that there are often limits to the effectiveness of even the most carefully drawn clause.

FUNDAMENTAL BREACH OF CONTRACT

How have the courts done this? First, they look at the contract between the parties and ignore the exemption clause. They try to see just what the contract is about – to disregard the details and the trimmings, so that they can discover the essential obligation. In a case such as *Andrews* v. *Singer*, the contract may be lengthy and complicated but the essential obligation is simple: to sell a new Singer car.

Having focused attention on the essential obligation, the courts can now turn to the exemption clause. The object of the exemption clause, it is agreed, is to exclude liability – but surely the parties cannot intend the clause, however widely drafted, to exclude the essential obligation of the contract itself? There is therefore a strong presumption that even the widest exemption clause is not intended to exclude liability if the supplier has *completely* failed to carry out his contractual obligations.

This then would be the modern answer to a case such as *Andrews* v. *Singer*: the exemption clause fails to protect the supplier, not because of any loophole in its wording, but because the supplier has failed to do what he contracted to do – because he has failed to supply a new Singer car. And it is clear from this reasoning that even if the clause had tried to exclude 'any *express* or implied condition' the result would have been the same. It would not be easy to convince the court that the parties intended the transaction not to impose any legal obligation on the supplier at all.

Thus, if the supplier has committed a *fundamental breach of contract*, no exemption clause is likely to be intended to enable him to escape liability. As long ago as 1838, in a case relating to the supply of 'Chanter's smoke-consuming furnace', Lord Abinger, the chief judge of the Court of Exchequer, explained that 'if a man offers to buy peas of another, and he sends him beans, he does not perform his contract' (*Chanter* v. *Hopkins*). The courts today follow that principle by saying that if a seller delivers goods that are fundamentally different from those ordered by the buyer, he cannot shelter behind an exemption clause which was not intended to go so far.

According to the House of Lords in a shipping case reported in 1966, *Suisse Atlantique Société d'Armement Maritime S.A.* v. *N.V. Rotterdamsche Kolen Centrale*, it seems that if an exemption clause is genuinely intended to exempt the supplier even if he has broken the contract in a fundamental respect it may be effective; but it is difficult to see how any clause can protect the supplier from a total non-performance of the contract unless it is conceded that the transaction is not in reality a legally binding contract at all but a mere expression of intent.

Some modern cases will show how valuable this doctrine of fundamental breach of contract has proved to the consumer.

In the first, *Karsales (Harrow) Ltd* v. *Wallis*, in 1956, a Mr Wallis wanted to take a second-hand Buick car on hire purchase. He inspected it at the dealers' showroom and gave it a trial run: it was in excellent condition. The car was then sold to a finance company who let it out on hire purchase to Mr Wallis (the mechanics of hire purchase will be explained in Chapter 6). There was a clause in the hire-purchase agreement which read: 'No condition or warranty that the vehicle is roadworthy, or as to its age, condition, or fitness for any purpose, is given by the owner or implied herein.' Shortly after the agreement was signed the car was delivered to Mr Wallis. It was left outside his house at night, having been towed there. The new tyres had been replaced by old ones, chrome strips round the body were missing, the valves were burnt out, and there were two broken pistons. In the words of the Court of Appeal, 'the car would not go'. It would have cost £150 to put the car into the condition in which Mr Wallis had first seen it. The Court ruled that though the hire-purchase agreement excluded liability for the condition of the car, Mr Wallis could nevertheless reject it since the car delivered was fundamentally different from the car contracted for. Indeed, Lord Birkett went so far as to say that 'a car that will not go is no car at all'.

This was admittedly an extreme case – the suppliers (though it was not the fault of the finance company) had delivered something quite different from what had been agreed. But the more usual complaint is not that the goods delivered are fundamentally different from the ones ordered; it is rather that they do not work, or break, or are of poor quality. Here we reach the borderland of the doctrine of fundamental breach, for there is room for argument as to whether or not a breach of contract is fundamental, and some breaches are more fundamental than others.

There can be no easy formula to guide the courts in situations such as this. All the circumstances are relevant, particularly the price paid, the suppliers' knowledge of the buyer's requirements, and the seriousness of the fault. It is clearly not possible, for example, to seize on Lord Birkett's graphic phrase – 'a car that will not go is no car at all' – as if that supplies the answer to every problem. *Why* will the car not go? A set of faulty sparking plugs, a loose electrical connexion, a flat battery – such defects are unlikely to amount to a fundamental breach of contract.

Other cases, however, show how a combination of faults can together bring the doctrine into play. In *Yeoman Credit Ltd* v. *Apps* (1961) the car did in fact go – but only just. It took one and a half hours to travel three or four miles, the brakes, clutch, and steering were described as 'terrible', and it was said to be 'in an unusable, unroadworthy and unsafe condition'. The cost of putting the car into good repair would have been about £100. It was held that the accumulation of defects constituted a fundamental breach of contract, and that the finance company could not take refuge behind an exemption clause. Mr Apps was awarded £100 damages.

In another case, *Farnworth Finance Facilities Ltd* v. *Attryde* (1970), Mr Attryde took a new motor cycle on hire purchase. It went back for repairs three times in the first four months. Then it broke down again and he refused to pay any more. The finance company repossessed the cycle and the question arose whether they had to repay the money, nearly £200, which they had received.

The hire-purchase agreement stated that the cycle 'is not supplied subject to any condition that the same is fit for any particular purpose.' The Court of Appeal said that this was not intended to exclude liability for a fundamental breach of contract, so the question arose whether the breach of contract was fundamental or not, for Mr Attryde had ridden the cycle for 4,000 miles. 'Any defect is serious,' said Lord Denning, holding that there had been a fundamental breach, 'if it is likely to cause an

accident or to render the vehicle unsafe on the road. It
may be easily remediable, yet, until it is remedied, it is a
serious defect.' Lord Justice Fenton Atkinson evidently
felt that although each defect, taken alone, might not
have amounted to a fundamental breach, yet there was
'such a congeries of defects as to destroy the workable
character of the machine' and, taken together, there was
a fundamental breach of contract. Mr Attryde was accordingly entitled to his money back.

This doctrine of fundamental breach of contract is not
limited to hire-purchase contracts, or to the buying of
goods. It is of general application. The courts have, for
example, been able to help the consumer in contracts for
carrying, storing, or cleaning goods. Indeed, the principle
was well established in its application to transporting
goods by train or ship long before it was first applied to
sale contracts.

A good illustration of the doctrine in this context is
afforded by *London and North Western Railway Co.* v.
Neilson, which came before the House of Lords in 1922.
A theatrical company, presenting a musical comedy
known as *My Soldier Boy*, was moving on a Sunday in
June 1920 from Llandudno to Bolton. The scenery and
props, including bagpipes and uniforms, were loaded
into a special van. Unfortunately, when the van arrived
at the Exchange Station at Manchester the label had
come off the van, so the contents were taken out. Some of
the luggage bore old labels, and this luggage was accordingly dispatched to places as far afield as Bath and Scarborough. The remainder was stored in the cloakroom.
Ultimately, everything was recovered, but the Monday
matinée had been missed and the railway company was
sued for £28 4s. 3d. The contract for the carriage of the
goods stated that the goods were carried at the owner's
risk and that the proprietor of the touring company
agreed 'to relieve you [the railway company] from all

liability for loss, damage, misconveyance, misdelivery, delay or detention of or to such goods during any portion
of the transit . . .' This widely-drawn clause did not protect the company, for it applied only to loss or delay
during the transit, and once the goods departed from the
usual route the railway had gone completely outside the
confines of the contract, and had broken the contract in a
fundamental respect. As Lord Summer pointed out, 'In
my opinion, neither on the findings nor on the printed
contract did the route from Llandudno to Bolton run
through the Manchester Exchange Station cloakroom.'

If a person agrees to store or clean goods and deliberately destroys, sells, or gives away the goods, he too has
committed a fundamental breach of contract: he is considered as having acted in a manner so repugnant to the
purpose of the contract that he is liable to the owner of
the goods despite a contractual clause excluding liability,
unless the clause permits the act complained of. In a case
heard in 1945, *Davies* v. *Collins*, an American Army Officer entrusted his uniform to cleaners to be cleaned and
to have certain small repairs done to it. The officer did
not read the printed conditions on the docket handed to
him but the Court of Appeal treated them as contractual
terms binding on him. They read thus: 'Whilst every
care is exercised in cleaning and dyeing garments, all
orders are accepted at owner's risk entirely and we are
unable to hold ourselves responsible for damage, shrink-
age, colour or defects developed on necessary handling.
The proprietors' liability is limited to ten times the cost
of cleaning.' The uniform was sent by the cleaners to
sub-contractors and it was never returned. Now there was
no mention in the docket about sub-contracting the work
and, indeed, the printed conditions began by saying that
'every care is exercised in cleaning and dyeing garments.'
The Court of Appeal took the view that these words
implied a promise by the cleaners to take care which

could only be fulfilled if the work was carried out by servants whom they could control and supervise. By sending
the uniform away to a sub-contractor, the promise to take
care was, as Lord Justice MacKinnon put it, 'manifestly
futile'. In the result, since farming out the work was
doing something not contemplated by the contract at all,
the Court refused to allow the cleaners to rely on the
printed condition limiting their liability, and made them
liable to pay the full value of the uniform.

But this case illustrates that there may be ways in which
an astute supplier of goods or services can get round the
doctrine of fundamental breach of contract. The key to
the doctrine is that the courts must determine the fundamental obligation of the contract. Once they have done
this the exemption clause may be unavailing, so the supplier must transfer his attention from the exemption
clause to the fundamental obligation itself: he must see
whether he can write his protection into the contract's
description of what he is to do.

This means that a suitable addition to the conditions
on a dry cleaner's receipt might remove the basis of the
decision in *Davies* v. *Collins*. Such an addition would be
the following: 'The cleaners may contract work out
wholly or in part, and these conditions shall apply to
goods entrusted to sub-contractors.' It seems that no customer could argue in the face of this condition that sub-
contracting was not contemplated by the contract. The
contract itself expressly contemplates it.

But the question would then arise: could the consumer
sue the sub-contractors themselves for negligence? It is
clear that, even though there is no direct contract between
customer and sub-contractors, the sub-contractors owe to
the customer a duty to take care of the goods. Can they in
their defence rely on an exemption clause in their contract with the cleaners? This is a question we will consider
shortly.

The discussion above demonstrates a simple way round the doctrine of fundamental breach of contract. This doctrine depends on the presumed intention of the parties. If their intention is made clear, there is no room for the presumption. So, in the *Andrews* v. *Singer* type of case, the contract need not be made out for the sale of a 'new car'. It can now relate to the sale of a 'new or used car'. Again, the cigarette slot-machine can be described as a 'metal object resembling an automatic machine but not necessarily capable of use as such'. And the car in the hire-purchase agreements could be described as a 'mass of machinery resembling in shape a motor-car'. But there are serious objections on the suppliers' part to such revealing frankness, and to these we will return later in this chapter.

MISREPRESENTATIONS

The narrow interpretation of exemption clauses, and the doctrine of fundamental breach of contract, are not the only weapons used in the assault on exemption clauses. Another illustration, also from the field of cleaners' contracts, is *Curtis* v. *Chemical Cleaning and Dyeing Co. Ltd*. Mrs Curtis took her white satin wedding dress to a shop for cleaning. A shop assistant gave her a piece of paper headed 'Receipt' which she was asked to sign. Before signing, Mrs Curtis asked the assistant why her signature was required and was told that it was because the shop did not accept liability for damage to beads and sequins. The assistant did not tell Mrs Curtis that in fact there was a clause in the receipt that excluded liability for *any* damage to articles accepted for cleaning, however caused. When the dress was returned to Mrs Curtis there was a stain on the dress and the cleaners denied liability, relying on the clause in the signed receipt. The Court of Appeal, however, ruled that as the cleaners, through their assistant, had misrepresented (albeit quite innocently) the contractual terms and misled Mrs Curtis as to the extent of the exemption from liability, they were not entitled to rely on the clause and must pay damages.

Here, too, a clause which has been used by some firms may enable a cleaner to argue that he has evaded this decision. It reads: 'None of our agents or employees has any authority to alter, vary or qualify in any way these terms and conditions.' If, in the future, a cleaner's assistant misrepresents the effect of the conditions on the receipt, will the cleaner be able to rely on such a clause? Can he say 'my assistant has no authority to alter, vary or qualify – or misrepresent – the conditions' and ignore the misleading statement? No one can be sure of the answer – and even the present authors differ in their views.

WHO IS PROTECTED BY THE EXEMPTION CLAUSE?

Another principle which has helped to limit the operation of exemption clauses is based on the view that contracts are worthy of enforcement because they have been *agreed* by the parties. Therefore no one who has not entered into the agreement can be made liable under the contract nor, it follows, can he take the benefit of the contract. Contracts can only benefit persons who are *parties* to the contract.

This was the principle applied in *Adler* v. *Dickson* in 1954. Mrs Adler was a first-class passenger taking a Mediterranean cruise on the P. and O. Line steamship *Himalaya*. The ship had docked at Trieste and gangways were placed between the ship and the shore to enable passengers to go ashore. Mrs Adler had been ashore, and while she was walking up one of the gangways on her way back to the ship the gangway moved and Mrs Adler was thrown some sixteen feet to the wharf sustaining serious injuries.

The contract between Mrs Adler and the shipping company was embodied in the ticket and contained this clause: 'Passengers . . . are carried at the passengers' entire risk . . . The company will not be responsible for and shall be exempt from all liability in respect of any . . . injury . . . to the person of any passenger.' Doubtless advised by her lawyers that a claim against the company was bound to fail in view of the contractual term quoted, Mrs Adler brought an action not against the company but against the master and the boatswain of the ship. The Court of Appeal upheld her claim on the basis that the master and the boatswain were negligent in setting up the gangway and had no right to rely on the exemption from liability contained in Mrs Adler's ticket. The conditions set out there were conditions of the contract between Mrs Adler and the company, and the company's servants were not parties to the contract.

A similar problem arises where, as in *Davies* v. *Collins* (p. 49 above), work is sub-contracted. In *Morris* v. *C. W. Martin & Sons Ltd*, heard by the Court of Appeal in 1965, Mrs Morris sent her long white mink stole to her furrier for cleaning. He telephoned her to explain that he did not do cleaning himself, and she authorized him to send the fur to the defendant company, a well-known cleaner of furs for the trade. The fur was stolen by an employee of the defendants, and Mrs Morris sued them for £350, the value of the fur. There was no contract between Mrs Morris and the defendants, who were under a duty irrespective of contract to take care of the fur, but the defendants relied on exemption clauses in their contract with the furrier from whom they had received the fur. There was no attempt to exclude liability in the contract between the furrier and Mrs Morris herself.

Lord Denning posed the problem in this way: 'Can the defendants rely, as against the plaintiff, on the exempting conditions although there was no contract directly between them and her? There is much to be said on each side. On the one hand, it is hard on the plaintiff if her just claim is defeated by exempting conditions of which she knew nothing and to which she was not a party. On the other hand, it is hard on the defendants if they are held liable to a greater responsibility than they agreed to undertake.' Lord Denning concluded that Mrs Morris would be bound by the defendants' conditions (which were those laid down by a trade association) because, when she authorized the furrier to send the fur on to the defendants for cleaning, she impliedly agreed to his making a contract for cleaning on the terms usually current in the trade.

Neither of the other two judges in the Court of Appeal were prepared to go as far as Lord Denning on this point for they, like Lord Denning himself, were of the opinion that even if the exemption clauses bound Mrs Morris they were ambiguous and not sufficiently clear to exempt the defendants from liability. In the final result, therefore, all three judges agreed that the defendants were liable. The case does not settle the question whether, if the clauses had been sufficiently clear, they could have been effective as against Mrs Morris who did not know of them.

One result of such cases is, as we have seen, that the traders concerned often act on an adverse decision of the courts by redrafting their contracts. It did not take the shipping companies long to alter their tickets in order to get round *Adler* v. *Dickson* (p. 52 above). Lord Denning, who himself delivered one of the judgements in that case, was equally quick to comment on their reaction. His trenchant remarks, delivered at a public lecture in 1955, deserve a full quotation:

They have promptly put a printed slip on all their tickets making it clear that the master and crew can avail themselves of the exempting conditions just as the company can. All the passengers have to accept this condition. They will not be allowed to travel unless they do. And what, I ask, does this printed slip come to? It is nothing more or less than legislation by the steamship companies to overcome decisions of the courts: and it is legislation which has never been put before Parliament or any other representative body but has been imposed by the companies themselves in their own interests. I do not suppose that the great shipping companies mean to be unreasonable or unfair. They will no doubt make *ex gratia* payments in deserving cases where passengers have been injured. I suggest that compensation should not be left to the discretion of the companies in this way. It is contrary to principle. It is done under the guise of freedom of contract but the freedom is all on one side. Freedom for the companies to impose what conditions they will. No freedom for the individual to object.

No one should be surprised that faced with a court ruling that is against the interests of a shipping company – or a cleaning company, or a distributor, or an insurance company – the company takes whatever steps are open to it under the law to evade the result of the decision. Nor need one condemn the company for trying to protect itself or its employees from liability to customers. What is to be regretted is the reluctance of the courts to jettison the pretence of freedom of contract when the freedom is 'all on one side' – though by a process of technical reasoning it might be held that even the new conditions are ineffective.

One cannot escape the conclusion that though the courts have endeavoured to put up a fight against the exemption clauses of suppliers, their struggle was doomed never to be completely successful. The reason is that the courts deny themselves any general power to reject a clause simply because it may be unreasonable. Only Lord Denning of modern judges has gone so far as to suggest that a condition in a standard-form contract should not be enforced by the courts if it is harsh or unfair. But Lord

Denning, a self-styled iconoclast, would be the first to admit that his views are not representative of those of his brother judges. The attitude of the law is still that people are free to make what contracts they wish, and once a contract is made it must be enforced. No account can be taken of the fact that so many contracts are not the result of free negotiation in any meaningful sense. In the words of Lord Devlin: 'The courts could not relieve in cases of hardship and oppression because the basic principle of freedom of contract included freedom to oppress.'

THE WAY AHEAD

The last chapter traced the ability of the common law – judge-made law – to develop over the centuries, to adapt itself to changing situations and to give new remedies where none previously existed. The common law has not stood still in this century, and one example – the doctrine of fundamental breach of contract – has been described in this chapter. Indeed, lawyers will speak with eloquence of the adaptability and wisdom of the common law of England and gladly endorse Sir Edward Coke's seventeenth-century aphorism that 'the Common Law itself is nothing else but reason'.

But the truth is that the common law has in some fields not shown itself sufficiently capable of radical development, and the field of consumer protection is the outstanding example. The doctrine of precedent – the notion that the judge's task is merely to apply the principles laid down in earlier cases – has inhibited it from playing a more creative role. The courts have not always felt free to move beyond *laissez-faire* conceptions that were appropriate in the nineteenth century but are outmoded in this, because those conceptions are embodied in the judgements of the past: they comprise the precedents which present-day judges feel bound to follow.

Thus in 1966 Lord Reid, in the *Suisse Atlantique* case, said that probably the most objectionable exemption clauses were those 'found in the complex standard conditions which are now so common. In the ordinary way the customer has no time to read them, and, if he did read them, he would probably not understand them. If he did understand and object to any of them, he would generally be told that he could take it or leave it. If he then went to another supplier, the result would be the same. Freedom to contract must surely imply some choice, or room for bargaining.' Where the parties were bargaining on equal terms, he went on, and an exemption clause was accepted for a quid pro quo or other good reason, this objection did not apply; yet the courts had not taken the power to consider whether the exemption was fair or was harsh and unconscionable, or whether or not it was freely agreed by the customer. 'This is a complex problem which intimately affects millions of people,' he added, 'and it appears to me that its solution should be left to Parliament.'

How should Parliament tackle this complex problem? One way, suggested in a radio talk by Lord Gardiner before he became Lord Chancellor, would be to confer on the courts a broad power to strike out conditions in contracts if they are unjust or unreasonable. Some judges would welcome the flexibility this would give in the interests of justice. Others would deplore it: it would make for uncertainty, for no one would know whether a clause was effective until the case had gone to court, and it would be open to the criticism made of section 7 of the Railway and Canal Traffic Act 1854. This section provided that, when a railway company carried goods, any condition limiting its liability for damage or loss caused by negligence could only be enforced if the court thought the condition 'just and reasonable'. As Lord Bramwell commented in one case:

It seems to me perfectly idle, and I cannot understand how it could have been supposed necessary, that it should be referred to a judge to say whether an agreement between carriers, of whose business he knows nothing, and fishmongers, of whose business he equally knows nothing, is reasonable or not.

Nevertheless the courts developed a way of testing whether such conditions were 'just and reasonable', based on the idea that the railway companies should offer their customers a fair alternative by quoting two prices: one, at a reasonable rate, accepting liability, and a lower rate subject to the exemption clause (see p. 263 below). This approach, it will be seen, incorporated what Lord Reid described as a 'quid pro quo' for the exemption clause – a reasonable reduction in price – and helped to ensure that the customer knew of the presence of the exemption clause.

The test of reasonableness has its modern counterparts. In all but one of the states of the United States legislation known as the Uniform Commercial Code has been adopted to replace earlier statutes based on the Sale of Goods Act. Under this Code the courts are given a specific power to refuse to enforce unconscionable clauses, though the exact scope of 'unconscionable' is still the subject of controversy. In England, section 3 of the Misrepresentation Act 1967 bans any clause excluding liability for misrepresentation (see pp. 66–73 below) 'except to the extent (if any) that . . . the court . . . may allow reliance on it as being fair and reasonable in the circumstances of the case.' How this will operate in practice is not yet known. Some commentators have attacked this vague criterion for exemption clauses as 'an abdication by Parliament of its proper responsibility in the formulation of policy for satisfactory law reform', but there is no reason to think that the judges will not apply the Act with common sense.

Other proposals have been made in the belief that certainty in the law is important. For example, it has been suggested that suppliers wishing to use a form of standard contract embodying an exemption clause might come before a special court such as the Restrictive Practices Court (see Chapter 12 below) to have the fairness of the clause decided in advance. Israel has had a procedure of this kind since 1964, but it does not seem to have been much used. In England this method is laid down in the Housing Act 1961, whereby in some cases obligations to repair can be excluded by landlords only if a court makes an order with the consent of both landlord and tenant.

Another proposal is that a number of standard forms of contract should be laid down for particular transactions, such as an official form of hire-purchase agreement. Unlike present standard form contracts, which are drawn up by one party to the transaction with his own interests in mind, these forms would try to hold the balance fairly between both parties. They would be drawn up by a committee representative of both consumers and businessmen and would be approved by some public body. All future dealings in the fields covered would be governed by these approved forms of contracts, and contracting out would not be permitted. There are already unofficial precedents for such standard forms which try to be fair to all, though not in the consumer field – building contracts approved by the Royal Institute of British Architects, for example, and standard conditions of sale laid down by trade associations such as the London Corn Trade Association.

A different method is for legislation to deal with a particular kind of contract and to lay down in advance what kinds of liability cannot be excluded. Thus section 151 of the Road Traffic Act 1960 (repeating a provision originally in an Act of 1930) says that a bus company (publicly or privately owned) may not negative or restrict its liability for the death of or injury to a passenger, and any term in a contract which tries to do so is void. A similar provision (introduced since the decision in *Thomson* v. *LMS Railway*, p. 37 above) covers railway passengers but, as we have seen, passengers by sea have no such protection as yet. Airline passengers are protected, but the position is more complicated and will be dealt with in Chapter 10.

This was the technique adopted also by the Hire-Purchase Act 1965. If goods were taken on hire purchase, and the total hire-purchase price was not more than £2,000, certain conditions set out in the Act are implied in the hire-purchase agreement and could not be excluded. Full discussion of the Act and its social and economic implications would anticipate Chapter 6 below but, as an example, the Act implied a condition that the goods would correspond with their description in the contract, and no words in the hire-purchase agreement could exclude or limit that condition.

In 1966 the Law Commission, in conjunction with its Scottish counterpart, commenced a wide-ranging study of how Parliament might deal with exemption clauses, aided by a Working Party whose membership included lawyers and representatives of business interests, industry and consumers. Their First Report on this subject (Law Com. No. 24), issued in 1969, dealt with the sale of goods and recommended a ban on exemption clauses in consumer sales. The Bill which is expected to become the Supply of Goods (Implied Terms) Act 1973 implements this Report and also replaces some of the sections in the Hire-Purchase Act 1965 (see Chapters 3 and 6 below).

A further report will deal with exemption clauses in other contracts. A working paper issued for consultation in 1971 recognized the difficulty of defining a 'consumer' for contracts other than those for the sale of goods; it canvassed the possibility of a general ban on exemption clauses, except where found to be reasonable by the court in the light of the particular circumstances, with an over-riding principle that clauses attempting totally to exclude liability for death or personal injury should be void. When the Law Commissions' report is published the 'urgent legislative action' called for by Lord Reid in 1966 will be in sight.

PUBLIC OPINION

It is trite to say so, but a final and very significant influence on exemption clauses is informed public opinion. This is not merely a pious hope. One of the real successes of the consumer movement in Britain has been its influence on standard form contracts containing exemption clauses.

The story of unfair guarantees will be told in a later chapter. For the moment, cleaners and laundries afford an excellent example of the 'consumer pressure group' at work.

In the summer of 1958, *Which?* published an article about standard form contracts which printed, side by side, a typical form of 'conditions of acceptance' issued by a large firm of dyers and cleaners, and a draft form drawn up for the Consumers' Association with the consumer's interests in mind. This led to correspondence with the National Federation of Dyers and Cleaners which drew up a new set of recommended conditions, but these went only a small way to meeting the objections of *Which?*

The publicity given to the conditions had, however, an important effect. It drew people's attention to the conditions and – more important – it told them what they meant. This, surely, is the real answer to the exemption clause: knowledge. Such clauses have been used for years simply because no one knew what they signified. A cleaner might happily issue a condition reading 'No liability is accepted for any delay, damage or loss howsoever arising'. But he would think twice before publicly announcing 'We do not agree to take care of your garments'. Once it is generally known that both mean the same thing, the cleaner who cares for his reputation is not likely to issue conditions which reveal such a lack of confidence in his own service.

And this has indeed been the result of the publicity. The National Federation of Dyers and Cleaners no longer recommends its members to use any conditions of accept-ance. In an allied field, a trade association, the Guild of Professional Launderers and Cleaners, has been formed under the auspices of the Institute of British Launderers. Members do not rely on exemption clauses, but instead proclaim their common law liability and, indeed, give the customer even greater protection:

We accept full responsibility for every article entrusted to our care. We undertake to re-process free of charge any article considered unsatisfactory and to compensate fairly in any case of loss or damage.

This, of course, is why the suggestion made above for evading the doctrine of fundamental breach of contract has not been acted upon. The seller of a new car cannot very well announce that he may supply a used car instead; the supplier of automatic machines cannot simply agree to sell 'a metal object'. The exemption clause is an excel-lent device, as long as it can be foisted on to an ignorant customer. But a blatant declaration is a poor advertise-ment.

CHAPTER 3

THE DUTIES OF A SELLER

MANY of the duties that a seller of goods owes to his customer are to be found in the Sale of Goods Act 1893. Set in a mould formed eighty years ago, it is not to be wondered at that the Act is not entirely adequate to the needs of the present day. To what extent the Act does protect the modern consumer, and how serious are its shortcomings, are questions that must be looked into in this chapter. But not all of the seller's duties to his customer are contained in Acts of Parliament; much of the law is to be found in the decisions of the courts, in precedents going back in many cases some hundreds of years.

UNACCEPTED OFFERS

What if a shopkeeper displays an article in his shop window, with a price ticket on it? Can one insist on having the goods at the marked price – is the seller under a duty to hand them over if the money is offered? It is clear law that a display of goods in a shop window is *not* an offer to sell them which can be accepted by a customer saying he will buy them. Instead, the display is known as an 'invitation to treat', an invitation by the shopkeeper to receive offers from potential customers. It is the customer who makes the offer, an offer to buy; the shopkeeper may accept that offer, in which case there is a contract binding on both of them, but the shopkeeper need not accept the offer, and without such acceptance it is impossible for the customer to insist upon the goods or to sue the shopkeeper for not letting him have them. It has been held by the courts that even in a self-service store the display is merely an invitation to the public to make offers; the customer makes an offer to buy when he takes goods down from the shelves and puts them in his wire basket, and unless the seller (or the cashier on his behalf) accepts the offer by taking cash from the customer, there is no duty on the seller to let him have the goods. There is an advantage in this for the customer, because until his offer to buy is accepted he is under no obligation and may freely replace the goods on the shelves. On the other hand, the seller may want to take them back from the customer because they have been displayed by mistake or had the wrong price tag on them, and he would have the legal right to do this. But under section 11 (2) of the Trade Descriptions Act 1968 it is a criminal offence for the shopkeeper to mark goods with a price below that at which they are in fact for sale.

Further protection for consumers is given by the Unsolicited Goods and Services Act 1971. It is not unknown for people to be sent goods like records or books which they have never ordered. At common law the recipient was not bound to pay for them unless he agreed to buy them or used them in some way, but many people were persuaded to pay in ignorance of the legal position. Under the 1971 Act a private person who receives unsolicited goods and does not agree to acquire them must let the sender take the goods back during the six months after receiving them; but after the six months, provided he has not agreed to return them, the goods become the recipient's property and he can use them, sell them, or give them away as if they were an unconditional gift to him. The recipient has the right to cut short the period of six months by giving written notice to the sender of the goods, stating his name and address and that the goods are unsolicited. The sender then has 30 days to collect the goods and, if he fails to do so, the goods become the recipient's property at the end of the 30 days. If the sender demands payment for unsolicited goods, or threatens proceedings, he is liable to a fine.

COMMENDATORY PUFFS

Sometimes people imagine that where, by advertisement or orally, a seller of goods makes some general commendatory reference to the goods or their performance, he can be sued if it is shown that the reference was knowingly exaggerated or frankly optimistic. Certainly, where a seller makes a statement of *fact* about the goods he is selling and the statement is untrue, the buyer may, indeed, have some remedy against him. There is undoubtedly a duty on the seller to refrain from making false statements of fact, but he is free to employ generalized or ambiguous sales talk, words which express opinion rather than fact, with impunity. Statements by a seller of goods that his product 'gives results' or is 'fully guaranteed' can hardly be gainsaid because they have no specific meaning: a seller's description of a second-rate house as 'a desirable residence for a family of distinction' is no more than a sales puff and because it cannot be pinned down as a statement of fact the buyer has no remedy. Some latitude must be allowed for a seller to indulge in sales talk of this kind – life in the market-place would be less colourful without it. The authors of a leading students' textbook give the generally accepted justification:

> Eulogistic commendation of the thing sold is the age-old device of the successful salesman, and it would be an impracticable and mischievous rule which permitted the rescission of contracts merely because expressions of a laudatory and optimistic nature, couched in the language of exaggeration, chanced to transcend the truth.

It may be, however, that existing law is over-generous

in the licence it gives, that the law is pushed to its limits and abused by modern advertising methods. As one writer has said:

The fact that the common law of puff remains the cornerstone of the industry of advertising which, in this aspect, may not unjustly be described as institutionalized dishonesty, simply demonstrates one of the natural limitations of the common law as an instrument of social control.

The problem will be more appropriately gone into further in the next chapter, since it is advertising by the manufacturer rather than by the retailer that is more important at the present time.

MISREPRESENTATIONS

One of the more difficult problems of law concerning a buyer's rights against a seller is whether a false statement of fact made by the seller about the goods is a substantial part of the contract, that is, a binding promise and a term of the contract, or is, instead, merely a statement which had helped to induce the buyer to make the purchase but which is not part of the contract itself. Suppose that in the sale of a washing machine the seller describes it as 'sound in every respect'. Is that an express term of the contract of sale, or is it merely a 'representation': something that may encourage the buyer to make the contract whose only express terms may be a sale of this washing machine for that price?

The question is an important one should the statement about the machine turn out to be false. If the statement is a term of the contract then the buyer will, at the least, be entitled to claim damages from the seller, and if he acts promptly he may be able to call off the deal and demand his money back. On the other hand if the statement is not a term of the contract, but only a representation, or rather a misrepresentation, the buyer may claim damages only if he can show the seller was fraudulent, i.e. that the seller knew his statement was false or made it recklessly not caring whether it was false or not, or if, under the Misrepresentation Act 1967, the representation was made negligently. It has always been notoriously difficult to establish fraud and, until the 1967 Act made it possible to claim damages in respect of a misrepresentation made negligently, the law was in a most unsatisfactory state. It was apparently the law that where there had been a misrepresentation made without fraud – that is, an innocent misrepresentation – the buyer could, if he acted reasonably promptly after taking delivery, reject the goods and demand his money back, but even that limited right was uncertain. Some decisions suggested that once the contract was completed the buyer could not have it set aside on the ground of innocent misrepresentation. If, however, there was such a right, certainly it had to be exercised promptly or not at all. If the buyer allowed even a few days to elapse before he sought to reject the goods because of some innocent misrepresentation made by the seller, he was undoubtedly too late to obtain any remedy at all; he could neither reject the goods nor have damages.

There is something to be said for a firm rule that once the buyer has had a reasonable opportunity to examine the goods, he should not be able to call off the whole transaction simply because the seller has made an innocent misrepresentation about the goods. In a 1950 case, *Leaf* v. *International Galleries*, Leaf bought a painting of Salisbury Cathedral for £85 after the dealer had told him that the picture was painted by Constable. Leaf only discovered that the painting was not a Constable when he tried to sell it to Christies some five years later. He endeavoured to return the picture and recover his £85 from the dealer on the ground that the dealer had made an innocent misrepresentation, but the Court of Appeal held that it was too late. Lord Evershed pointed out that, although in this particular case the picture could be returned in the condition and quality it had on the sale five years earlier, that might not always be the position; in the intervening time there might have been a change in the article sold through wear and tear or some other cause. A set of chairs attributed to Chippendale might, after being used for some years, be said to have suffered damage which might appreciably diminish their market value. Similarly, a change in fashion might reduce their worth. These possibilities, however, while they justified the rule that a buyer may not call off a deal after he has had the goods for some time, did not justify the old rule that he could not even obtain damages against a seller who has made an innocent misrepresentation, in reliance on which the purchase was made.

The Misrepresentation Act 1967 enables a buyer to claim damages for innocent misrepresentation unless the seller proves he had reasonable cause to believe and did believe that the facts represented were true. It also clears up the previous doubts about the buyer's right to reject the goods by enacting that mere performance of the contract is no bar to having the contract set aside for innocent misrepresentation. As the motoring organizations pointed out to the Law Reform Committee, whose recommendations inspired the Act, the accuracy of a representation about the quality and construction of a car is seldom apparent from an inspection by a person who is not an expert, or even from a short trial run. The same point applies to other articles of a mechanical nature. This new rule does not mean, however, that the buyer has an absolute right to set the contract aside on the ground of innocent misrepresentation where he acts reasonably promptly, because the Act gives the court a discretion to award damages instead. The court may award damages instead of rescission even where an innocent misrepresentation is made without negligence. Rejection would be an unduly drastic remedy for a minor misrepresentation, for example, as to the mileage done by a car since its engine was last overhauled.

THE CASE OF THE 1939 MORRIS

Even since the 1967 Act, it may still be necessary to determine whether a statement of fact made by the seller about the goods sold is a term of the contract or is a mere representation; only if it is a term of the contract can the buyer obtain damages as of right should the statement turn out to be untrue even though neither fraud nor negligence can be shown. It is often difficult to be sure whether a statement is a term of the contract or not. One test suggested by the courts is for the buyer to ask himself whether it is reasonable to assume that the seller is taking definite responsibility for the truth of what he is saying. Unless the answer is affirmative the courts will consider that his statement was only a representation.

In *Oscar Chess Ltd* v. *Williams*, heard by the Court of Appeal in 1956, a Mrs Williams of Port Talbot acquired a second-hand Morris car on the footing that it was a 1948 model. The car was used a good deal by Mrs Williams's son, and he later approached Oscar Chess Ltd, who were motor dealers, with a view to buying from them a new Hillman Minx car, offering the Morris in part exchange. Williams described the Morris as a 1948 car and the dealers checked that the car's registration book showed it to be a 1948 car. The dealers then looked up 'Glass's Guide', which gives current prices for second-hand cars according to the year of manufacture, and said they would make an allowance of £290 for the Morris. The transaction went through as planned, Williams selling the Morris to the dealers in part exchange for the Hillman Minx. Eight months later, the dealers discovered that the

Morris car was made, not in 1948 but in 1939. Apparently, the style and finish of such cars had not been changed between 1939 and 1948, but although outwardly a 1948 model looked the same as a 1939 one, the price was very different. If the dealers had known it was a 1939 model they would have given only £175 for it, not £290. Williams, in describing it as a 1948 car, was perfectly innocent; perhaps someone back in 1948 had fraudulently altered the car's registration book, but if so he could not now be traced. In these circumstances the dealers claimed as damages from Williams £115, the difference in value between a 1939 Morris and a 1948 Morris. Since there was no question of Williams having been fraudulent, the only ground on which the dealers could succeed in this claim for damages was if they could show that Williams's statement about the age of the car was a term of the contract and not a mere innocent misrepresentation. The Court of Appeal held that the statement was only an innocent misrepresentation and the claim for damages, therefore, failed. The only remedy the law allowed up to 1967 in respect of an innocent misrepresentation, a claim to call off the transaction, was not available because the dealers had allowed eight months to elapse. In the result the Court could give no remedy. The reason why the Court said that Williams's statement as to the age of the car was not a term of the contract was because he had no personal knowledge of the date of the car's manufacture. He was merely repeating what the registration book indicated. It was not reasonable, in these circumstances, to say that Williams was taking personal responsibility for the accuracy of his statement. The Misrepresentation Act 1967 gives a remedy in damages where the misrepresentation is negligent, but this would make no difference in a case like this as Williams had reasonable grounds for believing the car was a 1948 Morris. This reasoning would not necessarily apply to the sale of a car *by* a dealer.

OVER-SUBTLE DISTINCTIONS

Two earlier cases can be cited to show how, on closely similar facts, two different courts may easily come to different conclusions on whether a seller's false statement is a contractual term or not. In *Hopkins* v. *Tanqueray*, decided in 1854, a horse called California was sent to Tattersalls to be sold. The day before the auction the owner, going into the stables at Tattersalls, saw Hopkins kneeling down in a stall examining California's legs, and said to him: 'You need not examine his legs: you have nothing to look for: I assure you he is perfectly sound in every respect.' Hopkins replied: 'If you say so, I am perfectly satisfied,' and immediately got up. Hopkins bought California the next day for 280 guineas, but soon afterwards he found the horse to be unsound and resold him, obtaining only 144 guineas on the resale. The court held that the seller's statement was an innocent misrepresentation that may have induced Hopkins to make the purchase, but it was not a term of the contract of sale, so no damages could be awarded to him.

In 1913, the case of *Schawel* v. *Reade* was heard by the House of Lords on an appeal from Ireland. A stallion was required for stud purposes, and while the intending purchaser was inspecting a horse at the owner's stables the owner said to him: 'You need not look for anything: the horse is perfectly sound. If there was anything the matter with the horse I would tell you.' The examination was not continued with, and some three weeks later the horse was bought. In fact, the horse was totally unfit for stud purposes. The House of Lords held that the seller's statement did constitute a warranty, a term of the contract of sale, for breach of which damages should be awarded. Lord Moulton asked:

How in the world could a vendor more clearly indicate that he is prepared and intends to take upon himself the responsibility of the soundness than by saying: 'You need not look at that horse, because it is perfectly sound', and sees that the purchaser thereupon desists from his immediate independent examination?

One may think the same could be said of the seller's statement in *Hopkins* v. *Tanqueray*, yet there the decision was different.

IMPROVEMENT BY THE 1967 ACT

With such conflicting decisions in the law reports, difficult if not impossible to reconcile, it is no easy task for a buyer or, for that matter, a lawyer on his behalf, to predict with any real hope of accuracy whether a court will choose to treat a false statement made by a seller as a term of the contract of sale or not. It has been seen that the 1967 Act does not entirely eliminate the significance of this distinction, but a consideration of one typical case decided before the Act, *Long* v. *Lloyd* (1958), will show that the distinction will now have much less importance.

Long read a newspaper advertisement inserted by Lloyd offering for a sale a lorry described as being in 'exceptional condition'. On the telephone the same evening Lloyd resolved the ambiguity inherent in this phrase by saying it was 'in first-class condition'. A price of £750 was agreed shortly afterwards and, before leaving with the lorry, Long said: 'If I find anything wrong, your phone won't stop ringing,' to which Lloyd replied: 'It's quite all right.' Two days after the purchase, Long drove the lorry to Rochester. On this journey the dynamo ceased to function and Long noticed various other defects. Having told Lloyd about these matters, it was agreed that Lloyd should pay half the cost of a reconstituted dynamo. The following day, the dynamo was fitted and the lorry driven by Long's brother to Middlesbrough. It broke down during this journey and, on expert examination, the lorry was found to have many serious defects sufficient to make it utterly unroadworthy. In the view of the Court of Appeal, Lloyd's statement that the lorry was in first-class condition was not a contractual term but only an innocent misrepresentation. Since the buyer had a reasonable opportunity of examining the lorry before it broke down, it was too late now for him to reject it and get his money back. Furthermore, as the law did not permit damages to be awarded in respect of an innocent misrepresentation, Long was left without any remedy against Lloyd.

If a similar case occurred today, there is no doubt that the buyer would be able to claim damages against the seller. It would be very difficult for the seller to prove he had reasonable grounds for saying the vehicle was in first-class condition, and unless he could do so he would be liable in damages to the buyer if the statement were false.

In making its proposals for changes in the law, the Law Reform Committee recognized that if the right to claim damages for negligent misrepresentation and the extended right to reject goods could be defeated by a contractual clause, the improvements in the law would not be very far-reaching. It recommended that any clause excluding liability for misrepresentation should be void. The Act follows this view, subject to a discretionary power in the hands of the court or an arbitrator, in any proceedings arising out of the contract, to allow reliance on an exclusion clause if such reliance is 'fair and reasonable in the circumstances of the case'.

SALE OF GOODS ACT PROTECTION

Considered as a product of its time, the Sale of Goods Act 1893 appears as an admirable piece of legislation. As we saw in Chapter 1, it sought to describe the common law as it existed in the early 1890s, and it established beyond argument the important exceptions to the rule of 'let the buyer beware' which had been developed by the courts in the nineteenth century. It does in fact provide the consumer with a firm foundation of legal protection and the Act is sometimes spoken of as the consumer's charter. Moreover it was a model of clarity and precision for which well-deserved praise is customarily given to its draftsman, Sir Mackenzie Chalmers. But it must not be forgotten how limited were Chalmers's objectives. He was not attempting to produce a logical, coherent code which would attempt to foresee, and provide for, all future developments. He simply attempted to reproduce the existing state of the common law, and the blemishes and shortcomings of the Act reflect those of the law made by the judges up to that time: these imperfections have become more apparent over the years with the growing complexity of sale transactions and innovations in manufacturing and sales techniques undreamt of eighty years ago.

The Law Commissions' 1969 report on the Sale of Goods Act reviewed the recommendations for reform made by the Molony Committee seven years earlier and put forward firm proposals for redrafting several sections of the Act. The Supply of Goods (Implied Terms) Bill which is expected to become law in 1973 will put the Law Commissions' recommendations into effect by redrafting those sections in the Sale of Goods Act referred to below. If this Bill is passed the new sections should be compared with the original sections which are quoted here. It should also be noted that section 14(1) will become section 14(3) of the Sale of Goods Act after the reform takes effect.

FITNESS FOR PURPOSE

The main protection for the buyer against the delivery of faulty goods is to be found in section 14 of the Sale of

Goods Act. This section starts off with a terse expression of the principle of *caveat emptor*:

... there is no implied warranty or condition as to the quality or fitness for any particular purpose of goods supplied under a contract of sale, except as follows ...

As we saw in Chapter 1, it is what follows that is of supreme importance to the buyer: drafted as exceptions to the general rule, the provisions in this section considerably modify the *caveat emptor* rule and furnish the buyer with invaluable weapons for use against a dealer who has sold him defective goods.

First, section 14(1):

Where the buyer, expressly or by implication, makes known to the seller the particular purpose for which the goods are required, so as to show that the buyer relies on the seller's skill or judgement, and the goods are of a description which it is in the course of the seller's business to supply (whether he be the manufacturer or not), there is an implied condition that the goods shall be reasonably fit for such purpose, provided that in the case of a contract for the sale of a specified article under its patent or other trade name, there is no implied condition as to its fitness for any particular purpose.

It will be seen that before a buyer can rely on this implied condition that the goods will be reasonably fit for their purpose, two requirements must be satisfied: the buyer must make known the particular purpose for which the goods are required, and he must rely on the seller's skill or judgement. The courts have interpreted these rules favourably to the consumer. Thus very often the 'particular purpose' for which goods are required is obvious. The courts have sensibly taken the view that in these cases the buyer, merely by asking for the article, is 'by implication' making known the purpose for which he wants it. Nor is it difficult for the consumer to show reliance on the seller's skill or judgement. As Lord Wright put it, when goods are bought from a retailer 'a buyer goes to the shop in the confidence that the tradesman has selected his stock with skill and judgement'. The Law Commissions' view was that this reliance should normally be inferred without special proof, and that it should be for the seller to show, if he could, that the buyer did not rely, or that it was not reasonable for him to rely, on the seller's skill or judgement. The new Bill adopts this view.

THE CASES OF THE BATH BUN AND CRABS

Both the above points were brought out in the case of *Chapronière* v. *Mason*, decided in 1905. The plaintiff was a solicitor who practised in the Haymarket, London. One day he sent his clerk to Mason's bakery in Piccadilly to buy him a bath-bun and a meat pie. When Chapronière bit the bun, his teeth struck on a stone; one of his teeth was broken and an abscess formed in his jaw. The case was left to the jury who, somewhat strangely, did not give a verdict in the plaintiff's favour. However, the Court of Appeal thought there should be a fresh trial. The Master of the Rolls, in the course of his judgement, said: 'The presence of a stone of considerable size in a bath-bun is a very untoward incident, and speaking for myself, I should be inclined to say that such a bun is not reasonably fit for mastication.' Needless to say, Chapronière's clerk had not expressly said to the baker that the bun was wanted for eating; that was presumed. And simply going to that bakery rather than to another was sufficient to show that reliance was placed on the baker's 'skill or judgement' in carrying on his business.

The Irish case of *Wallis* v. *Russell*, heard in 1902, emphasizes that the buyer can make sure that he brings himself within the protection of section 14(1) by always adopting the technique of stating quite clearly exactly what he wants the goods for. The plaintiff sent a girl to a fishmongers for two crabs, and she told the manager that she wanted 'two nice fresh crabs for tea'. Two crabs were selected by the manager, paid for and taken away. The plaintiff was made seriously ill by eating these crabs. Maurice Healy recalls in his book *The Old Munster Circuit* the exchange between witness and judge in the case:

CHIEF JUSTICE O'BRIEN: Where were you educated?
BUYER: At the Ursuline Convent, my Lord.
CHIEF JUSTICE O'BRIEN: They teach you to buy food?
BUYER: Yes, my Lord.
CHIEF JUSTICE O'BRIEN: And they teach you: Never buy anything without telling the shopman what it is for, so that you can say you have relied on his skill and judgement?
BUYER: Yes, my Lord.
CHIEF JUSTICE O'BRIEN: What admirable nuns!

A buyer, however, has no remedy against a seller if the goods supplied are reasonably fit for their purpose even though, owing to some special factor affecting the buyer, they are not fit for him. In *Griffiths* v. *Peter Conway Ltd*, heard in 1939, Mrs Griffiths purchased from retailers a Harris tweed coat which had been specially made for her. Shortly after she began to wear it she contracted dermatitis. Apparently there was nothing in the cloth which would have affected the skin of a normal person, but Mrs Griffith's skin was abnormally sensitive. This fact had never been mentioned to the retailers so that they were held not liable: the coat was 'reasonably fit' for wearing and there was no breach by the retailers of section 14(1).

BRAND NAMES

From the provisions of section 14(1) of the Sale of Goods Act, quoted above, it will be noticed that there is no duty imposed on the seller if the goods are sold under a patent or other trade name, even if their purpose is known. The section reads as if this was an exception to the usual implied condition of fitness for purpose, but the courts have treated these words rather as an illustration of circumstances in which the buyer does not rely on the seller's skill or judgement.

In effect the final words of section 14(1) are limited to the situation where the buyer himself specifies the article under its trade name. It is true that, with the growing tendency of consumers to become brand conscious as a result of advertising, buyers tend to rely less and less on the individual seller's skill or judgement and more and more on the manufacturer's claims and reputation. Nevertheless, even though he relies on the manufacturer's advertising, in these days of mass production the buyer may still be said to rely on the seller's skill or judgement in selecting a particular specimen of the branded article which is fit for its purpose. The Molony Committee had no hesitation in saying that the 'patent or other trade name' provision ought to be deleted and the Law Commissions supported this proposal. The new Bill will carry this into effect.

MERCHANTABLE QUALITY

Section 14(2) of the Sale of Goods Act provides a buyer with this further protection:

Where goods are bought by description from a seller who deals in goods of that description (whether he be the manufacturer or not), there is an implied condition that the goods shall be of merchantable quality; provided that if the buyer has examined the goods, there shall be no implied condition as regards defects which such examination ought to have revealed.

This provision overlaps section 14(1). In many cases, not only is the buyer able to claim that goods bought are not fit for the purpose for which he wants them, but also that they are not of merchantable quality. Whether goods are of merchantable quality depends on whether a person who wanted goods of that description would be happy to accept them. If goods are not reasonably fit for the only purpose for which they are customarily used they are not of merchantable quality and the seller is clearly in breach of both section 14(1) and section 14(2). If a car will not go it is neither fit for its purpose nor of merchantable quality. If a television set breaks down through a manufacturing fault it, too, is unfit for its purpose and lacking in merchantable quality. Section 14(2) does, however, go a little further in the cause of consumer protection. A new car may be reasonably fit for use as a car but the paintwork may be so badly scratched or the bumper so dented that it is not of merchantable quality – no one buying a new car would want it.

Again, the 'fit for purpose' condition in section 14(1) cannot protect a buyer who has not relied on the seller's skill or judgement – for example, where goods have been specified under a trade name. But if they are not of merchantable quality the buyer can nevertheless claim under section 14(2). In *Wren* v. *Holt*, for example, decided in 1903, Wren frequented Holt's public house. He knew the pub was 'tied' and sold only Holden's beer, and he went there because he preferred Holden's beer to any other, but his choice was unwise because he suffered from arsenic poisoning as a result of drinking the beer. He could not rest his claim on section 14(1) because his insistence on Holden's beer was a purchase under a trade name; but arsenical beer is not beer of merchantable quality and he was awarded £50 damages against the seller.

The 'merchantable quality' condition only applied if the goods were 'bought by description'. We saw in Chapter 1 how the development of these warranties of quality was, at first, limited to cases where the buyer had not seen the goods before agreeing to purchase them. If the buyer bought a specific article which he had seen, the courts were loath to give him a remedy if it was defective, on the basis that he could have examined it before purchase – a reasoning exemplified by the case of *Chandelor* v. *Lopus* as long ago as 1606 (p. 18). This approach was breaking down in the nineteenth century, but its influence was still sufficiently strong for Chalmers, in his first draft of the Sale of Goods Act, to limit the warranty of merchantable quality to cases 'Where goods are ordered by description from a seller who deals in goods of that description ... *and the buyer has no opportunity of examining the goods.* ...' The later omission of the italicized words and their replacement by the sentence limiting the buyer's rights where he has actually examined the goods and ought to have discovered the defect was a conscious amelioration of the law, but unfortunately the reference to purchase by description was not removed.

The result is that whether there was any condition of merchantability turned on the use of words to describe the goods. In *Godley* v. *Perry*, in 1960, a six-year-old boy bought a plastic catapult for sixpence from a newsagent. Three days later it snapped as the boy pulled the elastic and he lost his left eye. The catapult was not of merchantable quality; but was there any implied condition under section 14(2) of the Sale of Goods Act? The judge found that the boy had asked for 'a catapult', so it was sale by description and the boy succeeded, obtaining £2,500 damages. Presumably if he had simply pointed to the catapult, or picked it up from the counter, he would have lost his claim under this head.

It can be seen that that use of words to describe goods may be quite fortuitous. It might be argued that in the absence of words an article is sold by description in the sense that, for example, the little boy wants a catapult and not just 'that thing', and buys the article because it looks like a catapult – it describes itself by its appearance just as a picture on the packet might describe the contents. The Law Commissions, following the view of the Molony Committee, recommended that the words 'by description' were inapt in modern conditions and should be deleted. The new Bill does delete these words.

SALE BY A DEALER

The historical account in Chapter 1 showed how these implied obligations were imposed only on dealers in the type of goods sold. Strangely enough Sir Mackenzie Chalmers used different words in the two subsections of section 14. In the first, dealing with fitness for purpose, he wrote that the goods must be 'of a description which it is in the course of the seller's business to supply'; in the second, dealing with merchantable quality, that the goods must be bought 'from a seller who deals in goods of that description'. Presumably these were intended to mean the same thing, but the Molony Committee criticized the idea expressed in the Act. 'We take the view,' they said, 'that if a retailer sells an article in the course of business he should be answerable for its merchantability . . . whether or not he has traded in the same line previously.' The Law Commissions supported this and recommended the same words should be used in both subsections and that the conditions 'should be implied into all sales other than those in which the seller sells in a private capacity. In other words, the [conditions] should be implied whenever the seller is acting in the course of a business even though he may not be a dealer in goods of the relevant description.' This will be the law once the Bill becomes the Supply of Goods (Implied Terms) Act 1973.

DUTIES OWED ONLY TO BUYER

An important limitation to the protection afforded consumers by the Sale of Goods Act arises from the theory that the duties are imposed on the seller, not by the general law, but as terms implied in the contract of sale. As we have already seen, the benefit of promises in a contract can be claimed only by a party to the contract. The contract of sale is between seller and buyer, and thus the seller can be made liable only to the buyer and to no one else.

In a case decided in 1903, *Preist* v. *Last*, a man bought a hot-water bottle from a chemist, for use by his wife. After a few days' use by the buyer's wife, the bottle burst and she was scalded. The buyer was successful in an action against the chemist to recover the expenses he had incurred in the treatment of his wife's injuries. The chemist was in breach of section 14(1) of the Sale of Goods Act because clearly the bottle was not reasonably fit for its purpose. But there was no question of the wife in such circumstances being able to sue the chemist to recover damages in respect of her injuries, because she had not bought the bottle – she was not a party to the contract. It is true that if she could have established negligence on the part of the chemist or the manufacturer she could have made a claim, but the important difference is that the *buyer* could claim in respect of *his* loss against the retailer without having to prove negligence at all. The retailer's liability to the buyer under the contract is a strict one; if the goods are not fit for their purpose, he must compensate the buyer for any loss he suffers even though the defect is one which the retailer could not be expected to have discovered; no carelessness on his part need be shown.

The same sort of problem might have arisen from the

facts of *Godley* v. *Perry* – the case of the sixpenny cata-pult. The little boy who bought the catapult was injured when it broke, and he was able to obtain £2,500 damages from the shopkeeper. As we saw (p. 80), the catapult was not of merchantable quality; nor was it fit for its purpose. The shopkeeper was therefore liable for breach of con-tract, although there was no suggestion that he was in any way to blame. (He, in his turn, had a similar claim against the wholesaler, his own supplier, and the wholesaler against the importer.) But six-year-old Nigel Godley, un-fortunate and tragic though his accident was, was at least lucky that he had bought the catapult himself, and that his mother had not bought it for him: if he had not been the actual buyer he would never have received compensa-tion from the shopkeeper. Or suppose that Nigel had lent the catapult to a friend, and the friend had been injured. *He* would have had no remedy under the Sale of Goods Act.

What if someone suffers an illness after eating at a restaurant a meal which someone else had paid for? In *Buckley* v. *La Réserve*, in 1959, the plaintiff suffered from food poisoning after eating snails at a restaurant. It was understood before the meal began that the plaintiff was the guest of another, so she was not the purchaser of the meal and had, therefore, no claim under section 14. Negligence was not alleged and, indeed, it may well be difficult in a case like this to prove the restaurant knew or should have known the harmful quality of its snails. The restaurant was in breach of the Food and Drugs Act 1955 for sup-plying food which was unfit for human consumption, but this Act merely imposes a criminal penalty – it apparently confers no right on the unfortunate customer to claim damages. The plaintiff's action failed. (In fairness to restaurant owners, it should be added that their strict liability to those customers who do pay for their own meals can involve them in dishonest claims. Dr A. L.

Goodhart has related that one man was found, after careful investigation by insurance companies, to have had the misfortune to find a beetle in his soup in twelve different restaurants!)

There is clearly a need, at least in the context of consumer protection, to reconsider the English rule that benefits under a contract can be enforced only by a party to the contract. This rule, which appears to have developed into its present rigid form during the nineteenth century, has been the subject of searching criticism on historical grounds by Lord Denning, though his points are not accepted by the legal profession. It is ironical that the rule was firmly entrenched in the law by a decision of the House of Lords as recently as 1915, in an important case which struck down the enforcement by a manufacturer of fixed resale prices on the ground that the retailer was not a party to the contract. Authoritative recommendations for the reform of the law were made by the Law Revision Committee in 1937, but they have never been acted on. In 1956, as we shall see in Chapter 11, the rule was abrogated in its application to resale price maintenance, but it remains in most other branches of the law. It has little to justify it beyond legal conservatism, and in its strict form it is virtually confined to the English legal system.

A notable illustration of a more just rule is to be found in the sale of goods provisions of the Uniform Commercial Code which has been adopted by most of the United States. This lays down that promises in the contract of sale, whether they are expressly entered into or are implied under the Code, 'extend to any ... person who is in the family or household of the buyer or who is a guest in his house if it is reasonable to expect that such person may use, consume, or be affected by the goods.' Indeed, with the young borrower of a faulty catapult in mind, we could go a stage further and prescribe that the duties laid on the seller by the Sale of Goods Act should be owed to anyone who might use, consume, or be affected by the goods. The Law Commissions discussed whether to recommend such an extension, but their consultations showed that many lawyers felt that a fuller study of the problems was needed, so no recommendation was made.

THE SELLER'S NEGLIGENCE

There is one way in which the actual user of goods may, if he is injured by them, be able to claim against the seller. He cannot rest his claim on the contract of sale, but he may be able to rely on a more general duty owed to a wider circle. The basis of such a claim is the seller's negligence. For example, in *Kubach* v. *Hollands*, decided in 1937, a thirteen-year-old schoolgirl lost an eye in an accident in the chemistry laboratory. Her teacher had purchased some black powder from retailers. The retailers had labelled it as manganese dioxide but it was in fact another chemical which was dangerous when heated. The manufacturers had not been negligent for they had given notice to the retailers that the powder must be tested before use. But the retailers had not carried out any test, nor had they warned the teacher that a test was necessary. They were therefore negligent and the schoolgirl, although not a party to the contract of sale, was able to obtain £3,000 damages from them. As Lord Hewart, the Lord Chief Justice, said, if they had taken the simple precaution they had been warned to take, no mischief would have followed.

More recently sellers were held liable when the contents of a plastic container of jewellery cleaner unexpectedly shot out and injured the user's eyes: *Fisher* v. *Harrods Ltd* (1966). The sellers had purchased a quantity of the cleaner from a small manufacturer and had not tested or examined it sufficiently closely to become aware of its dangerous qualities or the unsuitability of the container, which bore no warning. They were found to have been guilty of negligence.

The principles which govern a claim based on the seller's negligence are those following from *Donoghue* v. *Stevenson*, the case of the snail in the ginger-beer bottle. They will be considered in more detail, in relation to the manufacturer's liability, in Chapter 4. The mere fact that there are many instances where lack of care on the retailer's part cannot be established, however, means that this liability for negligence is no substitute for an extension of the seller's duties under the Sale of Goods Act which we have advocated above.

INADEQUATE REMEDIES

If there is something wrong with the goods, three possible remedies might reasonably be expected by the buyer: repair or replacement of the faulty goods; money to compensate him for the fault and for any loss it has caused; or his money back and the right to refuse or return the goods.

The first of these remedies he may well obtain as a matter of practice. Many shopkeepers will not hesitate to repair defective goods, or to replace them with a perfect specimen, in order to secure their customer's goodwill, and at least one multiple store has built up a nation-wide reputation with its policy of exchange with no questions asked. But the buyer is completely in the seller's hands, for there is no legal obligation on the seller to repair or replace.

The other two remedies *are* recognized by the law. Indeed, money to compensate the buyer, or 'damages', is the normal and original remedy obtainable from the common law. The object of the award of damages is to put the buyer into the position he would have been in had the seller properly performed the contract, so far as money can do so. Thus if an electric fire is delivered with a faulty element, the cost of repair (which need not be carried out by the original seller) represents the buyer's loss, and can be recovered as damages. If the defect causes other loss or damage, then damages must compensate for that too: it is on this basis that the little boy recovered £2,500 for the injuries caused by his faulty catapult.

Damages were the only remedy available from the common law courts in their early days. In the eyes of the judges there was no injury so bad that money could not make it better, and thus the only remedy for the breach of a 'warranty' given by the seller was money. But sometimes the buyer did not want money to compensate him. If he had been sold inferior goods, the damages would represent the difference in value between perfect goods and the goods he had been sold. In effect he need only pay the true value of the inferior goods – but he would have to keep them, whether he wanted them or not. Unless the goods were completely and literally valueless he could not get his money back – and he never had the right to reject the goods for breach of a warranty, not even if the warranty was given expressly.

It was therefore necessary for a buyer who wanted to call off the purchase completely to treat the seller's promise not as a warranty but as something more important. He could do this by making the contract, or his own performance of it, conditional on the performance of the seller's promise. Thus instead of a mere promise or warranty by the seller that the goods were of merchantable quality, the contract might take the following form: 'If the goods are of merchantable quality, I will buy them. If they are not, I won't.' In this way the term as to merchantable quality would become a *condition* of the contract, and if the condition was not fulfilled the buyer could refuse to pay (or recover his money if he had already paid), and refuse to take the goods.

Even if the seller was in breach of a condition of the contract, the courts would not permit the buyer to keep the matter open indefinitely. The law has always striven for certainty and finality, and once the buyer had discovered the breach of condition, or if he ought to have discovered it, he had to make up his mind what he wanted to do. If he continued to treat the contract as being in existence he would lose his right to reject the goods for breach of condition. Logically, no doubt, he would then be left without any remedy at all, but the courts seem always to have recognized that breach of condition was a greater legal wrong than a breach of warranty and that the greater included the lesser; thus although he may have lost his special rights for breach of a condition, he could still exercise his rights as if the condition had been a warranty – in other words, could claim damages for the breach.

The cases hammered out the detailed rules which showed when the buyer lost his right to reject goods. If the contract was for the sale of a specific, identified article – that plough, for example, or that black mare – the buyer had virtually no right of rejection at all. We have seen that the courts were loath to imply warranties except where the buyer could not have seen the goods he was agreeing to buy; they made it even more difficult for him to rely on conditions, for they took the view that the proper time for the buyer to ensure that the goods were what he wanted – that they were fit for their intended purpose, or of merchantable quality – was *before* the contract was made. Once a contract for a specific article was entered into, the buyer would become the legal owner of it even before delivery; and if he had become its owner, it was too late for the buyer to claim that there was no contract. There was, of course, a logical flaw in this reasoning, but the courts acted on it and Chalmers, in what was perhaps the most unsatisfactory section in his Sale of

Goods Act, accepted it as the law. Until the italicized words were deleted by the Misrepresentation Act 1967, section 11(1) (c) read as follows:

Where ... the buyer has accepted the goods ..., *or where the contract is for specific goods, the property in which has passed to the buyer*, the breach of any condition to be fulfilled by the seller can only be treated as a breach of warranty, and not as a ground for rejecting the goods and treating the contract as repudiated, unless there be a term of the contract, express or implied, to that effect.

Loss of the right to reject by a deliberate act of acceptance, or even by lapse of time, is fair and just. But the attempt to link the loss of important rights with the legal technicalities governing the passing of ownership from the seller to the buyer was both unnecessary and unsatisfactory.

But even before the legislature stepped in, the courts did not always apply the old rule literally. In *Varley* v. *Whipp*, in 1900, Whipp met Varley in Huddersfield and agreed to sell him a 'self-binder' reaping machine then at his farm at Upton. He described the machine as having been used one season and having cut only fifty or sixty acres. When the machine was delivered Varley found it was a very old one, much used and repaired. Varley claimed to reject it: under section 13 of the Sale of Goods Act there is an implied condition that the goods shall correspond with the description, and the condition had plainly been broken. The difficulty was Whipp's argument that the machine fell into the category of 'specific goods', and that under the general rule laid down in the Act the buyer had become the owner of the reaper the moment the contract was made. The court could, perhaps, have launched into a detailed analysis of the law to demonstrate where the fallacy in Whipp's argument lay; but the judges contented themselves with the general statement that they did not think the rules applied to this case. Accordingly, Varley was able to get his money back.

The decision was eminently reasonable, and in keeping with the cases before the Sale of Goods Act which dealt with the sale of goods which the buyer had never seen, but it was difficult (though not impossible) to justify in the light of the statutory provisions. Moreover, its reasoning applied just as strongly to goods which the buyer could not properly examine at the time of sale, even if he could see or handle them. Chalmers, drafting the Act in 1889, did not foresee the purchase of mass-produced, pre-packed articles, or of complicated electrical machinery. In law, a tin of soup may be specific goods, but the buyer cannot discover whether the contents are fit for consumption until he opens it; a washing-machine may be specific too, but its defects are unlikely to reveal themselves until it is in use in the buyer's home.

It became clear that the law was out of touch with trading conditions. Although strictly speaking outside its terms of reference, the Law Reform Committee (in its report on Innocent Misrepresentation) recommended that the buyer should not lose the right to reject goods for breach of condition until, having had a reasonable opportunity fully to examine the goods, he voluntarily accepted them. This recommendation was implemented by the Misrepresentation Act 1967 by repealing the words above in italics in section 11(1) (c) of the Sale of Goods Act.

The real reason for the unsatisfactory state of law was perhaps that the Sale of Goods Act of 1893 came at too early a stage in the development of the legal rules. The courts had already, in many decided cases in the nineteenth century, come to protect the interests of the consumer by saying that the seller owed certain duties to him, and the 1893 Act sought to put those decisions into statutory form. Probably the judges would have continued in the twentieth century to develop the law in the direction of consumer protection but for the strait-jacket of this Act, which gave statutory force to an interim stage in the development of the case law. However, any optimism on this might-have-been of legal history must be tempered by the knowledge that, in the parallel field of hire purchase, the courts failed to give consumers even a modicum of protection and Parliament had to intervene and pass the Hire-Purchase Act of 1938.

EXEMPTION CLAUSES

Another major defect in the protection afforded by the Sale of Goods Act has already been discussed: the perpetuation in the Act of the principle of freedom of contract, so that the implied conditions could, in many cases, be effectively excluded by a simple clause in a contract or order form.

Exemption clauses are not common in cash sales. They are to be found in 'guarantees' of electrical and similar goods, of doubtful legal effect as we shall see in Chapter 4, and they are common in the sale of cars. In the motor trade it is usual for the seller to require the buyer to sign an 'order form' which contains conditions of sale. Among these conditions, almost invariably, is to be found something like 'All conditions and warranties, express or implied, statutory or otherwise, are hereby excluded.'

The Molony Committee recognized that the consumer is entitled to a minimum standard of protection from the law, and in order 'to improve the quality of consumer goods by increasing the liability, and thereby heightening the interest in quality, of those who sell them to the consumer' proposed that sellers should no longer be free to exclude all their obligations, though they saw that it was difficult to justify a general ban on contracting out of implied conditions. If one large industrial concern sells goods to another the contract will usually be studied by lawyers, engineers, and other experts on both sides. The buyer might be prepared to take the risk of faulty goods if the price is reduced to compensate for this. Accordingly the Law Commissions' recommendation in 1969 was that it should not be possible to exclude or restrict any of the implied conditions or warranties under the Sale of Goods Act in consumer sales. A consumer sale would be a sale of consumer goods by a seller in the course of a business where the goods are sold to a buyer in his private capacity (i.e., to a person who does not buy them in the course of a business). The Commissions agreed that in some circumstances business buyers might deserve some protection against exemption clauses. The Supply of Goods (Implied Terms) Bill adopts the view of some of the Commissioners that even in business sales the Court should have the power to strike out an exemption clause if it would not be fair or reasonable to allow the seller to rely on the clause.

The effect of the new Bill, if it becomes law, on exemption clauses in consumer sales is that exemption clauses will be void. The implied condition of merchantable quality in section 14(2) of the Sale of Goods Act 1893 will, however, not operate as regards defects (a) if the defects were specifically drawn to the buyers attention before the contract was made or (b) if the buyer examined the goods before the contract was made and the examination ought to have revealed the defects. The implied condition of fitness for purpose in what will become section 14(3) of the 1893 Act will not operate if it is shown that the buyer did not rely, or that it was unreasonable for him to rely, on the seller's skill or judgement.

SELLER NOT THE OWNER

It sometimes happens that, unwittingly, a buyer purchases goods that are not the seller's to sell – they may be stolen goods, or the seller may merely have possession of them under a hire-purchase agreement. Often a person who has goods on hire purchase really believes he has a right to sell them, but in reality he has no such right until he has paid up the final instalment and become the owner of the goods.

What remedies has a buyer when he discovers the seller had no right to sell to him? On the face of things, a buyer is well provided for by the existing law. Although normally the buyer will have to hand the goods back to the true owner, section 12 of the Sale of Goods Act does give him a right to recover his money from the seller. Other provisions in that Act, in the Factors Act 1889 and in the Hire-Purchase Act 1964 even entitle the buyer, in some circumstances, to retain the goods and enjoy the ownership of them although he has bought them from a non-owner.

Section 12 says that there is an implied condition on the part of the seller of goods that he has a right to sell the goods. *Rowland* v. *Divall*, heard by the Court of Appeal in 1923, shows how useful this provision can be for a buyer. Divall sold a car to Rowland, a motor dealer, for £334, and Rowland resold it to a customer two months later for £400. After a further two months, the police took possession of it because it was a stolen car and Rowland refunded his customer the £400. The Court of Appeal held that Divall, although perfectly innocent, had been in breach of section 12 of the Sale of Goods Act, and Rowland was therefore entitled to recover the £334 he had paid. The Court felt that Rowland could recover the *whole* of the price he had paid without any allowance made for the fact that he or his customer had had four months' use of the car, because he had paid the price not merely to have the use of the car but to become its owner. As Lord Justice Bankes put it: 'he did not get what he paid for – namely a car to which he would have title.'

Reporting in 1966 the Law Reform Committee considered this decision and suggested that it was unjust not to permit the seller to retain part of the price representing the benefit the buyer had had from the use of the car for four months. But it might be equally unjust to the buyer unless he could, after the four months, buy a similar car for a corresponding amount of money less than he originally paid. The Law Commissions, in their 1969 report, thought that the practical problems involved prevented early legislation to change the law in this respect.

SALES IN MARKET OVERT

Although, generally speaking, if a buyer purchases goods from a non-owner, he has no rights to the goods and they must be returned to the original owner, there are instances where the buyer is allowed to retain the goods and to become their owner. One example is where the sale is made in 'market overt', that is, in an 'open, public and legally constituted market.' Provided the buyer is in good faith and does not know of any want of title on the part of the seller, he will be entitled to the ownership even though the seller was not the owner. When is a sale in market overt? Within the ancient City of London all shops are market overt for the goods they usually sell. Thus if stolen jewellery is sold by a jeweller in Fleet Street, which is in the City of London, an innocent buyer will become the owner if the sale is in the normal business hours on a business day in a public part of the shop. But a similar sale by a jeweller in the Strand, which is outside the ancient City, will not be a sale in market overt. Outside the City, shops are not within this principle at all: market overt is limited to the market place in one of England's market towns, where the market was established by an Act of Parliament or in some other legally recognized way, such as Royal Charter. And even then, sales in market overt can only take place on the recognized market days. There is no market overt in Wales or Scotland.

A modern example is the case of *Bishopsgate Motor Finance Corporation* v. *Transport Brakes Ltd*, decided by the Court of Appeal in 1949. A man had possession of a Hillman car under a hire-purchase agreement with a finance company. Very soon after making the agreement, he took the car to Maidstone market on a market day and sold it there to a dealer who reconditioned it and sold it to the defendants. The finance company brought an action to recover the car. The Court of Appeal, however, held that the dealer had purchased the car in good faith in market overt and therefore obtained a good title to it which he had passed on to the defendants. Evidence showed that there had been a market in Maidstone at least since the time of Elizabeth I, established by Royal Charter.

The historical merit of giving this protection to purchasers of goods in market overt was that it helped to stimulate trade; people were encouraged to attend fairs and markets by being able to buy goods without being concerned whether the seller was the owner or not. If the goods were openly displayed the buyer was entitled to assume the seller did own them, and people could attend fairs assured that goods they paid for would belong to them. It was not thought unfair to the original owner whose goods may have been stolen and put on display in the market because, since the goods were openly on display, he always had a fair chance of tracing them. One may wonder now, when there is such a profusion and diversity of retail outlets, and the owner's chance of tracing his goods is, therefore, remote, whether this old rule should be retained.

Professor E. R. Hardy Ivamy, in a public lecture on the revision of the Sale of Goods Act in 1956, asked why a purchase in a shop in the Strand should not be protected while one in a shop in Fleet Street is. He thought that there was little justification for the retention of shops in the City of London within the principle of market overt. On the other hand, in a dispute between the original owner of goods and their innocent purchaser the protection of the purchaser may seem more important, not least because the original owner is better able to protect himself by insurance. If this is accepted, the answer might be to retain the concept of market overt in its application to shops, and to extend it from shops in the City of London to shops throughout the country.

This suggestion is adopted by the Law Reform Committee in its 1966 Report on the Transfer of Title to Chattels. It recommends that a person who buys goods by retail at trade premises or by public auction should acquire the ownership of the goods provided he buys in good faith and without any notice of want of title on the part of the seller.

SALE BY DEALER IN POSSESSION

There are other instances where a buyer's rights are protected although he buys from a non-owner. By virtue of the Factors Act 1889, section 2, if the seller is a dealer who is in possession of goods, say furniture, with the owner's consent, the buyer will obtain a good title to the furniture provided he does not know of any lack of authority to sell on the part of the dealer. As a result of the somewhat curious decision of the Court of Appeal in the 1951 case of *Pearson* v. *Rose and Young Ltd*, if a car dealer is in possession of a motor vehicle with the owner's consent, but is not in possession of the registration book or not in possession of it with the owner's consent, then the purchaser from the dealer will not obtain a good title. Sensible car purchasers do normally ask to see the registration book, but according to this decision even if the dealer is able to produce it, that is no guarantee the dealer obtained it with the owner's consent. If the owner is able to show he did not willingly give the book to the dealer, the purchaser will not obtain a good title to the car. In any legislation designed to amend the existing law, this decision would be a good candidate for statutory reversal so as to protect the innocent purchaser, though if the Law Reform Committee's proposal that a retail purchaser from trade premises should get a good title is implemented, this case will lose its importance.

SALE BY HIRE PURCHASER

As we shall see in Chapter 6, the concept of hire purchase was devised in the late nineteenth century to protect the security of the trader. If he sold goods on credit, he might agree with the buyer that the goods should be returned on non-payment of any part of the price. What if the buyer resold the goods to some innocent purchaser who knew nothing of the original agreement?

Originally the trader could get the goods back, wherever they were, provided his original agreement specified that the ownership of the goods was to remain his until all the price was paid. In order to protect the innocent purchaser in this situation the Factors Act 1889 provided in section 9 that he would acquire the ownership of the goods as long as he knew nothing of the original owner's rights. The hire-purchase agreement was devised to evade the provisions of this Act, and as a result partly of court decisions and partly of the Hire-Purchase Act 1965, the present position is that the trader (or finance company which has taken over the trader's rights) can get the goods back from an innocent purchaser provided that the price is payable by instalments and that the agreement expressly provides that the ownership of the goods is not to pass from the trader until the last instalment is paid.

But there is one important exception to this principle, to be found in Part III of the Hire-Purchase Act 1964. This applies to motor vehicles – cars, vans, lorries, motor-cycles and all mechanically propelled vehicles for use on public roads – held under hire-purchase agreements. If a private purchaser – someone who does not carry on the business of buying and selling vehicles or providing finance for their hire purchase – buys such a vehicle in good faith, not knowing of the hire-purchase agreement, he will acquire the ownership and thus be protected against the original owner. (This protection applies even if the hire-purchase agreement is for more than £2,000.) This is an important inroad into the security afforded to traders and finance companies by hire-purchase agreements, and an important concession in the law in favour of innocent purchasers of cars. It could well be extended to all kinds of goods.

TRADING STAMPS

For many years some shops have tried to attract customers by offering money or gifts to regular patrons. For example, metal tokens used to be given with purchases, each token representing sixpence or a shilling spent: when a specified number of tokens was collected they could be exchanged at the shop for money or goods. Again, we have been familiar with stamps or coupons on packets of tea or breakfast cereal which can be returned in quantity to the manufacturer for money or goods.

Schemes of these kinds take time and money to organize, and are not readily available for smaller shops. In recent years, therefore, companies have been formed to promote such schemes and to offer them to many different shop-keepers. The administration is carried out by the promot-

ing company, which prints the stamps, books in which
to collect them, and catalogues detailing the 'gifts' which
can be purchased with specified quantities of stamps. The
shopkeeper buys the stamps from the promoter, and gives
them to his customers with their purchases. When a
customer has sufficient stamps, he can exchange them with
the promoter for cash or goods.

Much money has been spent on advertising these
schemes and in persuading shopkeepers to participate,
and at one time they seemed to attract more public attention than they rationally deserved. From the shopkeeper's
point of view it seems like a method of cutting prices; but
whereas prices on individual items cannot be cut by less
than half a penny, the price cut or rebate represented by
the trading stamps amounted to much less than that.
Some of the stamps in use at the time of writing, for
example, are said to have a cash value of ·033p each. Thus
1000 of these stamps can be redeemed from the promoter
for 33p in cash. As one stamp represents $2\frac{1}{2}$p spent, 33p
worth of stamps represents £25 spent. Looked at in this
way, stamps scarcely seem a sufficient reason for preferring
one shop to another. It is said that if enough stamps are
saved and they are then exchanged for goods rather than
for cash the customers will find the stamps are worth
more than the advertised cash value; no doubt this is so,
but perhaps the chief attraction of the scheme to the
customer is the pleasure of receiving goods without the
mental association between acquiring the goods and
spending money for them. If all other things are equal – if
the goods are the same quality and price, and the service
and convenience are equal – the shop offering stamps does
afford something which its rival without stamps does not
offer; but the difficulty lies in ascertaining whether all
other things are indeed equal, and not surprisingly an
investigation carried out by the Consumer Council
showed that few shoppers who collected stamps had

worked out their advantages in a rational way. After all, it is difficult enough to compare advertised prices and alleged price cuts between different shops; it is virtually impossible when shopping to compare the prices of everything purchased and then to compensate for the value of trading stamps.

Several legal problems arise from trading stamp schemes of this kind. For example, suppose a scheme is closed down. Does the collector of the stamps, who may have scores of filled books, have any right against the promoter? The difficult question is to decide whether collecting the stamps creates any contract between the collector and the promoter. Or suppose goods supplied in return for stamps are unsatisfactory: what are the promoter's responsibilities? Here the difficulty arises from the fact that if no money changes hands between the stamp collector and the promoter, the supply of goods by the promoter is not a sale to the customer. Thus the implied conditions of fitness for purpose and merchantable quality under the Sale of Goods Act 1893 do not apply.

To some of these questions the Trading Stamps Act 1964 supplies an answer. Although the Act does not entitle the collector to demand goods from the promoter, it does entitle him (or her) to demand cash, and for this reason all stamps issued today must state their cash redemption value. Stamps of the face value of 25p or more may be redeemed for cash on demand. When goods are obtained in exchange for stamps, there are now implied warranties of title and merchantable quality. And the Act also requires certain information – like a notice in shops stating how many stamps customers are entitled to – to be made available. The Act does not apply to stamp or token schemes operated by one shop or group of shops, or by one manufacturer such as the tea or cereal coupons mentioned above. Nor does it apply to the dividend paid by Co-operative Societies, which in law are equated to company dividends payable to shareholders rather than to trading stamp schemes. As a result of amendments to the law proposed by the Supply of Goods (Implied Terms) Bill expected to come into force in 1973, it will not be possible for trading stamp promoters to exclude the warranties of title and merchantable quality implied by the Trading Stamps Act 1964.

In some respects the Act does not go far enough. Its most important omission is its failure to regulate the solvency of trading stamp promoters. In the light of the financial failure of some companies promoting stamp schemes, it does not seem to be unreasonable for the law to ensure that these companies have sufficient financial reserves for them to be able to redeem stamps already being collected.

CHAPTER 4

THE DUTIES
OF A MANUFACTURER

How has the law kept in touch with the changing position of the manufacturer? At a time when craftsmen made their wares and sold them to the user at a face-to-face meeting, the law had no need to lay down special rules: the relationship between the seller and the buyer was a contract, and this contract, described in the previous chapter, formed the basis of legal duties. The direct sale from manufacturer to consumer is now the exception rather than the rule, so that some other basis must be found for the manufacturer's duties to the consumer.

We have seen in Chapter 1 how in the great case of *Donoghue* v. *Stevenson* (1932) the House of Lords, by a majority of three judges to two, established the principle that in certain circumstances a manufacturer owes to the ultimate consumer a duty to be careful. In this chapter we must consider this liability in more detail. But first we must look at the relationship between these two parties to see whether we can spell out any form of agreement between them when the manufacturer does not sell direct to the consumer.

CONTRACT BETWEEN MANUFACTURER
AND CONSUMER

The broad principle is clear. There is no contract, no legally-enforceable agreement, between manufacturer and consumer where there is no direct sale. But this does not mean that there can never be a contract between them. In the modern world of mass-marketing and advertising, brand-images and nation-wide sales campaigns, it is obvious that the manufacturer often plays a far more important role in influencing the consumer than does the retailer; and this role has on occasion been reflected in judicial decisions.

Sometimes there is an express contract, usually entered into after the goods have been purchased. A good example is a contract to service a vacuum cleaner or a washing machine for which the consumer will agree to pay so much a visit. This sort of contract will not be discussed in this chapter, but the relevant principles will be mentioned in Chapter 7. Our immediate concern is a contract the existence of which is not so obvious. There are, in fact, two business activities which might lead to such a contract: an advertising campaign, and a promise to repair or replace contained in a manufacturer's guarantee or warranty.

ADVERTISING

There has been no general acceptance by the law of the idea that an advertising campaign, aimed by the manufacturer at the consumer and designed specifically to influence the consumer, brings the manufacturer into a legal relationship with the consumer. Decided cases in which it has been held that a contract exists between the two parties have been regarded, not as milestones in the development of the law, but as isolated instances. If, in any particular case, an attempt is made by the consumer to claim against the manufacturer, he will have to show that all the necessary elements of a contract exist. The elements relevant to the present context are: an offer by one party, precise and unambiguous enough to warrant enforcement by the courts, which has been accepted by the other party; the intention of being legally bound; and consideration. These technical ideas will become clearer from the examples given below.

There are three main ways in which an advertising offensive may be launched: an itinerant salesman calls on the prospective customer; as a substitute for the salesman, letters are sent by direct mail or by door-to-door delivery; or, most common and least personal of all, space is taken in newspapers, on television or films, or on poster sites.

(a) The Salesman Calls

These are the circumstances which may most easily lead the courts to accept that a direct legal relationship exists. The manufacturer's representative calls on the consumer and makes statements relating to the goods or services to be supplied. If the consumer were then to buy the goods from the manufacturer himself there would be a contract of sale between them and the statements made by the salesman might well have some legal effect: either as representations inducing the consumer to enter into the contract, or as promises which form part of the contract. The distinction between these two concepts was discussed in the previous chapter. It need not be repeated here, but it is clear that in view of the relationship between the parties and of the fact that the manufacturer can be assumed to have more knowledge of his product and of its capabilities than the consumer, there is every probability that such statements would be treated as contractual promises, at least if they were not so vague and imprecise as to be meaningless.

But this is not the problem under consideration. What if the consumer acts on the sales talk by buying the goods, not from the manufacturer himself, but from a local supplier? There is no contract of sale between the manufacturer and consumer, but there may be some other contract.

A good example is afforded by *Shanklin Pier Ltd* v. *Detel Products Ltd*, which came before the High Court

in 1951. As a result of an inquiry they had received, a
director of Detel Products Ltd visited the popular resort
of Shanklin in the Isle of Wight and called on the manag-
ing director of the company which owned the pier. There
he explained the advantages of using a paint, known as
D.M.U., manufactured by his company and recommended
for use on ships. He suggested that two coats should be
used on the pier and promised that it would have a life
of at least seven to ten years.

Persuaded by these statements, the pier company
ordered their painting contractors to use D.M.U. paint,
and the painters bought the paint from the manufacturers and used it. The paint proved to be unsatisfactory
and, so far from lasting seven to ten years, it lasted only
about three months. The expense of repainting almost
immediately amounted to over £4,000.

What remedies did the pier company have? They had
not bought the paint themselves, so that they could not
claim against the manufacturers under the implied condition in section 14(1) of the Sale of Goods Act that the
paint was reasonably fit for its known purpose. Nor could
they claim against the painting contractors, for although
the paint used was not fit for its purpose, the pier company had not relied on the painters' skill or judgement
– indeed, they had themselves specified the paint to be
used.

Mr Kenneth Diplock, k.c. (now Lord Diplock), appear-
ing for the pier company, argued that although there
was no contract of sale between the manufacturers and
his clients there was another contract, created by the
words used by the director of the paint company when
commending D.M.U. paint. Mr Justice McNair accepted
this argument: the promise that the paint would last
seven to ten years became a binding contract when the
pier company accepted it by ordering the painters to use
the paint. Nor was it a gratuitous promise, for the manu-

facturers benefited by the sale of their paint to the contractors.

Nothing turned on the fact that the salesman held a responsible position in the manufacturers' company: he was in fact a director, but the result would no doubt have been the same if he had been an employee, for example a commercial traveller.

(b) Direct Mail Advertising

In principle there should be the same result where the manufacturer's promises are conveyed to the consumer, not by a personal visit but by a letter or a printed brochure. From one point of view the consumer should be in a stronger position, for there can be no argument (as there was in the *Shanklin Pier* case) about the exact words used.

There has been no English decision on the legal effect of this form of advertising, but this may be at least in part due to the vague and non-committal words in which advertising leaflets are often couched. In the *Shanklin Pier* case the judge's finding that the words were spoken was certainly strengthened by the production of a printed pamphlet which claimed that D.M.U. paint would keep a ship free from corrosion for over four years, though the pier company did not seek to base its claim on this pamphlet.

The stumbling block where sales literature is concerned is, no doubt, to find a sufficient intention on the part of the manufacturer to be legally bound by his statements. It is, for example, well-established that the issue of a catalogue listing goods for sale is not an offer to sell the goods advertised, but an invitation to readers of the catalogue to make offers to buy the goods. The effect of this is that the seller need not fulfil an order if he does not wish to do so, or cannot do so. But if he does fulfil an order, it is almost certain that the descriptive terms in the catalogue will form part of the contract. In the same way, if the goods are bought on the faith of a descriptive leaflet, not from the manufacturer who issued the leaflet but from some other supplier, the terms in the leaflet could have contractual force on the same basis as in the *Shanklin Pier* case; to translate the words used from plain English, if they had been written by a lawyer they would no doubt read: 'In consideration of your buying our goods from your local dealer, we promise that...'

An American decision shows that sales pamphlets are capable of having legal effect. The (American) Ford Motor Co. published a catalogue in the 1930s saying that its windscreens were 'shatterproof'; Ford windscreens, it claimed, would 'not fly or shatter under the hardest impact'. Mr Baxter bought a new Ford car from a dealer in the State of Washington, having carefully studied the catalogue. When driving the car a pebble hit the windscreen: it shattered, and Mr Baxter lost an eye. In *Baxter* v. *Ford Motor Co.* (1934) the Washington court held that the statements in the catalogue were intended to be relied upon by intending purchasers; the liability was based on the words used, not on negligence, so Ford's evidence that there was no better or safer windscreen available did not help them.

(c) 'Mass Media' Advertising

Advertising in the press, on television, and so on, is less personal than the advertising we have been considering, but it, too, can create a contract between the manufacturer and the consumer.

If you ask a lawyer whether a consumer can sue a manufacturer in reliance on a newspaper advertisement, you are unlikely to get an immediate, positive 'Yes'. Yet every law student knows the case of *Carlill* v. *The Carbolic Smoke Ball Co.* which entertained the Court of Appeal in 1893.

The story began during the influenza epidemic of 1889–92 with the advertisement which appeared in the *Pall Mall Gazette* of 13 November 1891 (see below).

Mrs Carlill paid her ten shillings to a chemist for a carbolic smoke ball and used it as directed, three times a day, for two months. Then she caught influenza. She sued the manufacturers. They raised every possible legal point to avoid paying and, having lost in the High Court,

---

£100 REWARD

WILL BE PAID BY THE

CARBOLIC SMOKE BALL CO.

To any person who contracts the increasing Epidemic,

INFLUENZA,

Colds, or any diseases caused by taking cold, AFTER HAVING USED the BALL 3 times daily for two weeks according to the printed directions supplied with each Ball.

£1,000

Is deposited with the ALLIANCE BANK, REGENT-STREET, showing our sincerity in the matter. During the last epidemic of Influenza many thousand CARBOLIC SMOKE BALLS were sold as Preventives against this Disease, and in no ascertained case was the disease contracted by those using the CARBOLIC SMOKE BALL.

One **CARBOLIC SMOKE BALL** will last a family several months, making it the cheapest remedy in the world at the price—10s., post free. The BALL can be RE-FILLED at a cost of 5s.   Address :—

CARBOLIC SMOKE BALL CO.,

27, Princes-street, Hanover-sq., London, W.

---

appealed to the Court of Appeal. But they had to pay the £100.

Some of the defences need not detain us – the plea that this was a gambling contract, for instance, or that Mrs Carlill had failed to notify the company that she proposed to use her smoke ball. But three of the arguments are of more general interest.

First is the argument that the advertisement was too

vague to be enforced as a contract. '£100 reward will be paid' was clear enough, but was everyone who used the smoke ball for two weeks permanently protected? There was no time limit and, they argued, 'it cannot be supposed that the advertisers seriously meant to promise to pay money to every person who catches the influenza at any time after the inhaling of the smoke ball'. But the judges did not think the protection would go on for ever. An ordinary person reading the advertisement would think that protection would last for a reasonable period after using the ball, or possibly only while the ball was being used: either way, Mrs Carlill succeeded, for she was still using the ball when she became ill.

Next is the suggestion that the manufacturer's promise was not supported by 'consideration' – that it was a gratuitous promise, the offer of a free gift, and could not therefore be enforced at law. No, said the judges: the inconvenience of using the ball was sufficient, for the law is not concerned with the *adequacy* of consideration – in other words, whether £100 was a fair recompense for the trouble of using the smoke ball. 'But,' added Lord Bowen, with a flash of insight into the purposes of advertising, 'I think also that the defendant [the Smoke Ball Co.] received a benefit [from Mrs Carlill's use of the ball], for the use of the smoke ball was contemplated by the defendants as being indirectly a benefit to them, because the use of the smoke balls would promote their sale.'

Finally, there is the defence that there was no intention to be legally bound by the advertisement – that it was a 'mere puff'. As we saw in the last chapter, the common law gives advertisers a generous (some would say, a too generous) leeway. But the Smoke Ball Co. had been too precise in their terms. Their intention was not to be judged by the courts on the basis of what they said they intended, but on the basis of what they actually said, and what a reasonable man would think that meant. Here they foundered on the £1,000 deposited with a bank, 'showing our sincerity in the matter'. There could be no doubt what a reasonable man would make of that.

How far can we draw from this fascinating case general principles applicable to all advertisements? The decision certainly disposes of the argument that promises contained in advertisements are not supported by 'consideration', but two features in the carbolic smoke ball advertisement stand out and are not often to be found in modern advertising (for, as E. S. Turner put it in his book *The Shocking History of Advertising!*, the case 'is a red light over the desk of the advertising copywriter').

They are the precise, unambiguous promise: '£100 WILL BE PAID'; and the bank deposit as a token of sincerity.

Although the Court pointed to the deposit of £1,000 to support their decision that the advertisement was to be taken seriously – that there was an intention to be legally bound – this is almost certainly not an essential element. In *Wood* v. *Lectrik Ltd*, in 1932, the makers of an 'electric comb' advertised 'What is your trouble? Is it grey hair? In ten days not a grey hair left. £500 Guarantee.' Mr Wood found that after ten days his hair was still grey and that the only result was that the comb had scratched his head. Although there was no bank deposit, Mr Justice Rowlatt held that there was a contract, and Mr Wood won his £500.

But the offer of a precise sum of money is the feature common to these two cases. It is probably true to say that the courts would recognize a contract arising out of a manufacturer's advertisement only if the promise can be spelled out in equally unambiguous terms, though the promise of a sum of money is no doubt not essential. Among enforceable promises, it is thought, may be included 'Money back if not satisfied' (the consumer must act reasonably in being dissatisfied), and a recent adver-

tisement announcing that a well-known paint 'lasts at
least five years'.

If a manufacturer negligently makes a false statement
in an advertisement it could, since the decision of the
House of Lords in *Hedley Byrne & Co.* v. *Heller & Partners* (1963; see p. 231), be argued that the manufacturer is
liable quite apart from any contract. But Professor Harry
Street, a leading authority on this branch of the law,
writes in his Pelican book *Freedom, the Individual and
the Law* that 'in all probability it remains the law that
advertisers will not ordinarily be liable for their false
statements, however carelessly made. Only in the rare
case where the victim could show that the advertiser had
such special skill or knowledge that he would know that
the victim was relying on his statement, so that the advertiser would assume responsibility for its accuracy, would
the victim have a remedy against the advertiser.' One may
wonder whether it is really rare for the manufacturer to
have special skill or knowledge of his own products, yet
it must be conceded that the courts are unlikely to impose liability on this ground except in rare cases.

GUARANTEES

The other way in which a direct contract may come into
existence between a manufacturer and the consumer
stems from the manufacturer's 'guarantee' or 'warranty'.
These are now common with all types of what are known
as 'consumer durables', and especially with electrical and
mechanical goods, ranging from electric toasters to cars.

Much the same principles as those we have discussed in
relation to advertisements apply to guarantees. Indeed,
many guarantees are simply a form of advertisement or
sales gimmick. There can not usually be room for argument as to whether the manufacturer intended to be
legally bound – after all, the guarantee is useless if it is

not to be taken seriously. How far the manufacturer is bound, however, depends on precisely what the guarantee says. Some guarantees are, no doubt, so vague that they could not possibly be treated as contracts.

But the major legal problems in connection with guarantees are concerned with the question whether there is 'consideration' for the manufacturer's promise. 'Consideration' has been defined as a benefit accruing to the party making the promise, or a detriment to the party receiving the promise. Sir Frederick Pollock (1845–1937), a great and prolific legal writer, described consideration as 'the price for which the promise . . . is bought', and it is not always easy to see just what price a buyer has paid to the manufacturer in return for the guarantee.

Where the terms of a guarantee are publicized before the buyer decides to buy, so that the guarantee is a factor which influences the purchaser, Lord Bowen's comment in *Carlill* v. *Carbolic Smoke Ball Co.* would seem to apply: the guarantee promotes the sales of the manufacturer's product and so benefits him. This reasoning would clearly apply to the swing-ticket type of guarantee which is prominently exhibited on the article in the shops.

On the other hand, many guarantees are not evident at the time of purchase; they may, for example, be tucked away in envelopes with instruction cards. Even here, though, the existence of a guarantee with the products of a particular make may be well-known, or there may be mention of a guarantee in advertising literature seen by the buyer, so that the buyer may have been influenced by the guarantee.

The difficult case is where the buyer does not know of the guarantee until after he has bought the goods. The result is that he has paid no price for the guarantee: it did not influence his decision to buy, so that it cannot be said that he suffered the 'detriment' of buying, nor did it benefit the manufacturer directly, for his sales have not been increased by the presence of the guarantee. It may be argued that subsequent discovery of the guarantee tends to advance the manufacturer's reputation and, indirectly, to increase his sales but this would not appear to create a contract between them.

It should be added that the English doctrine of 'consideration' – that a promise, seriously made and made, presumably, for a reason which seemed sufficient at the time, is unenforceable in the courts unless it is supported by this benefit or detriment – has been the subject of considerable legal controversy, and of criticism by distinguished lawyers. It often serves no useful purpose save to enable a person to evade an obligation willingly incurred. But there are many guarantees where the consumer suffers a detriment much more significant than the mere purchase, and much more closely connected with the guarantee, for it is written into the guarantee itself: here it can clearly be described as the price paid for the manufacturer's promise and, without doubt, furnishes consideration.

THE CONTENTS OF GUARANTEES

The contents of most guarantees can be divided into two parts: the manufacturer's promise itself, and the conditions and qualifications which delimit and hedge about the promise. The positive part of the guarantee is usually quite short, and the form suggested to manufacturers of domestic appliances by the British Electrical and Allied Manufacturers' Association may be taken as typical:

The — Company guarantees its domestic appliances for a period of one year from the date of purchase or hire-purchase agreement against mechanical and electrical defects. ...

Accordingly, the Company undertakes to exchange or repair, free of charge, any part found to be defective within the specified period. ...

It will be seen that the manufacturer's obligation under this clause is quite different from that of the seller under the Sale of Goods Act, described in Chapter 3. The seller is under no legal obligation to repair or to replace: instead, he may have to return the price paid or, more often, to pay the cost of repair. The manufacturer's undertaking on the other hand is at the same time wider – he commits himself to doing work on the goods or to replacing faulty goods or parts – and narrower – he need not pay the cost of repairs done elsewhere, and the guarantee puts him under no obligation to pay compensation for damage caused by the defect.

The other part of the guarantee varies more from manufacturer to manufacturer. The guarantee card taken from an electric kettle manufactured by A.E.I.-Hotpoint Ltd is illustrated opposite; this is particularly favourable to the consumer, for it contains an express obligation to pay all costs of carriage and labour. Not all guarantees are as satisfactory as this from the consumer's point of view, however, and a variety of clauses attempting to limit or exclude the consumer's rights can be found.

For example, many guarantees purport to make the manufacturer the sole judge in any dispute which arises with the consumer, as in the following:

Our decision on all questions relating to alleged defects shall be conclusive.

Such clauses are no doubt useful to the manufacturer in fortifying his argument with a customer, but they do not in law take away the consumer's right to go to court to settle a genuine dispute. In the striking words of Lord Justice Scrutton (1856–1934) in 1922, 'There must be no Alsatia in England where the King's writ does not run,' and any attempt to exclude the jurisdiction of the courts is held to be against the policy of the law and completely ineffective. Another legal maxim supports the consumer:

'No man shall be a judge in his own cause.' Not even a judge may try a case in which he has a direct personal interest – and few manufacturers would claim the conscious impartiality of one of Her Majesty's judges.

GUARANTEE

We, A.E.I.-Hotpoint Limited guarantee that should any defect in workmanship or material occur in this Hotpoint Hi-Speed Kettle within TWELVE MONTHS from the date of purchase we will repair or, at our option replace the defective part FREE OF ANY CHARGE for labour or for materials, or for carriage on condition that the appliance:

(a) has been used only on the supply circuit or voltage range stamped on the rating place.

(b) has been used only for normal domestic purposes and has not been tampered with or been subject to accident.

(c) has not been taken apart, except by a person authorised by us.

(d) has not been used outside Great Britain and Northern Ireland.

A.E.I.-HOTPOINT LIMITED
33 GROSVENOR PLAGE, LONDON, S.W.1

But perhaps the most important of these clauses is one which deliberately sets out to take away from the consumer the rights he has under the general law. Sometimes this says:

This guarantee excludes all express and implied conditions and warranties, statutory or otherwise.

Such wording seems to have no legal effect, for apart from the guarantee there is normally no contract between the manufacturer and the buyer and therefore no conditions and warranties to be excluded. In so far as the manufacturer's promise contained in the guarantee itself may be regarded as a condition or a warranty, this clause could hardly exclude it (the principles were discussed in Chapter 2), though it might conceivably be argued that this clause excludes a manufacturer's liability for statements in his advertisements, if any. 'Conditions and warranties' are, of course, apt to describe the seller's liability under the Sale of Goods Act, but unless he too is made a party to the guarantee, and the terms of the guarantee are accepted by the buyer *before* he buys the goods, such a clause could not take away the buyer's rights against the seller. Perhaps the only common example where this is done is on the sale of a new car, and this is usually effected by putting the clause cited into the order form (representing the terms of the contract between the buyer and the seller) rather than (or as well as) in the guarantee (or 'warranty') given by the manufacturer.

Another form of wording (which may be additional to that just referred to) is, however, more serious:

This guarantee is in lieu of, and expressly excludes, all liability to compensate for loss or damage, howsoever caused.

The effect of this, if it forms part of a contract between buyer and manufacturer, is to exclude the manufacturer's legal liability for loss or damage caused by his negligence. Paradoxically, however, this very clause – because it takes away rights the buyer would otherwise have – can furnish the 'consideration' necessary to render the manufacturer's obligation to repair or replace into a legally-enforceable contract. The effect of such a clause is, it should be emphasized, not as far-reaching as it may at first appear, for the manufacturer's liability for negligence extends, as we shall see, to other people as well as the buyer personally, whereas this clause can only take away the rights of the buyer, the person who becomes a party to the contract.

NEGLIGENCE

The manufacturer's liability for loss or damage caused by his negligence – or by the negligence of his employees – does not arise out of a contract or agreement, but out of a duty imposed by the law. It is a civil wrong, or 'tort'. But negligence does not simply mean 'carelessness': if you are injured, physically or financially, as a result of someone else's carelessness it does not necessarily follow that you can sue that person for negligence. For you must show three things in order to succeed: (a) that the defendant owed you a *duty* to take reasonable care; (b) that he *broke* that duty by failing to take reasonable care; and (c) that his breach of duty resulted in foreseeable *damage*.

The importance of *Donoghue* v. *Stevenson*, the 'snail in the ginger-beer' case which came to the House of Lords in 1932 (described on p. 30), was the decision of the majority judges that the manufacturer of goods owes a duty to the ultimate consumer, with whom he is not in any contractual relationship. In striking words which are often quoted Lord Atkin expressed his conception of the philosophy which lies behind the civil wrong known as 'negligence':

The rule that you are to love your neighbour becomes in law, you must not injure your neighbour; and the lawyer's question, Who is my neighbour? receives a restricted reply. You must take reasonable care to avoid acts or omissions which you can reasonably foresee would be likely to injure your neighbour. Who, then, in law is my neighbour? The answers seems to be – persons who are so closely and directly affected by my act that I ought reasonably to have them in contemplation as being so affected when I am directing my mind to the acts or omissions which are called in question.

Not only does the manufacturer owe a duty to the buyer of his goods, therefore; he owes the duty to all persons whom he ought reasonably to have in contemplation. In *Donoghue* v. *Stevenson* itself, Mrs Donoghue was not the buyer (if she had been, she could have sued the café proprietor for breach of contract); nevertheless, the manufacturer of the ginger-beer ought to have contemplated that persons other than purchasers would drink the beer, and that they would be closely and directly affected by his acts in making and bottling the ginger-beer. He therefore owed her a legal duty to be careful. In another case, *Stennett* v. *Hancock and Peters* (1939), the flange on the wheel of a lorry came off, mounted the pavement, and injured a passer-by. It was held that the owner of the garage which had negligently fixed the flange ought reasonably to have contemplated that a passer-by might be injured, and so owed him a duty of care.

The second element in a claim of negligence is a failure to take reasonable care – a breach of the duty of care. The failure to be careful might arise at almost any stage in the manufacturing process, from the original design until the final inspection, packing, and labelling. The most difficult problem here arises from the rule that it is for the plaintiff in a civil law suit to prove his case. Often the consumer can do no more than to say: 'This is what happened. This doesn't usually happen, isn't supposed to happen, and wouldn't have happened if the manufacturer had taken reasonable care.' It is likely that such an argument would have been successful in *Donoghue* v. *Stevenson* itself, for the very presence of a snail in a bottle of ginger-beer leads one to think that reasonable care was lacking. (Strangely enough, we cannot be quite sure that

Mrs Donoghue would have won her case in court: the appeal to the House of Lords was decided on the legal issues, without calling evidence, assuming for the sake of the legal argument that she could prove all the facts she alleged. She won on the point of law, and the case was then settled out of court for £100 before evidence was given.)

This sort of argument was subsequently successful in *Grant* v. *Australian Knitting Mills Ltd* (1936), where Mr Grant contracted dermatitis from an excess of chemicals in a pair of underpants he bought. He could not show how the chemicals got there, but he could show that when he bought them the pants were still in their wrapping as they had left the manufacturer. The Judicial Committee of the Privy Council (hearing his appeal from the High Court of Australia) thought that the only inference was that the manufacturer had not been sufficiently careful.

More recently, in *Steer* v. *Durable Rubber Manufacturing Co. Ltd* (1958), a six-year-old girl was scalded by a faulty hot-water bottle. She could not sue the chemist who sold it, even though it was not reasonably fit for its purpose, because her father had bought the bottle and she was not herself a party to the contract. She therefore sued the manufacturers, claiming that the defect in the bottle was due to their failure to take reasonable care. How could she prove this?

She was able to show that a hot-water bottle was expected to last for at least three years, and that this bottle had split after only three months. That evidence, said Lord Jenkins, called for an explanation by the manufacturers of how a bottle which was defective and dangerous was allowed to get into the hands of an unsuspecting member of the public. In other words, the onus of proof had shifted, and it was for the manufacturers to show that they had not been negligent, or to give some explanation of the cause of the accident which did not connote negligence. Although they proved that this accident was quite unprecedented and that they had produced nearly a million bottles, all satisfactory, in the previous year, no explanation of how the fault occurred without negligence was given. The manufacturers were therefore held liable, and the Court of Appeal affirmed the award of £75 damages to the little girl.

It must be emphasized that whereas the seller's liability under the Sale of Goods Act does not involve any imputation of fault on the seller's part, the manufacturer's liability is essentially based on fault. If the manufacturer can show the court that the defect was not his fault – if he can prove that the defect occurred in a way which could not reasonably have been foreseen or guarded against – he will not be liable. 'The duty owed to the consumer by the manufacturer,' said Mr Justice Lewis, 'is not to ensure that his goods are perfect. All he has to do is to take reasonable care to see that no injury is done to the consumer.' In *Daniels and Daniels* v. *R. White & Sons Ltd and Tabard* (1938), from which these words are taken, the consumer had drunk a bottle of lemonade which contained a large quantity of carbolic acid. This probably came from the manufacturer's washing and disinfecting plant, but the judge accepted their evidence that their system was 'foolproof' and that *reasonable* care had been taken to prevent such an occurrence. On the other hand, one must bear in mind that whether the care taken in a particular case is reasonable depends, among other things, on how serious is likely to be the effect of a want of care. Over thirty years have passed since *Daniels* v. *White and Tabard* and if a similar accident occurred today the manufacturer might find it harder to convince a court that he had taken reasonable care.

It may not always be easy to convince the court that the defect was caused by the manufacturer's fault. In *Evans* v. *Triplex Safety Glass Co. Ltd* (1936) the plaintiff bought a car fitted with a windscreen manufactured by the defendants. A year later occupants in the car were injured when without warning the windscreen shattered. The defendants were held not liable, for the breaking of the glass might have been caused by something other than a fault in manufacture, and a long time had elapsed since the windscreen left the factory.

The first elements of a claim based on negligence have been discussed: the existence of a duty to take care, and breach of that duty. The third element is damage resulting from the breach of duty. Here the law is still in the process of developing, and there is some uncertainty as to the exact circumstances in which a claim may be brought.

If the defective goods cause physical injury to the consumer, as in all the examples so far cited, this type of damage can clearly be made the basis of a negligence claim. So, too, if physical damage is caused to property: if, for example, a faulty electrical appliance causes a fire which damages curtains and furniture. On the other hand, if no injury or damage is caused – if, let us say, the faulty hot-water bottle split without hurting anybody – it is arguable that the manufacturer is under no direct liability to the consumer for the cost of repair or replacement of the bottle itself. As Lord Atkin put it in *Donoghue* v. *Stevenson*, a manufacturer owes the consumer a duty to take reasonable care where the absence of care 'will result in an injury to the consumer's life or property': whether this includes the financial injury caused by damage to the article itself is still uncertain.

Another limit is to be found in the notion of foresight: the manufacturer is not liable for all loss caused as a result of his negligence, but only for loss which he could reasonably have foreseen. Thus the manufacturer of a car can reasonably foresee that a defect in the steering mechanism might cause an accident, that it might injure the driver of the car, passengers, and other road users (including the occupants of other cars and pedestrians); he can, moreover, foresee that such injuries might involve not only pain and suffering but also medical and nursing expenses; but he cannot reasonably foresee that one of the injured parties was on his way to a business meeting and might lose a profitable deal as the result of the accident. That sort of damage would be too remote from the manufacturer's negligence to entitle the businessman to compensation for his business losses.

THE VALUE OF THE TORT OF NEGLIGENCE

The idea that there is a general legal principle enjoining reasonable care developed comparatively recently, but it is today the most important of all torts. Perhaps the fundamental social value of liability for being negligent is that this liability encourages the taking of care. Who can doubt that, in all walks of life, some people would be less careful if there were no sanctions visited on carelessness? Furthermore, once there has been damage or injury caused by carelessness, the legal liability seeks to place the financial burden (it can do nothing about the burden of pain and inconvenience) on the person who caused the damage rather than on the person who suffered it.

Thus the tort of negligence serves useful purposes in our society: we should be worse off if this liability did not exist. Yet, as we have seen, it is possible for a manufacturer to enter into a contract with the consumer – typically, in a 'guarantee' – whereby the consumer agrees to exclude the manufacturer's liability for negligence. Although the courts view such contracts with disfavour, as shown in Chapter 2, they have recognized that a suitably drawn clause can exclude liability for negligence (though so far the courts have never had to consider such a clause in a manufacturer's guarantee).

If this principle of negligence has such a valuable function, why should not an Act of Parliament prohibit clauses excluding or restricting liability? The Molony Committee did not support this idea, but the English and Scottish Law Commisions are now studying this question. In a Working Paper published in 1971 they put forward for consultation the suggestion that manufacturers should not be permitted to exclude liability for negligence by a clause in a guarantee.

Underlying the Molony Committee's conclusions on guarantees was an unrealistic attitude to the relationship between consumer and manufacturer. The Committee recognized that, more and more, the consumer relies on the manufacturer rather than the retailer. Advertising, the impact of brand names, and the complexity of so many mechanical and electrical goods all tend to encourage the consumer to look to the manufacturer for quality, performance, and the rectification of complaints. Despite this development, the Committee said: 'We are in no doubt, however, that the consumer should be encouraged to regard the retailer as the person primarily responsible for the soundness of goods bought.' This was the premise from which the Committee made its recommendations, rather than the conclusion at which it arrived after considering the evidence.

Yet common sense will tell the consumer that if a new car has brakes which are poorly designed for the job they have to do, or if a washing machine has incorrect electrical connections, it is the manufacturer who is responsible. Not merely should the manufacturer not be permitted to shelter behind an exemption clause in a guarantee if damage is caused: there is much to be said for a far more fundamental change in our legal concepts, even if no damage or injury results. It would be possible, for example, to jettison our emphasis on the parties to a particular contract of sale which gives the buyer (and no one else) rights under the contract against the seller (and no one else). We could recognize that the manufacturer sells the goods – to a wholesaler or other distributor – intending them to be re-sold one or more times until they ultimately reach the consumer, and enable the consumer to enforce directly the obligations in the contract of sale by the manufacturer even though the consumer is not a party to that contract. Clauses excluding liability in that contract would, of course, be forbidden. Some of the United States of America (each State has its own system of law) have indeed achieved this result; in New Jersey, for example, it has been held (quite apart from the Uniform Commercial Code, referred to on p. 84 above) that there is an 'implied warranty of merchantability' on the part of the manufacturer of a car which benefits not only the ultimate buyer but also members of the buyer's family and other persons occupying or using the car with his consent.

Perhaps a radical change in the legal position of manufacturers is on its way. In December 1972 the Government announced a Royal Commission, to be chaired by Lord Pearson, to inquire into the basis of civil liability for causing death or personal injury. As we have seen, the main bases of that liability are at present a direct contract or negligence; without a contract, few claims can succeed unless negligence is proved. Among other matters the Pearson Commission is to consider the basis of liability for death or injury caused 'through the manufacture, supply or use of goods or services'. It will be some years before its report is available.

The Molony Committee's one positive suggestion was that 'the consumer must be left to secure protection by his own vigilance'. The consumer might, for example, delete from any guarantee card which he is asked to sign a clause excluding the manufacturer's common-law duties. If the manufacturer accepts the altered guarantee it will be effective in its amended form. But if the manufacturer does not accept it, or fails to reply at all, the guarantee will be ineffective for all purposes.

Nevertheless, until exemption clauses are controlled by Act of Parliament, action such as this may be worth while. It is one of the ways in which consumers can make their influence felt, and it may encourage manufacturers themselves to revise their guarantees. For many years guarantees were accepted uncritically, and only lawyers realized that some guarantees tried to take away more than they gave. Then both *Which?* and *Shopper's Guide* published articles which explained just what these documents meant. Some consumers struck out offending clauses. Manufacturers became conscious of public feeling, and many of them set about revising their guarantees. The British Electrical and Allied Manufacturers' Association recommended to its members who make domestic appliances a guarantee which does not take away rights, and the Retail Trading-Standards Association, whose members are retailers and manufacturers, also approved a similar form. The Advertising Association's *British Code of Advertising Practice* recommends, in a rule laid down by the Advertising Standards Authority in 1966, that: 'No advertisement should contain a direct or implied reference to a guarantee which purports to take away or diminish the statutory or common-law rights of the purchaser.'

These developments highlight the Molony Committee's succinct comment: 'The consumer's first safeguard must always be an alert and questioning attitude. This in itself will supply a valuable stimulus to commerce.' Whether this is enough is, unfortunately, open to doubt.

CHAPTER 5

CRIMES AGAINST THE CONSUMER

DESPITE the criticisms which can be made of the law described in the previous chapters, it is evident that there is a substantial amount of protection already afforded to the consumer. Yet however complete and favourable the framework of legal protection is, it might as well not exist if the rules are not adequately enforced, if they can be ignored with impunity. And, sad to relate, they often can be ignored without fear of the consequences.

The law we have described is the civil law: the branches of the law concerned with individual rights. If a person's rights are infringed – if, for example, the goods he buys are not of merchantable quality – it is up to him to take action in the civil courts. If he is successful, he will obtain damages from the party held liable – compensation for his loss in the form of a money payment. In exceptional cases the result of a civil action may be an order that the other party must carry out his contractual promise (a decree of specific performance) or that he must stop doing something (an injunction).

But there is little incentive for the individual consumer to take civil proceedings when there is not much money at stake. Civil actions over small sums are an expensive luxury. Moreover the consumer, as an individual, suffers from inertia, lack of energy, an unwillingness to cause trouble and, very often, lack of interest because only a few pounds are involved. In this lies the temptation to suppliers of goods and services, a temptation not necessarily to be dishonest, but to depress standards of care and quality; the profit from each individual consumer may be tiny, but the aggregate profit could be substantial.

Thus the need to protect the public as a whole, rather than as individuals, must be met by some machinery which does not rely on action by isolated individuals. And it is to the criminal law that we can look for proceedings, taken by public officials at the public expense, which maintain high standards of moral conduct in trade. The individual who has been wronged may not perhaps benefit financially from the court proceedings, for the object of a criminal case is not compensation for the injured party but punishment for the guilty party, although he shares in the benefit to the community as a whole.

The main target of the criminal law is dishonesty, and for centuries it has offered some protection against the most blatant kind of cheating. For example, in 1705 two men, one calling himself a 'broker', and the other a 'Portuguese merchant', purported to sell Port wine; their ware was in fact beer mixed with vinegar and coffee grounds. They were convicted of a criminal offence. In 1877 a door-to-door hawker called on a Leicestershire housewife and offered her 'good tea' at 2s. 3d. a pound. The county analyst showed that the bags he sold contained a mixture of tea, sand, quartz, and iron oxide. The hawker was sentenced to six months imprisonment for obtaining money by false pretences. In 1971 a magazine salesman went from house to house in Sussex falsely saying that he was a student taking part in a competition and that the student who sold most magazines would win a trip to the Far East. He was convicted under the Theft Act 1968 of dishonestly obtaining money by deception and sent to prison for five months.

These were merely applications of the ordinary criminal law to dishonest trading. But special legislation to restrain trading abuses has also been with us for a very long time. The regulation of weights and measures, and control of gold and silver, date back to the Middle Ages. The Assize of Bread and Ale in the thirteenth century prescribed measures for those two commodities, and the Statute of the Pillory soon afterwards laid down that:

If a Baker or a Brewer be convict, because he hath not observed the Assize of Bread and Ale, ... if the Offence be grievous and often, and will not be corrected, then he shall suffer Punishment of the Body, that is to wit, a Baker to the Pillory, and a Brewer to the Tumbrel ...

The same statute also punished the use of false weights and measures, and the sale by butchers of 'contagious flesh', and it controlled bakers' profits.

For many centuries this sort of detailed control was concerned with staple commodities such as bread, corn, ale, and wine, and with the very important wool trade. The only standards of quality which have been protected continuously from medieval times to the present are those for gold and silver, platinum being added more recently. The object of much of this legislation was not to protect the consumer, but to protect honest traders. Thus, the force behind the hall-marking system has always been goldsmiths and silversmiths, who have sought to prevent the importation of poor quality wares, and undercutting by the sale of inferior goods. But such legislation – and notably weights and measures statutes – served to protect the consumer as well.

Not until the nineteenth century did the modern pattern of legislation take its shape. The stimuli were, of course, the industrial revolution, leading thousands of workers into the towns, and the growing population of this country. The prime considerations were the health of the community, the fear of epidemics and disease, and the prevention of malnutrition. Even today much of the legislation is concentrated on the sale of foodstuffs.

Important though it is, there will be no account here of the controls exercised by the Ministry of Agriculture, Fisheries and Food over the production of milk and dairy products, nor of the regulation of dangerous drugs. The topics to be dealt with are: weights and measures; standards of quality and composition; and false or misleading trade descriptions.

WEIGHTS AND MEASURES

The control of the use of weights and measures takes three main forms:

    (*a*) inspection of weighing and measuring devices by Weights and Measures Inspectors;

    (*b*) penalties for giving short weight or measure;

    (*c*) the labelling of quantity on packages.

Until relatively recently a great deal of the law was contained in the Weights and Measures Act 1878, though there had been important amendments through the years, notably in the Sale of Food (Weights and Measures) Act 1926. For many years there had been a growing feeling that the law was out of date and inadequate, and in 1948 the then President of the Board of Trade appointed a committee to consider the whole problem. The committee (known as the Hodgson Committee, after its chairman) reported in December 1950, and called for many changes in the law. Not until 1963 was a new Weights and Measures Act passed by Parliament, embodying some (but not all) of the recommendations of the Hodgson Committee. Small wonder that the Molony Committee expressed the hope that their own recommendations would not suffer the same 'monumental delay'.

(a) Inspection

The earliest aim of weights and measures legislation was to establish national standards: to ensure that a pint of ale was the same in York as it was in London. Magna Carta itself laid down that 'One measure of Wine shall be throughout our Realm, and one measure of Ale, and one measure of Corn'. But not until 1878 was a full-scale national system of control and inspection established.

Weights and measures inspectors are employed by local authorities but must qualify by passing examinations administered by the Department of Trade and Industry. One of their functions is to inspect regularly all equipment for weighing and measuring – scales, weights, pint measures, rules, petrol pumps, to name but a few – which is 'in use for trade'.

All weights and measures in use for trade must be verified and stamped by an inspector of weights and measures, and the use of unstamped appliances, or even the mere possession of them for use, is an offence. But the stamping of equipment depends on detailed regulations made by the Department of Trade and Industry, and there are many appliances in existence for which no regulations have been made, such as fabric measuring instruments found in draper's shops, milk-measuring instruments, and 'bulk flowmeters' for petrol and fuel oil. This is what the Hodgson Committee said in 1950:

> In the absence of regulations. no penalties are incurred by the use of unstamped appliances of these types; and there is in effect no direct control over their accuracy. This is a most unsatisfactory state of affairs; and we strongly recommend that the Department should, as a matter of urgency, undertake the revision of all the existing regulations and the promulgation of such new regulations as are necessary.

No new Act of Parliament was needed to do this: but no regulations have been made in response to this urgent call. Perhaps they will one day be made under the powers contained in the 1963 Act.

(b) Short Weight

The protection of the public against short weight or measure is a comparatively recent development but, to consumers, it is the keystone of weights and measures control. The inspection and testing of weights, scales and measures is, of course, of great importance in this protection. But accurate equipment is one thing; careful and honest use of that equipment is another.

To some extent the consumer can, and should, protect himself. It is a small matter to watch the actual weighing process to see whether, for example, the pan has come to rest before the goods are whipped into a bag. But what protection does the law give against short weight or measure? Since 1878 wilful fraud in the use of weights or measures has been a criminal offence. In 1926 it became an offence to sell less food than was purported to be sold. There were separate statutes for certain commodities such as coal and sand. But not until the Weights and Measures Act of 1963 was there a general provision in the law prohibiting the giving of short weight, even where no fraud can be proved. The rule is now to be found in section 24(1) of the 1963 Act:

... any person who, in selling or purporting to sell any goods by weight or other measurement or by number, delivers or causes to be delivered to the buyer a lesser quantity than that purported to be sold or than corresponds with the price charged shall be guilty of an offence.

It will be seen that this vital provision only applies where goods are sold by weight or other measurement, or by number. The 1963 Act lists many goods which must be sold in this fashion, including solid and liquid fuels, soap, ribbon, nails, paint, polishes, and many foodstuffs. For all these goods the quantity must be made known to the buyer. Sometimes this will be done in writing, but the Act is complied with if the goods are weighed, measured or counted in the buyer's presence. A controversial provision permitted the Department of Trade and Industry to authorize a 'do-it-yourself' weighing procedure: this envisages that a weighing machine will be kept available in a convenient position so that the buyer can weigh the goods himself if he wishes; the Act requires a prominent notice, but not necessarily a prominent weighing machine. The major weakness of the Act, however, is that there is no express requirement that the buyer must be told the price per pound or per pint. Without this, knowledge of the weight or measure affords relatively little protection.

If goods must, under the 1963 Act, be sold by weight, it is an offence to expose them for sale otherwise than by weight. In *Lucas v. Rushby*, which came before the Queen's Bench Divisional Court in 1966, the Home and Colonial Stores Ltd at their Scunthorpe branch displayed in the shop window cuts of meat, bacon and ham, each labelled with a price but not stating the weight. When a customer chose a cut it was taken from the window and weighed in his presence. It was nevertheless held that an offence had been committed by the manager of the shop as the meat had been exposed for sale otherwise than by weight.

The Hodgson Committee refused to support a proposal that all articles must be sold by weight, measure, or number: a rule such as this, they felt, 'might well result in a raising of the price or a lowering of the quality to the consumer; and the attempt at protection would thereby have defeated its own ends.' The reasoning here (if, indeed, this comment was a reasoned one) is muddled. Apart from milk there is no control on price nor, with some exceptions, on quality. There is therefore nothing to stop fluctuations in price or quality whatever the legal rules. Moreover, such a rule would permit knowledge of, and comparison of, the price, which is not always possible at the moment. Price fluctuations would no longer be hidden. Fortunately the Act does now specify that many pre-packed articles must be marked with the weight or measure.

(c) Pre-packed Goods

Much of the food we buy these days is pre-packed. It is rare to see a shop assistant weighing sugar or tea for the individual customer, or patting butter into shape on the scales. Many foods, including, of course, the whole range of tinned and frozen foods, are packed by machinery on a large scale; other foods may be delivered in bulk to the retailer, but packed before sale to save time or to make them available for self-service.

As we have seen, not all goods must be sold by weight or measure. But if foods are stocked by a shopkeeper in bulk, they will normally be sold in specified quantities – by the pound or by the pint – no matter what the law says. In practice, therefore, the consumer obtains some protection. The same foods, however, may be sold by the packet or by the tin if pre-packed. And for this reason it can be taken as a general rule that (with some exceptions) pre-packed food must be marked with the weight or measure of the contents. The weight must usually be the net weight – the weight of the food itself; but for certain foods, such as butter (when sold from bulk) and similar commodities, the weight marked may be the gross weight – the weight of the packet as a whole, including the wrapper or container, provided the wrapper itself does not exceed the weights laid down.

The 1963 Act also lists a number of other pre-packed articles which must be marked with their weight or measure, including perfumes and toilet preparations, toothpaste, soap, and detergents.

STANDARDS

The control of standards of quality and composition or construction is more detailed for foodstuffs than for other goods. False or misleading trade descriptions, including descriptions of quality, will be considered later, but for most goods no standards are laid down by law.

Where standards do exist for consumer goods other than food or drugs they are generally imposed in the interests of health or safety. Exceptions include the statutes prohibiting the sale of gold, silver, and platinum unless hallmarked (designed to protect the trade, the economy and, originally, the currency), the Seeds Act 1920 (imposing standards for seeds, including some used in the garden) and the Fertilizers and Feeding Stuffs Act 1926 (regulating the composition of fertilizers); these last two were passed primarily to benefit British agriculture. The Gun Barrel Proof Acts of 1868 and 1950 prohibit the sale of guns by any person unless the gun has been examined and tested by one of the proof houses in London or Birmingham and bears a proof mark: these Acts, introduced into Parliament by gunmakers in the interest of public safety, are private Acts of Parliament not to be found in the ordinary collections of statutes, yet they bind all persons.

Modern safety legislation is, however, of limited scope at the moment. The Rag Flock and Other Filling Materials Act of 1951, replacing earlier Acts, regulates the purity and cleanliness of fillings used in cushions, upholstery and mattresses. The Fabrics (Misdescription) Act 1913 is narrower in its effect than its title suggests: it prohibits the sale of any textile fabric, whether in the piece or made up into garments, to which is attributed expressly or by inference the quality of non-inflammability or safety from fire, unless it conforms to prescribed standards. These standards were brought up to date in 1959 to take account of new research by the British Standards Institution. Under the Road Traffic Act 1972 it is an offence to sell or hire crash helmets for motorcyclists, or rear lights or reflectors, unless they comply with the appropriate British Standards specifications; nor may a

car or other vehicle be sold unless it measures up to the
Motor Vehicles (Construction and Use) Regulations 1969
(some of the details of which can be found summarized in
the Highway Code).

Until recently each new standard required a fresh Act
of Parliament. The Molony Committee issued an interim
report in 1960 dealing solely with hazards to life and limb
caused by consumer goods and expressing concern at the
possible delays when legislation was needed. They recommended that statutory power to deal with dangerous
goods 'should exist in advance of the demonstrable need'
and advocated early legislation to this effect. This resulted
in the Consumer Protection Act 1961 which gives the
Home Secretary a general power to make regulations
about any goods in order to protect the public from the
risk of death, injury, or disease. The regulations may deal
with composition, design, or construction and with labels
or instructions. Not many regulations have been made.
Gas, electric, and oil fires must not be sold or hired unless
fitted with a guard tested in a specified way to ensure that
it will prevent clothes touching the flame or element (it
offers only limited protection against children's prying
fingers); these regulations were originally made under an
Act of 1952. Other regulations deal with oil heaters burn-
ing paraffin; since 1962 these must bear a warning and
comply with the detailed safety tests laid down in the
regulations. Children's nightwear must be made of non-
flammable material. Stands for carry-cots must be of
specified dimensions and strength. The lead content of the
paint on toys is controlled, and toys must not be made of
celluloid (though this does not apply to ping-pong balls).
The colour coding for wiring in electrical appliances must
comply with that laid down in regulations, and until
1977 they must be sold with a label explaining the code.
As from 1972 standards and warning labels for electric
blankets are prescribed.

In its final report in 1962 the Molony Committee drew
attention to dangers in the sale of electrical toys: the
danger of shock unless the voltage was limited to twenty
volts, and the dangers from electrical transformers used
with toys if they failed to comply with recognized safety
standards like those in the relevant British Standard. The
Committee called for action under the Consumer Protection Act, but the Government has not yet acted. Unfortunately the enforcement of the Consumer Protection
Act is irregular and patchy, for no clear duty is imposed
on local authorities to enforce the regulations. However,
since 1971 the prosecution procedure has been improved:
if a retailer is brought to court it is now possible to take
proceedings against the manufacturer or importer as well
as a result of the Consumer Protection Act 1971.

Foodstuffs are subject to much more control than other
goods. Since the 'Act for preventing the Adulteration of
Articles of Food and Drink' in 1860, fourteen sections
long, legislation has been of enormous importance, and
the present Food and Drugs Act of 1955 (137 sections
and twelve schedules), and the regulations made under it,
give considerable protection to the consumer. The main
object is, of course, to ensure that food is pure and whole-
some and fit for human consumption. But in addition the
important section 2 lays down that 'If a person sells to the
prejudice of the purchaser any food or drug which is not
of the nature, or not of the substance, or not of the quality
of the food or drug demanded by the purchaser, he shall
. . . be guilty of an offence.' In effect, this section adds the
sanctions of the criminal law to the purchaser's right
under the Sale of Goods Act 1893 to take civil proceedings against the seller if the goods do not correspond with
the description in the contract.

In proceedings under section 2 of the Food and Drugs
Act the court usually has to decide whether the food supplied is or is not of the nature, substance or quality de-

manded. Sometimes there can be no real argument: if beef is demanded and horseflesh supplied, or if margarine is supplied when butter is ordered, an offence has been committed. But the answer is not always so clear. May a confection not made with egg-white be sold as 'meringue'? May a concoction tasting of strawberries but not in fact containing any fruit be sold as strawberry jam? May dogfish or cat-fish be sold as 'rock salmon'?

These questions are not all easy to answer. For some goods – the list is slowly growing – regulations have been made under the Food and Drugs Act prescribing firm standards of composition and quality. For example, the Food Standards (Preserves) Order, 1953, lays down that jam must contain at least 65 per cent of 'soluble solids', and must have a minimum quantity of fruit varying from 25 per cent for blackcurrant jam to 40 per cent for some mixed jams; strawberry jam must contain at least 38 per cent of strawberries, so an offence is committed if a jar is sold as 'strawberry jam' with less than this proportion. The meat content of pies is prescribed by the Meat Pie and Sausage Roll Regulations 1967, ranging from not less than 10½ per cent of meat for uncooked sausage rolls to at least 25 per cent for cooked meat pies ('Scotch pies' being permitted to contain less meat than 'meat pies').

For foods not the subject of food standards regulations the court must decide, in the light of evidence presented. Public health inspectors will often give evidence of the meanings usual in the trade, and public analysts are familiar with the usual composition of a wide variety of foods, though in the last resort the decision is based on what an ordinary purchaser expects to get. An important source, however, is to be found in a number of codes of practice which were agreed, mainly between 1945 and 1950, between the then Ministry of Food and representatives of the trade concerned. These codes of practice are not law, but as they represent the standards generally observed in the trade they are frequently accepted by the courts. For example, a coconut biscuit must contain coconut 'in a readily recognizable quantity' and a date biscuit must contain dates, but a wine biscuit indicates the use of the biscuit, not its ingredients. It is recognized that 'Cheese Assorted', 'Cheese Biscuits', and 'Cheddar Assorted' need not contain cheese, but any other use of the word 'cheese' – or the name of any particular cheese – indicates the presence of cheese in the biscuit. A voluntary code issued by the Meat and Livestock Commission in 1970 requires that certain meats should be labelled with information such as the price per pound and, in some cases, weight, description and origin. Under the Agriculture Act 1967 the Commission has power to make this code compulsory, but despite the requests of consumer bodies it has declined to do so.

Sometimes the codes of practice fill in the gaps in food standards regulations. For example, the Fish and Meat Spreadable Products Regulations 1968 distinguish between spreads and pastes. Thus 'Salmon Spread' must contain at least 70 per cent of salmon; 'Salmon Paste', on the other hand, must contain at least 70 per cent of fish, but the Regulations say no more than that salmon must 'characterize' the paste; however, the code of practice agreed with the Food Manufacturers' Federation says that there should be at least 25 per cent of salmon in 'Salmon Paste', the remaining 45 per cent being of any (unnamed) fish. 'Smoked Salmon Paste', on the other hand, need have only ten per cent of smoked salmon.

It must be confessed that for most food products the housewife can rarely rely on her own judgement: even if she knows of the existence of a food standards Order, even if she knows of its details, chemical analysis is often necessary to determine whether a food complies. And for the majority of foods no food standards Order exists. Nevertheless further protection is given by the Labelling of Food Regulations 1970, which come into operation on 1 January 1973, and improve the protection given under earlier regulations. Pre-packed foods must be labelled with the common or usual name of the food, or a description of the food sufficiently specific to indicate its true nature, and bear a list of the ingredients; unless the quantity or proportion of each ingredient is specified they must be listed in order of importance according to weight (greatest first) – though water need not be mentioned. Several products are exempted from the need to list ingredients, including bread, pastries, biscuits, ice cream, chocolates and sweets. Where foods are sold by retailers without being pre-packed a ticket must be displayed near them, clearly visible to customers, stating the name or description of the food; the main exceptions are foods containing only one ingredient, bread, pastries, chocolates, sweets and drinks. There are special rules governing certain foods: for example, processed peas must not be referred to as 'fresh' or 'garden' or 'green' peas; tenderized meat must be called 'tenderized', whether the tenderizing agent was added to the meat or to the animal while it was still alive; 'liqueur chocolates' must contain 'a significant quantity' of liqueur.

MISLEADING DESCRIPTIONS

The rules laid down by successive Food and Drugs Acts effectively controlled false or misleading descriptions of food. For other commodities control lagged behind. In 1862 legislation was passed to enable traders to protect their trade marks from use by unscrupulous competitors. The Merchandise Marks Act of 1887, which replaced and extended the Act of 25 years earlier, remained in force, with some amendments, until 1968: during this long period the emphasis changed from trader protection to consumer protection, but the Act of 1887 was not well suited to this purpose, and the Molony Committee in 1962 condemned it as being outmoded in form and language and obscure in meaning. Moreover, although local authorities were permitted to prosecute, the Committee reported that 'We accept the widespread view that the . . . Acts have not been adequately enforced. We are firmly of the opinion that the number of prosecutions undertaken bears no relation to the number of offences committed.' The Committee's valuable proposals for the reform of the Act were implemented in 1968.

Perhaps the most important change brought about by the Trade Descriptions Act 1968 is that it imposes on local authorities a positive obligation to enforce the Act. It is this which makes it capable of being an effective instrument for consumer protection, and weights and measures inspectors have been assiduous in enforcement: during the first three-and-a-half years of the Act's life there were 3,870 prosecutions, and over 3,400 convictions; the publicity given to the Act resulted in a very large number of complaints being received, many of which resulted in warnings or cautions given by inspectors.

The main offences created by the 1968 Act appear in section 1: 'Any person who, in the course of a trade or business, (a) applies a false trade description to any goods; or (b) supplies or offers to supply any goods to which a false trade description is applied; shall . . . be guilty of an offence.' What is a 'false trade description'? 'False' includes misleading. The definition of 'trade description' is in section 2 and includes any indication of any physical characteristics such as quantity, size, method of manufacture (e.g., 'hand-made'), composition (e.g., 'leather') and fitness for purpose, of the name of the manufacturer and the place and date of manufacture, and of the history of the goods, including previous ownership and use (e.g., 'brand new' or 'one owner'). It also includes the results of any testing or approval of the goods by anyone. The

section covers any indication as to any of these or certain
other matters, whether direct or indirect, and 'by whatever means given': thus sheep shown on a label on a
blanket not made entirely of wool led to a conviction,
and many prosecutions have resulted from the display or
sale by second-hand car dealers of vehicles whose mileage
recorders ('odometers') carried false readings. Oral mis-
statements are also covered by the Act – a notable advance
on the previous law: this recognizes the essential fact that
statements made by word of mouth may well influence
the shopper more than written statements and therefore
need just as much control.

MISLEADING PRICES

An easy way of making a £5 dress look more attractive is
to pin on it a ticket reading 'Formerly £15. Now £5'. The
earlier law did not regulate this practice, and even the
new definition of trade description may not catch it. It is
true that a false statement about the history of the goods
is an offence, but what does 'Formerly £15' mean? That
other dresses of the same design were once sold for £15?
(This is probably not a statement about the history of the
goods now being sold, and so not caught by the definition
of trade description.) That similar dresses were sold for
£15 in a shop of a different character in a more exclusive
shopping district? That similar dresses were formerly
priced £15, but that the price was excessive and none
were actually sold at that price? That this individual
dress was formerly priced £15? That this dress carried a
£15 price ticket for one day when the shop was closed?
    The Molony Committee recognized that fraudulent
price claims of this nature were sufficiently widespread
and deceptive to call for repression, but perceptively fore-
saw 'difficulty in the phrasing of the prohibition and its
enforcement'. They saw no need to restrain claims that

goods were 'worth' more than the stated price. The result is section 11 of the 1968 Act, much amended on its way through Parliament and still far from satisfactory. This makes it an offence to give any false indication to the effect that the price at which goods are offered is equal to or less than a recommended price or the price at which the goods, or goods of the same description, were previously offered by the present seller. In order to pin down the seller who quotes a previous price, this is taken (unless the contrary is expressed) to mean that the goods were offered at the higher price for a continuous period of not less than 28 days during the preceding six months. The difficulty for the prosecution is emphasized by the decision in *House of Holland Ltd* v. *London Borough of Brent* (1971). Evidence was brought showing that an advertisement, 'All prices FURTHER REDUCED', quoted prices no lower than those quoted about two months earlier; but the Divisional Court found that no offence had been proved in the absence of evidence as to prices during the whole of the six months before the advertisement, for higher prices might have been charged for a period of 28 days during the six months and it is for the prosecution to prove its case, not for the seller to prove his innocence. In order to enforce section 11, many weights and measures offices continuously record current prices at many shops in their area; but with a company with many branches in different areas the prosecution would not find it easy to prove that none of the branches had offered goods at a higher price for 28 days during the previous six months.

Section 11(2) forbids a false indication that goods are being offered at less than the price in fact being asked (see p. 64 above). Thus in one case a poster stuck on the window of a Tesco supermarket advertised a special cut-price offer of Radiant washing powder. Inside the shop, however, all the special price packets had been sold and the shop was charging the regular price. In the absence of the defence described below this would have been an offence under section 11(2) of the Act.

DEFENCES

All these provisions of the 1968 Act impose a strict liability, in the sense that a seller or manufacturer can be found guilty of making a false statement without proof of dishonesty. Proof that the statement was made, and that it was false or misleading, is all that is required of the enforcing authority. But the Act mitigates this strictness by providing for some special defences, which it is for the accused to prove. If a person who did not himself apply the false description proves that he did not know, and could not with reasonable diligence have found out, either that the description was false or that it had been applied to the goods, he must be acquitted. And it is a defence to any charge under the Act to prove that the offence was due to a mistake, or to reliance on information supplied by someone else, or to the act or default of someone else, or to an accident, or to some other cause beyond the control of the person accused, provided he can show that he took all reasonable precautions and exercised all due diligence to avoid the commission of an offence. 'Person' includes a company, and in *Tesco Supermarkets Ltd* v. *Nattrass* in 1971 (the Radiant washing powder case referred to above) the House of Lords held that the default of the manager of one of Tesco's stores could be relied on by the company as the 'default of another'; thus the company itself was relieved from criminal responsibility once the company had shown that it had instituted an efficient system to try to prevent any offence being committed.

SERVICES

The Merchandise Marks Act had no application to services as distinct from goods. Even now, though section 14 of the 1968 Act partially extends the law to cover services, it is only an offence to make a false statement about services, accommodation or facilities provided in the course of a trade or business if the statement is made by a person who knows it to be false, or if he makes it recklessly (such as an answer given without checking by a person who does not know whether his answer is true or not). This section is undoubtedly responsible for some improvement in the standard of accuracy of travel agency brochures. An estate agent's misleading description of a house offered for sale is, however, almost certainly not covered by section 14, whether made knowingly or not.

ADVERTISEMENTS

Before the Trade Descriptions Act 1968, there was virtually no liability for misleading advertisements unless they were covered by the Food and Drugs Act (see below) or goods were bought by mail order by reference to an advertisement. Now, every false or misleading trade description contained in an advertisement is governed by the 1968 Act, irrespective of whether goods are ordered by reference to the advertisement or whether there is any evidence that anyone actually relied on it.

There is, of course, a problem in proving that the description is false – how can one link a television advertisement for, say, a washing-up liquid containing lanolin with a container of liquid sold under the same name but without lanolin, which might have been manufactured some time earlier? And how long does an advertisement remain effective? Could stocks manufactured after the

advertisement safely omit the lanolin? The Act lays down
that a trade description in an advertisement is taken to
refer to all goods of the class to which the advertisement
relates, whether or not they are in existence at the time the
advertisement is published. In determining whether goods
are of the class to which the advertisement relates, regard
is paid not only to the form and content of the advertisement but also to the time, place, manner and frequency
of its publication, and to all other matters making it
likely or unlikely that a customer would think that the
goods belonged to the class of goods referred to in the
advertisement.

Legislation on matters which affect our health has been
with us longer. The Food and Drugs Act 1955 prohibits
advertisements which may mislead as to the nature, substance, or quality of food or drugs, including a misleading
statement as to the nutritional or dietary value of a food.
Under this provision local authorities in different parts
of the country have been able to keep an eye on advertising campaigns, including those in national newspapers
and magazines, which, for example, describe foods containing carbohydrates as 'slimming' or 'non-fattening'
when what is meant is that they are not as fattening as
larger quantities of some other foods.

The Labelling of Food Regulations 1970 control misleading claims in provisions based on a report of the
Food Standards Committee. The guiding principle is
'that the consumer has the right to know that the claims
which are made are true and are not phrased in such a
way that, although literally true, they are likely to mislead.' As an example of such a claim the Committee referred to claims that foods or drinks 'replace energy'. This
may be true in the sense that nearly all foods provide
calories, and calories give energy. Yet it may be quite
misleading to the consumer: 'he will assume that the food
is a particularly good source of energy, whereas it will

probably provide no more energy in any sense of the word than the normal components of his diet and might indeed provide no energy at all in the everyday sense.' Similarly the Committee recommended that no food or drink should be permitted to claim that it has 'tonic' properties, for there is no scientific justification for claims of this kind. At the other extreme, no claim that a food is a slimming food or has intrinsic weight-reducing properties is allowed: 'All foods contain energy and so can be fattening.'

False or misleading advertisements of medicinal products are banned by the Medicines Act 1968 and, if it is thought that a particular word or phrase is likely to mislead the public, regulations may ban the use of that word or phrase in relation to medicines. There is no general ban on the advertising of preparations for the treatment of illnesses or diseases, but under the Medicines Act the Social Services Minister can make regulations prohibiting advertisements of alleged cures for diseases named in the regulations. These regulations will, when made, supersede the Cancer Act of 1939 and the Pharmacy and Medicines Act of 1941 under which advertisements may not be published if they may lead to the use of the product for the treatment of cancer, Bright's disease, cataract, diabetes, epilepsy or fits, glaucoma, locomotor ataxy (a lack of control of the arms of legs), paralysis or tuberculosis, or for procuring an abortion. An Act of 1917 deals in the same way with venereal diseases. Another legal control relates to advertisements which claim that vitamins or minerals are present in a food: not only must the food contain the substance claimed, but the Labelling of Food Regulations 1970 provide that the advertisement or the packet must state the minimum quantity of each of certain specified vitamins or minerals per ounce (or fluid ounce or hundred grammes or hundred millilitres) of the food.

There are other restraints imposed on advertising by

different Acts of Parliament, including the Advertisements (Hire-Purchase) Act of 1967 (described in Chapter 6) and the Moneylenders Acts. The Television Act of 1964 (repeating the original Act of 1954) gives the Independent Broadcasting Authority power to enforce its 'Code of Advertising Standards and Practice'. Also of importance are the advertising industry's own British Code of Advertising Practice and the British Code of Standards relating to the Advertising of Medicines and Treatments: these have no legal force, but members of the industry often try to observe the rules. The trade has set up its own 'court', called the Advertising Standards Authority, to consider complaints that the rules have been broken; with an independent chairman and a number of members drawn from outside the advertising world it has no authority in the legal sense, but its decisions, if ignored, might lead to expulsion from trade associations.

The present control over misleading advertisements is better than it was, but it could be even more effective. A general prohibition on advertisements containing false or misleading statements of fact would not impose excessively high standards on an industry on which vast sums of money are spent each year. An essential feature of such control would be to limit the facts which the prosecution need prove if an offence is alleged. Once the publication of the advertisement is proved, it should be for the defendant to prove positively that the statements in the advertisement are true and not false or misleading. This would not merely relieve the prosecution of what may be a difficult and unnecessary burden; there are many statements used in advertisements which cannot be disproved in a way which would satisfy a court of law but which equally cannot possibly be proved. The law should frown on the use for commercial profit of unprovable assertions of a factual nature. It is not asking too much of an advertiser to ensure, before he launches an advertising campaign, that he can prove every statement he makes in it; if a statement cannot be justified it should not be used.

CIVIL REMEDIES

The statutes and regulations described in this chapter all operate through the medium of the criminal law. The individual consumer need not launch a court case and no initiative is needed beyond informing the appropriate official of the local authority. Enforcement by a public authority, at the public expense, is of enormous benefit to consumers in general. But the consumer as an individual benefits less. How far can the specific laws referred to in this chapter entitle an individual to obtain compensation?

A contravention of the Trade Descriptions Act 1968 does not of itself entitle the consumer to make a claim in the civil courts. A claim for damages arising out of the same facts that led to a conviction under the Act must depend on a separate action under the Sale of Goods Act 1893 or the Misrepresentation Act 1967. The only link between civil and criminal law here is that under the Civil Evidence Act 1968 proof of the criminal conviction affords prima facie proof of the facts on which it was based in a subsequent civil action. Of course, sometimes intervention by a weights and measures inspector does result in the shopkeeper informally giving the consumer a cash refund.

The Consumer Protection Act 1961 expressly provides for civil liability. In a very interesting provision, section 3(1) states that any obligation imposed by the Act on any person not to sell or have possession of goods which do not comply with the regulations

is a duty which is owed by him to any other person who may be affected by the contravention of or non-compliance with the requirement in question, and a breach of that duty is actionable (subject to the defences and other incidents applying to actions for breach of statutory duty).

Thus any person injured by goods which do not comply with the regulations – by a fire caused by a faulty oil heater, for example – can sue the seller for damages. This right to sue is not based on the contract of sale, because the person injured need not be the buyer himself, nor is it based on the seller's negligence, for he may have taken all possible care. It is based on his breach of the duty imposed by the Act of Parliament, and he may be liable for having broken the duty without any fault on his part.

The provision in the Consumer Protection Act is interesting simply because it is unusual. Many Acts of Parliament impose duties enforceable by criminal proceedings. The Factories Act of 1961 is an outstanding example: if the occupier of a factory fails to provide and maintain safe premises and equipment, or to fence dangerous machinery, he can be prosecuted in the criminal courts. Nothing is said, however, about civil actions by employees injured, for example, by unfenced machinery; yet the courts have held that the object of the Factories Act is to protect the employees, so that they can sue for damages if injured by a breach of the duties imposed by the Act. On the other hand, sometimes the courts have said that duties of this nature are intended by Parliament to protect the community at large, or to discourage undesirable conduct, without giving persons injured by a breach of the duty any right to claim compensation. For example, in *Square* v. *Model Farm Dairies (Bournemouth) Ltd*, in 1939, the family of the plaintiff became ill with typhoid fever as a result of infected milk. It was alleged that, under what is now section 2 of the Food and Drugs Act of 1955, the sellers had sold a food not of the nature demanded, that the duty under the Act was imposed for the benefit of buyers of foods, and that the plaintiff could therefore sue for damages. The Court of Appeal rejected the plaintiff's claim: the statute was not intended to add to the buyer's remedies under the civil law (where he could already sue if there was a breach of contract or negligence) but to provide machinery for preventing the forbidden acts. We saw in Chapter 3 how a similar claim failed in *Buckley* v. *La Réserve* (1959) where a restaurant supplied snails; in that case, it was argued that the seller was in breach of section 8 of the Food and Drugs Act 1955 in selling food unfit for human consumption, but the reasoning was the same as in *Square's* case even though the plaintiff could not have sued successfully in contract or for negligence.

How do the judges decide whether Parliament intended to permit persons injured to sue (as under the Factories Act) or did not intend to create new civil rights? 'The only rule which in all circumstances is valid,' said Lord Simonds in 1949, 'is that the answer must depend on a consideration of the whole Act and the circumstances, including the pre-existing law, in which it was enacted.' In other words, there is no way of predicting what view the judges will take and they can equally well justify a decision in favour of, or against, civil liability. Here lies the great merit of the Consumer Protection Act: Parliament has expressly said that a breach of the duty is to lead not only to criminal liability but also to civil rights for the person injured. Parliament has now clearly expressed that view in the Consumer Protection Act; exactly the same considerations apply to the Food and Drugs Act. The House of Lords is not bound by the precedent laid down by the Court of Appeal in *Square* v. *Model Farm Dairies (Bournemouth) Ltd* and could now decide that persons injured by a breach of the Food and Drugs Act might recover damages for breach of statutory duty. But we need not wait for litigation to reach the highest court, with all the expense and delay that would entail. Parliament ought at once to add to the Food and Drugs Act a provision, similar to that in the Consumer

Protection Act 1961, giving injured parties the right to sue for damages. Indeed, the Law Commissions recommended in 1969 that there should be a general statutory presumption that breach of an obligation imposed by an Act of Parliament is intended to be actionable at the suit of any person who suffers loss by reason of that breach, unless the Act imposing the obligation expressly excluded a civil action.

For a long time there have been procedural difficulties in the law, applicable *inter alia* to the Trade Descriptions Act and the Consumer Protection Act. A criminal prosecution under these Acts is brought, at the public expense, in the criminal courts. If the person injured wished to obtain damages he would have had to bring a seperate action in the civil courts at his own expense (unless he obtained legal aid). Two different courts at two different times would have had to consider substantially the same question – and they were not bound to come to the same conclusions.

The Criminal Justice Act 1972 goes a good way towards reducing this duplication of court proceedings. Section 1 supersedes a number of earlier scattered provisions and gives a criminal court power to make a compensation order requiring a convicted person to pay compensation in respect of any personal injury, loss or damage caused by the offence. This section enables the court hearing a criminal prosecution – for example, under the Trade Descriptions Act 1968 – to order compensation to be paid, even if the victim does not make a special application. If the trial is by jury there is no limit to the amount of compensation awarded, but a magistrates' court may not order more than £400 compensation for each offence. The compensation is in addition to any fine or other penalty imposed, but under section 4 any money paid under a compensation order is taken into account in civil proceedings in respect of the same injury, loss or damage.

FAIR TRADING

A considerable enlargement of the existing protection of the consumer against unfair trade practices may result from the Fair Trading Bill which was given a second reading in the House of Commons in December 1972. The Bill creates a new watchdog, the Director General of Fair Trading (whom we will call 'the Director'), supported by his own staff and by a Consumer Protection Advisory Committee. This new official is to have the task of keeping under review trade practices which may adversely affect the economic interests of consumers, as well as to keep under review commercial activities which involve monopoly or restrictive practices. His latter responsibilities will be referred to briefly at the end of Chapters 11 and 12.

Unlike the Trade Descriptions Act 1968, the Fair Trading Bill does not actually create any new offences. What it does is to provide the machinery whereby new offences may be created by order of the Secretary of State for Trade and Industry. There are several stages in the process. First of all, the Director has to consider whether a trade practice has the effect, or is likely to have the effect, (a) of misleading or confusing consumers with regard to the nature, quality or quantity of goods or services, or (b) of misleading consumers as to their rights and obligations, or (c) of subjecting consumers to undue pressure, or (d) of causing the terms of consumer transactions to be so adverse to consumers as to be inequitable. (Professional services and the nationalized industries are excluded.) If the Director does think the trade practice has or is likely to have such an effect, he may refer the matter to the Advisory Committee and, if he thinks fit, he may include proposals for recommending an order forbidding or regulating the practice. Any such reference to the Advisory Committee must be published, so that an opportunity is given for objections to be raised. The Advisory Committee will include people with knowledge or experience in the supply of goods or services to consumers, people with knowledge or experience in the enforcement of legislation such as the Trade Descriptions Act, and people with knowledge or experience in consumer protection organizations or activities. Normally it will have only three months in which to make a report and if it agrees with the Director's proposals, perhaps with modifications, the Secretary of State may make an appropriate order. This order may, for example, prohibit the trade practice, prohibit exemption clauses in specified consumer transactions, or require that contracts relating to specified consumer transactions should include certain terms. The order can take effect only if both Houses of Parliament approve.

Potentially there is plenty of scope for the banning or regulation of unfair trade practices, but there are a number of hurdles to be surmounted before an order is effective, and it remains to be seen how much use is made of the new machinery. In its favour is the greater flexibility enabling a new abuse to be dealt with without the need for fresh legislation. The valuable work of the weights and measures authorities in enforcing the Trade Descriptions Act is recognized by giving them the task of enforcing any new offences that may be created by order. As we have seen (p. 151), the Criminal Justice Act 1972 enables a criminal court to make a compensation order in favour of anyone who has incurred loss or damage as a result of an offence, and this will apply on conviction for any new offence made under the Fair Trading Act 1973. However, unless it is amended on its way through Parliament, the Bill allows the same defences as the Trade Descriptions Act, so that a trader may be able to shift responsibility on to an employee as in *Tesco Supermarkets Ltd* v. *Nattrass* (referred to on p. 143).

Interesting provisions are contained in Part III of the

Bill, giving the Director a general power to seek orders from the Restrictive Practices Court against persons who persistently maintain a course of conduct detrimental to the interests of consumers by breaking the criminal law or by breaking civil obligations, such as under the Sale of Goods Act, and who refuse to give written assurances that they will desist. These provisions clearly reinforce the existing criminal and civil obligations of the suppliers of goods and services. Thus, if a trader has persistently flouted the Trade Descriptions Act, despite perhaps many prosecutions by the weights and measures authority and fines imposed by the courts, the Director can, after due warning, take him to the Restrictive Practices Court which may make an order directing him to refrain from continuing the course of conduct objected to. Breach of such an order of the Court would be a contempt of court and render the trader liable to imprisonment. Similarly if a trader persistently breaks his civil obligations, perhaps by selling non-merchantable goods. Very often today the trader may 'get away with it' because it is left entirely to the individual consumer to exercise his right to take the trader to the county court for breach of the Sale of Goods Act, and the individual consumer may not think it worthwhile to sue and certainly not worth the expense of legal representation. Of course, if these powers of the Director are to be a reality, there will be a need to ensure that consumers are aware of his powers, and for local advisory services to channel complaints to Whitehall.

CHAPTER 6

HIRE PURCHASE

WITH an outstanding hire-purchase and credit-sale debt in Britain today of well over one thousand million pounds, instalment buying is of enormous importance to the economy and to both producer and consumer. The current scale of credit buying in the United States is even greater, and one does not need to be a prophet to say that in neither country has the peak yet been reached.

There are still people who regard buying on the 'never-never' as not quite respectable, and the better-off consumer who is unable to pay ready cash for some large item of expenditure may prefer – and may be wiser – to obtain an overdraft from his bank or to tap some other source for a loan. These factors, however, militate only very slightly against the steady growth of hire purchase. To more and more people, it is seen as a means of enjoying sooner than otherwise a higher standard of living. It is seen as a convenient way of equipping a home or obtaining a car – paying for them over a period while having at once the possession and use of the goods. As living standards rise, hire purchase is bound to go on expanding. It is this predictable expansion that makes it particularly urgent to probe the legal aspects of hire purchase, to see whether the legal form in which hire purchase is moulded approximates to social needs and whether it operates fairly so far as the consumer is concerned. To do this, we must first look at the origins of hire purchase and see how it has developed over the years.

The Singer Company claims the honour of being the pioneer of hire-purchase trading, back in the 1860s. The Institute of Economic Affairs publication *Hire Purchase in a Free Society* shows how the sewing machine had certain merits for this type of business. It was not only an asset with a long life against which money could be advanced with some security, it was directly productive, yielding tangible income to the hirer while the instalments were being paid off. Sewing machines were let out to housewives and tailors on a small initial payment with the balance payable by instalments for up to two years. Traders in pianos, furniture, and household equipment were quick to grasp the new idea and followed suit. They realized that people who could not afford spot cash for relatively expensive goods would be lost as customers if cash was insisted on, but it would be a different matter if they were allowed to pay over two or three years. Of course, there was a risk involved in allowing the customer to have the goods without paying in full. In order to exert pressure on the customer if he failed to pay instalments the trader wished to preserve his ownership of the goods so that he could threaten to take them back; usually the threat would be sufficient but, if not, the trader would seize the goods which he could then dispose of to another customer. There was a further risk, that the customer might wrongly sell the goods: but at common law, as we saw in Chapter 3, no one can give a better title to goods than he himself has. The result was that the trader could take the/goods back if he could trace them, no matter how innocent the buyer was and however great the hardship.

The Factors Act of 1889 introduced in section 9 a new principle into the law with its provision that enabled a customer who had agreed to buy goods, if he was permitted to take possession of them, to pass the ownership to an innocent buyer even if the trader had attempted to retain ownership under the original agreement. In *Lee* v. *Butler* (1893) it was held by the Court of Appeal that even if the agreement purported to be a hiring agreement, an obligation imposed on the customer to pay the whole price meant that he had agreed to buy the goods, so that a person who had purchased the goods from him in good faith secured the protection of the Factors Act. If the customer, instead of selling the goods, pledged them with a pawnbroker, the trader could only get them back by paying off the pawnbroker.

To avoid this possibility, the trader had to adopt a form of agreement which did not commit the customer to pay the whole price. Instead, the customer would hire the goods and be given an *option* to buy them, which he need not exercise if he did not wish to do so. This is the modern 'hire-purchase agreement' which is thus sharply differentiated from a sale of goods on credit: the trader retains his security in the goods and does not lose his ownership unless the customer has paid up all his instalments.

THE TRADER'S SECURITY

The House of Lords confirmed the effectiveness of this device in 1895 in *Helby* v. *Matthews*, a case which is the foundation of modern hire purchase law, and which explains the preference of traders for hire purchase rather than credit sale. Helby, a trader in Baker Street, London, agreed to let a piano on hire purchase to a Mr Brewster. Brewster agreed to pay 10s. 6d. on the date of the agreement and then to pay thirty-five monthly instalments of 10s. 6d. each. If Brewster punctually paid the full sum of £18 18s., it was agreed that the piano would become 'the sole and absolute property of the hirer', but unless and until that full sum was paid, the piano would continue to be the sole property of Helby, the owner. Brewster had the right to end the hiring and return the piano if he wished. Some four months after this agreement was made, Brewster, without Helby's consent, pledged the piano with pawnbrokers. The House of Lords held that Helby could recover the piano from the pawnbrokers without having to repay the loan the pawnbrokers had made to Brewster. If, instead of taking it on hire purchase, Brewster had agreed to buy the piano, then the Factors Act would have come into play and the result would have been different, but he had never agreed to buy the piano – 'Brewster might buy or not just as he pleased', said the Lord Chancellor.

Hire purchase has never looked back since *Helby* v. *Matthews*. The judgement gave traders just that assurance they wanted to go in for hire purchase in a big way. They could now dispose of goods on hire purchase confident that, if the customer did not keep up his payments, the goods could be recovered wherever they might be. Provided the goods were durable, and readily identifiable, this right to repossess them represented a very real safeguard.

It has been said that the first motor vehicle to be supplied on hire purchase was a charabanc in 1912, though public records are scanty. It is easy to see why the advent of cars and motor-cycles provoked an acceleration in the growth of hire purchase. To the customer, hire purchase enabled him to have the immediate use of an expensive article and to pay for it over a period of two or three years, less than the lifetime of the goods. To the trader, a car was something which could be easily repossessed and resold if the customer did not keep to his agreement. Other newly invented articles, like gramophones and radios, television sets, tape recorders, and washing machines had similar characteristics, and they too became typical subjects for hire-purchase agreements.

THE SNATCH BACK

Whatever its advantages to the trader, however, the form of hire purchase sanctioned by the House of Lords decision in *Helby* v. *Matthews* was not an unmitigated bless-

ing to the consumer. Since the hirer only had an option
to buy the goods, he did not become the owner till he
paid up all his instalments. A suitable clause in the agreement could ensure that, if the customer failed to pay
punctually any particular instalment, the goods could be
repossessed by the trader. It made no difference that he
might have paid twenty-two out of the twenty-four
monthly payments before defaulting – the goods could be
'snatched back' and all the instalments already paid were
forfeit. If the goods still had a good resale value, this
might well mean that the trader actually did better as a
result of the customer's default than if the agreement had
been carried through to its normal conclusion.

One of the common criticisms of hire purchase has
always been that it encourages feckless people to take
more goods than they can really afford to pay for – people
imagine that so long as they can find the initial deposit,
the instalments will somehow take care of themselves. But
whether the hirer was reckless or over-optimistic, or
whether he suffered a blameless and unexpected financial
difficulty because of illness or unemployment, the law
operated equally harshly: it gave no relief against the
repossession of goods and the forfeiture of instalments
paid if the hirer fell into arrears.

Another criticism commonly levelled against hire purchase is that aggressive sales techniques, to which housewives are supposed to be particularly prone, ensnare
people into signing for things they cannot afford and may
not even want. A county court judge is credited with the
remark that hire purchase consists in being persuaded by
a man whom you don't know to sign an agreement you
don't read to buy furniture you don't want with money
you haven't got. Until Parliament intervened in 1938, the
law virtually encouraged the more unscrupulous trader.
It encouraged him because he did not need to concern
himself at all with the ability of the customer to meet his

commitments. Indeed, as we have seen, the trader might well gain a profitable windfall if the customer defaulted, preferably towards the end of the contract period.

An early example is the case of *Cramer* v. *Giles*, heard in 1883. A trader let out a piano to Giles on the terms that if Giles paid twelve quarterly instalments of five guineas, the piano would become Giles's property. Until the full payment of sixty guineas, the piano remained the sole property of the trader. In a provision that was to become common form in hire-purchase agreements, default in the punctual payment of any instalment entitled the trader to resume possession of the piano and the instalments previously paid were forfeit. Giles did pay the first ten instalments, amounting to fifty guineas, but failed to pay punctually the last two instalments. Before the trader sought to recover the piano, Giles offered to pay the remaining ten guineas, but this was refused. The Court of Appeal upheld the trader's right to repossess the piano.

Neither in that case nor in later cases was the court prepared to give any relief to the hirer against the full and rigorous application of the repossession provisions in a hire-purchase agreement. There was no question of the hirer being allowed by the court further time to pay or to recover any portion of the instalments he had paid. The courts' failure to give the hirer any protection is merely another example of their uncompromising attitude towards the sanctity of contractual terms. If the hire-purchase agreement allowed for immediate repossession and forfeiture of instalments when a hirer failed to make punctual payments, that was the end of the matter.

Mortgages of land or houses have a longer history than hire purchase, as have leases of land or houses. But it is worth comment that while the courts have long protected mortgagors from foreclosure when they default in their payments, and tenants have been protected from immediate forfeiture if they default in rent payments, no simi-

lar protection was given by the courts to hirers under
hire-purchase agreements.

Another ground for complaint about the law, before
the Hire-Purchase Act 1938 provided a measure of reform, was that hire-purchase agreements frequently ab-
solved the owner from any liability for defects in the
goods. Although the common law, left to itself, would
read into a hire-purchase transaction an implied condition that the goods were reasonably fit for their purpose,
rather similar to that implied in contracts of sale, hire-
purchase agreements were invariably in writing. And they
were invariably prepared by the owner. The temptation
was too strong, the opportunity was not to be missed.
Inevitably, therefore, hire-purchase agreements would
contain a clause excluding implied conditions and warranties.

FINANCE COMPANIES

Since the early days of hire purchase, the parties to a hire-
purchase agreement have very often been, not the trader
(or dealer) and the consumer, but a finance company and
the consumer. How does it come about that a consumer
often finds that although he has dealt with, say, Mr Smith,
a dealer, and signed hire-purchase forms at Mr Smith's
office, the other party to the actual agreement turns out to
be a finance company with which he has had no direct
dealings at all?

When the amount of hire-purchase business done by a
trader was relatively small, he could himself provide the
required credit. But as hire purchase grew, and particularly when the amount of hire-purchase business done by
car dealers expanded, traders were not able to carry this
financial burden themselves. Finance companies, some of
which – the wagon companies – had been formed in the
nineteenth century to provide the money for colliery

companies to obtain railway trucks for carrying coal on the new permanent way, filled the gap. At present about 65 per cent of the credit outstanding on hire-purchase transactions is owed to finance companies.

The real function of the finance company is, of course, to lend money. It would have been perfectly possible, then, for the role of the finance company in the supply of goods to parallel that of the building society in the supply of houses. The consumer would borrow money from the finance company in order to buy the goods from the trader. Having bought them, he would then mortgage them to the finance company. If he failed to repay the loan, they would have rights against the goods. This is in fact the way the transaction is carried out in some parts of North America, where it is known as a 'chattel mortgage'.

There are two reasons why the chattel mortgage is not used by English finance companies. They are the Acts of Parliament passed in order to protect borrowers from unscruplous money-lenders. The Moneylenders Acts 1900 and 1927 impose severe restrictions on the way a money-lending business is carried on; the Bills of Sale Act (1878) Amendment Act 1882 regulates mortgages (technically known as 'bills of sale') on goods, laying down the form of document to be used and requiring registration of these documents at the Law Courts in London. The result is that, in order to avoid these restrictions, finance companies so carry on business that they do not, technically, lend money; rather, they buy goods.

The machinery is as follows. When a potential customer tells his car dealer that he wants to take a car on hire purchase, the dealer arranges to sell the car to the particular finance company with which he has built up a connection. The customer's deposit is retained by the dealer and the finance company advances to the dealer the difference between the deposit and the cash price of the car. The dealer, therefore, gets his price at once and often a commission from the finance company for introducing the customer to them. The hire-purchase agreement is then made between the customer and the finance company, now the legal owner of the car, and it is to the finance company that the customer pays his instalments, though exceptionally the dealer may act as collecting agent for the finance company.

The importance of all this to the customer is that his agreement is not with the dealer but with the finance company. If he defaults with his payments, it will be the finance company who will repossess the goods, and if the customer has any complaints about the goods, normally no claim can be made against the dealer because the customer has no contract with him. In theory a claim in respect of faulty goods may be made against the finance company but in practice, subject to what we shall say about the effects of the Hire-Purchase Act, the agreement will purport to exclude any express or implied terms as to the merchantability of the goods or fitness for their purpose.

The disadvantage of this transaction is that it hides the true function of the finance company. Although they call themselves 'finance houses' or 'industrial bankers', the way they have chosen to do business means that they become dealers in goods. Moreover, if the hirer defaults in his payments the finance company cannot bring a simple claim for the repayment of money lent. As Lord Diplock said in 1963:

hire-purchase companies cannot eat their cake and have it. If they choose to conduct their business by entering into contracts of hire of chattels instead of entering into money-lending contracts secured by chattel mortgages, their legal rights will be governed by the terms of the contracts into which they enter, and by the general principles of law applicable to contracts of that nature.

THE HIRE-PURCHASE ACTS

We have seen that the courts gave the hirer no kind of relief against harsh enforcement of repossession provisions in a hire-purchase agreement. In the depression and unemployment of the 1920s and 1930s many people found they could not meet the commitments they had entered into, and 'snatch backs', at any rate by some traders and finance companies pursuing their legal rights to the limit, were common. This practice, together with that of excluding liability for faulty goods, led to the Hire-Purchase Act 1938. It represents the successful outcome of a private member's Bill, sponsored by Miss Ellen Wilkinson, later Minister of Education, and supported by most of the trade associations.

The 1938 Act has been of great importance as an Act deliberately designed to interfere with 'freedom of contract' in order to redress the balance in favour of the individual consumer dealing with a company using a standard-form contract. In its original form it gave protection only in respect of relatively inexpensive goods taken on hire purchase. Apart from provisions about livestock inserted for the protection of farmers, it only applied if the price did not exceed £100, and for motor vehicles the price was as low as £50. By an amending Act of 1954 these financial limits were extended to cover all agreements (including those concerned with motor vehicles) where the price did not exceed £300, again with a higher limit for livestock agreements.

The Molony Committee, reporting in 1962, thought it wrong that the money limit should be so low, with the result that a high proportion of consumer trade – covering particularly, of course, cars and caravans – fell outside the ambit of the Acts. It considered whether to recommend merely an increased figure – say, agreements up to

£1,000 – and came to the conclusion that any limit was bound to be arbitrary: protection for the consumer taking a car on hire purchase might well depend on how much was obtained on a 'trade-in' (which might affect the interest charges), whether a heater was ordered, and whether repayment was over two or three years. It therefore proposed that there should be no money limit and that the protection of the Acts should apply to all 'consumer transactions', that is, all transactions where goods are taken on hire purchase for private use or consumption and not for use in any trade or business.

In 1964 came the first major reform of the law of hire purchase since 1938. Many of the recommendations of the Molony Committee were adopted, and other opportunities were taken to improve the law which, as a result of many court decisions, was in a state of chaos. It was an excellent opportunity to re-shape the whole of hire-purchase law. But the Committee's advice that financial limits should be removed from the Hire-Purchase Acts was rejected, and instead the 1964 Act raised the money limit to its present level of £2,000 for all kinds of goods, including livestock. Thus, while it is now accepted that the common law of hire purchase is fundamentally unsatisfactory and unfair to the hirer, and that it is not merely for low-price goods that protection is needed, if the goods are too expensive the statutory protection is forfeited. The £2,000 barrier is quite illogical. Since the important figure is the hire-purchase price, which is larger than the cash price as it includes the amount of interest or 'hire-purchase charges', goods with a cash price of £1,700 are likely to escape the Act's provisions if taken on hire purchase. There is no sensible reason why the hirer of a Triumph 2000 car with manual transmission should receive protection, while the hirer of a Triumph 2000 automatic should not: the one has no more negotiating power than the other, and is no more likely to consult his solicitor before signing. The only reason for having this rigid barrier between unfair law and fair law is one which is familiar to any student of political decisions: it represents a compromise between opposing factions. (The Supply of Goods (Implied Terms) Bill, if it becomes law in 1973, will at least remove the £2,000 limit so far as implied terms and exemption clauses are concerned: see below, p. 177.) As a further compromise, the 1964 Act excluded from the Acts any agreement where the hirer is a corporate body, a term which includes all limited companies, no doubt in an attempt to exclude many transactions of a business rather than a private nature.

While the 1964 Act improved the content of the law within its scope, it left the words of the law to be found in three complex Acts of Parliament. A further change was therefore called for, and the Hire-Purchase Act 1965, which is now the operative statute, has replaced the earlier Acts. Some of its provisions have been in force since the 1938 Act, others were introduced by the 1964 Act. The protection it affords to the hirer covers a wide field and, where it applies, many of the defects of the common law have been remedied.

THE SNATCH BACK ENDED

One of the principal features of the Act is that it gives the hirer a stake in the goods when he has paid one-third of the total hire-purchase price. If he has paid this proportion and then falls into arrears with his instalments, or breaks the agreement in some way, the owner (whether the original dealer or a finance company) may not 'snatch back' the goods, no matter what the actual agreement may say. In agreements to which the Act applies, if the hirer has paid one-third of the price before he falls into arrears, the owner's only recourse is to take him to the local county court – and before even that he must give

seven days written notice of default, thus giving the hirer
a further opportunity to pay.

There is one exception to the need to go to court, designed to save the expense of court proceedings if the hirer
no longer wishes to keep the goods. He may voluntarily
agree to return the goods, for what the Act says is that
the owner 'shall not *enforce* any right' to get the goods
back. The trap that lies in store for the hirer who fails
to get legal advice is well demonstrated by *Mercantile
Credit Co. Ltd* v. *Cross* in 1965. Having fallen seriously
into arrears with his instalments, the hirer of a motor-
cycle received a notice from the owners terminating the
hire-purchase agreement: this is the normal preliminary
to the commencement of county court proceedings. The
notice ended: 'we require you to give up possession to us
of the vehicle which is the subject of the said agreement.'
Believing that he had to comply with this notice, the
hirer got his wife to telephone the finance company. She
was told that the machine should be taken back to the
shop where it had been obtained. Although he did not
want to part with the cycle the hirer did as he was told.
But that did not end the matter, for soon after the finance
company sued for all the arrears of instalments which had
fallen due up to the time when the notice terminated the
agreement. At that stage the hirer sought legal advice
and learnt that, having paid more than one-third, he had
been under no obligation to return the motor-cycle. The
Act imposes a severe penalty on an owner who enforces
his rights without going to court after one-third has been
paid: the hirer is released from all liability under the
agreement, and every penny he has paid must be returned
to him. So in this case the hirer argued that he was no
longer liable to pay the arrears, and that all the money
he had already paid should be refunded. The Court of
Appeal rejected his claim. The finance company had done
nothing wrong in demanding the return of the cycle:

they had not forced the hirer to return it, and the hirer had voluntarily surrendered it. The fact that he was ignorant of his legal rights could not, said the court, alter the legal position. He therefore remained liable for the arrears.

Where the hirer does not consent to return the goods the next step is usually the issue by the owner of a summons in the county court demanding the return of the goods. This gives the county courts considerable work: in 1970 there were 57,248 summonses claiming the return of goods let under hire-purchase agreements. Those were the cases where at least one-third of the price had been paid; there were a further 11,559 summonses where less than one third had been paid. At the hearing the judge is given a number of powers under the Act. If the hirer clearly has no satisfactory reason for not paying his instalments, the judge may order the goods to be returned to the owner without giving the hirer any further time to pay for them. Such orders are rare. The most common result is a 'postponed' order. This is an order that the goods be returned, but the operation of the order is postponed so long as the hirer pays the balance of the price by such instalments as the judge thinks fit, bearing in mind the means of the hirer. This power enables the judge to take into account, for example, some temporary financial embarrassment, such as short-time working or illness; in effect he can vary the requirements of the hire-purchase agreement by giving the hirer more time to pay. The judge may vary his order at any time.

The view was put forward in the Institute of Economic Affairs publication *Hire Purchase in a Free Society* that these provisions in the Hire-Purchase Act should be amended:

In the changed circumstances of today, the question is whether the scales have not been tilted too heavily against the trader. The wider use and experience of consumer credit since prewar days should be expected to reduce the need for special protection. ... Provided all hire-purchase agreements set out clearly the terms of payment and conditions of repossession, the individual should accept the responsibility of deciding whether to make use of this form of credit. Having entered into the agreement, he ought to be held to the instalments, and in the event of default should be prepared to face the consequences, including surrender of the merchandise which the customer is 'hiring' until the final payment is made.

This view, however, ignored the point that the hirer has no real choice or say in the 'terms of payment and conditions of repossession'. Surely the main justification for statutory intervention on the hirer's behalf is to redress the imbalance of bargaining power. No one has suggested that judicial control of mortgages, dating from the Middle Ages, should be ended. The authors went on to criticize the practice of county court judges, under the Hire-Purchase Act, of allowing hirers more time to pay:

There is now a strong case for the view that the law should be amended to place the onus of proof more clearly on the customer. In particular, the courts might be directed to give favourable consideration to a claim for repossession where the trader or finance company can show that it took 'reasonable' care to enquire into the credit standing of the customer before extending credit to him. This is increasingly done, and, in view of the probable extension of instalment credit, there has long been a need to extend the information and records about the credit standing of members of the public.

Certainly, greater care by traders and a greater use by them of credit bureaux would tend to reduce the number of bad debts and the number of hirers taken to court for non-payment of instalments. But if a hirer is taken to court it seems right, as the Act provides, that the hirer's present means and circumstances should be the criteria for the judge's order, not whether the finance company or trader took care when giving him credit. Otherwise, we would be back in the pre-1938 situation of people losing both the goods and their instalments because of some temporary financial difficulty late in the contract period. Indeed, in our view the present law is still unduly harsh in that the 'snatch-back' is only prohibited under the Hire-Purchase Act when the hirer has paid one-third of the total hire-purchase price. If, for example, the hirer takes a car on hire purchase with a total price of £1,800, the car may be repossessed without court proceedings even if he had paid as much as £599. The Scots courts do not permit the snatch-back in any circumstances: a court order is always necessary if the hirer does not voluntarily surrender the goods. English law could well emulate Scottish law in this respect.

PENALTY CLAUSES

Now that the owner cannot 'snatch back' the goods where the agreement is within the £2,000 limit and at least one-third of the price has been paid, the harsh old rule that all money already paid must be forfeited has lost much of its former importance. If the judge in the county court permits the hirer to retain the goods by paying smaller instalments, credit will of course be given for money already received by the owner. If the hirer is unable to pay anything more – a rare situation – the judge has power to divide the goods, where this is possible (for example, where several items of furniture are comprised in a single hire-purchase agreement), so that the hirer may receive at least some benefit for what he has paid.

Where the hirer himself terminates the agreement, or voluntarily returns the goods, there is still no judicial control over the forfeiture of sums paid, nor over the rule that the hirer must pay all instalments which have fallen due up to the time when the agreement is terminated. But usually the owner is not satisfied with these amounts, and includes in the agreement a clause requiring the hirer to pay more money if the agreement is terminated before it reaches its natural conclusion. This clause is known as the 'minimum payment clause', and may be drafted to come into operation whether the agreement ends as a result of the hirer's breach of contract or at his express request.

One can understand the owner who wishes to impose a minimum payment clause. The goods may depreciate in value while the hirer has them, perhaps because time has passed, perhaps because the once-new goods have become second-hand. The money paid by the hirer as deposit and instalments may not cover the fall in value, in which case the owner naturally wants to claim some more. But this does not explain clauses which go far beyond any attempt to prevent loss to the owner, like the clause in *Cooden Engineering Co. Ltd* v. *Stanford* which said that if the agreement was terminated for non-payment of any instalment, the whole of the balance of the hire-purchase price should become payable. Thus the hirer would be liable to pay the whole price even though he had had to return the goods. When this case came before the Court of Appeal in 1953 they refused to enforce it.

This decision hardly seems surprising today, but surprising it was at the time. Until this case was decided, it was not thought that the courts had power under the common law to intervene even in patently unfair minimum payment clauses. The way in which they were able to do so was by holding that the sum payable by the hirer as a result of his breach of contract was not a fair attempt to estimate the loss likely to be caused to the owners by his breach. It was rather a 'penalty', hanging over the hirer's head as a threat, a device to force him to carry out the contract rather than to compensate the owners. For centuries the courts have refused to enforce penalty clauses in contracts, and in 1953 this doctrine was extended by the courts to hire-purchase agreements. This is one of the few respects in which the courts have been prepared to clamp down on harsh provisions in hire-purchase agreements without any prodding from Parliament.

Another example occurred later in 1953, in the case of *Lamdon Trust Ltd* v. *Hurrell*. A hire-purchase agreement for a car (total price £558 – then outside the Hire-Purchase Act) provided that if the agreement was terminated as a result of default by the hirer, he must make up his payments to 75 per cent of the price as 'compensation for depreciation'. After paying £302, the hirer defaulted and the finance company, having terminated the agreement, resold the car for £270. The company, therefore, had already recouped the whole of the total hire-purchase price and a little more. Not content, however, it claimed a further £122 under the so-called 'compensation for depreciation' clause. Lord Denning rejected the claim on the ground that 75 per cent of the price was not a genuine pre-estimate of the damage likely to be caused by the hirer's breach – it was a penalty, 'an extravagant and extortionate sum held *in terrorem* over the head of the hirer'.

It is not always easy to predict whether the minimum payment clause in a hire-purchase agreement will be struck down as a penalty, and in some cases such clauses have been upheld. Where the Hire-Purchase Act applies, however, there is a statutory minimum payment. The hirer must pay all instalments due to the date of termination of the agreement. If then the total amount he has paid under the agreement, including any deposit and any credit for goods he has parted with in part-exchange, comes to less than one-half of the hire-purchase price, he must pay more to bring his total payments up to one half. This statutory minimum payment of 50 per cent may be reduced in two ways: the agreement itself may specify a smaller amount (a very unlikely possibility!); and the court may reduce the hirer's payment to an amount sufficient to compensate the owner for his loss as a result of the termination, if the court is satisfied that this is less than the 50 per cent. But the agreement cannot impose a higher minimum payment.

This 50 per cent minimum payment in agreements within the Hire-Purchase Act applies however the agreement comes to an end – whether as a result of the hirer's breach of contract, or by his voluntarily returning the goods. Under the Act the hirer is entitled to terminate the agreement at any time. In the present state of the law, however, the courts' control over 'penalty clauses', still important where the agreement is not within the Hire-Purchase Act, only operates when the hirer breaks the contract. The harsh clause which the courts are prepared to strike out is thought of as a penalty for breaking a contract – a device to discourage the hirer from breaking the terms of the agreement. It is inherent in a hire-purchase agreement, however, that the hirer has an *option* – an option to buy or, if he prefers, to terminate the agreement and return the goods. Exercise of his option is not therefore a breach of contract, but rather the exercise of a right given by the agreement: and, judges have said, there is no reason why the agreement should not prescribe the price to be paid for exercising this right by a minimum payment clause.

If this is indeed the law, it produces the extraordinary result that the honest hirer may be in a worse position than the defaulter. A hire-purchase agreement outside the Act might for example provide that on termination, however this arises, the hirer must bring his total payments up to 90 per cent of the total hire-purchase price, regardless of the value of the goods returned to the owner. If the hirer finds himself unable to continue paying, the honourable thing to do would surely be to tell the owner that he wishes to terminate the agreement and return the goods. But he will then be bound by the 90 per cent clause, and the courts will grant him no relief. If, on the other hand, he simply falls into arrears, the owner may – rather than let the agreement drag on and the goods depreciate further in value – terminate the agreement. Now the minimum payment clause operates as a penalty for breach of contract, and the courts may disregard it.

Whether the law really does make this strange distinction is not certain. There are several decisions in the Court of Appeal which hold that no question of a penalty can arise on voluntary termination by the hirer. In *Bridge* v. *Campbell Discount Co. Ltd*, in 1962, the hirer had written to the finance company telling them he was unable to continue his instalments. The Court of Appeal treated this as an exercise of his option to terminate the agreement and held that he was bound by the minimum payment clause. On appeal the House of Lords took a different view of the facts, holding that the letter was rather a notification of his intention to break the contract. Then the minimum payment clause became unenforceable as a penalty. But the five judges in the House of Lords could not reach agreement as to what the result would have been if the hirer's letter had really been a voluntary termination: two of them thought the Court of Appeal's decision, with all its anomalies, was right; two of them thought it wrong, and that the courts *did* have power to regulate minimum payment clauses however they came into operation; the fifth judge expressed no firm view. The result is that the Court of Appeal ruling stands as a precedent, binding on that court and all lower courts, but that the question is still open in the House of Lords. Here is surely an issue in which Parliament should intervene even for agreements outside the scope of the Hire-Purchase Act, to extend the doctrine of penalties to all such clauses.

THE GOODS AND THEIR QUALITY

As we have seen, it was the practice in hire-purchase agreements for the owner to exclude conditions and warranties which would otherwise be implied. These exemption clauses were so common that the courts had few opportunities to consider what were the owner's obligations in respect of the goods comprised in the agreement. Thus an essential feature of the 1938 Act was to lay down a number of conditions and warranties to be implied in hire-purchase agreements and to provide that these could not be excluded by the wording in the agreement itself. They were a big advance on the terms implied by the Sale of Goods Act because, as we have seen in Chapter 3, those terms could be excluded by the provisions of the sale contract, though the Supply of Goods (Implied Terms) Bill expected to become law in 1973 will prevent this in consumer sales. The implied terms in the Hire-Purchase Act were amended in 1964, many of the criticisms of the Molony Committee being taken into consideration, and became sections 17 and 19 of the 1965 Act. These are now being replaced by the latest Bill in terms identical to those in the redrafted sections of the Sale of Goods Act. The description of the law that follows is of the law under the sections of the Hire-Purchase Act 1965 which are in force at the time of writing, but an account of the new proposals follows on p. 177.

The most important implied conditions are those of merchantable quality and fitness for purpose (the meaning of these terms is discussed in Chapter 3). The condition of merchantable quality is implied in all hire-purchase agreements within the Act except that where the hirer has examined the goods (or a sample of them) before the agreement is entered into, the condition does not apply to defects which the examination ought to have revealed to him. As a general rule no clause in the agreement can exclude the condition of merchantable quality – it is implied 'notwithstanding any agreement to the contrary'. But exemption clauses are permitted in two cases: where the goods are second-hand, and described as such in the agreement; and where specific defects are described in the agreement and brought to the hirer's notice. In both these cases, it is not enough for the agreement to contain a clause expressly excluding the condition of merchantable quality: in order to rely on such a provision the owner must prove that before the agreement was made the clause was brought to the notice of the hirer and its effect made clear to him.

The condition that the goods will be reasonably fit for their purpose comes into operation whenever the hirer has made known the particular purpose for which the goods are required; the purpose may be made known to the owner or to the dealer, or to the servant or agent of either, and may be made known expressly or by implication. Exclusion of this implied condition is always possible, but again only if the clause was brought to the notice of the hirer and its effect made clear to him before the agreement was made. The courts do not take kindly to attempts to exclude these conditions unless it can be shown that the hirer really appreciates the implications of the exemption clause. *Lowe* v. *Lombank Ltd*, decided by the Court of Appeal in 1960, demonstrates this. In June 1958 a sixty-five-year-old widow, Mrs Lowe, agreed to take a second-hand car on hire purchase. The total price was £223. The car dealer sold the car to Lombank Ltd, a finance company, and the hire-purchase agreement was entered into between the company and Mrs Lowe. She had never seen the car, but was content with the dealer's assurance that it was 'in perfect or almost perfect condition'. She never read the agreement before she signed it, but in it was a clause which said that she had 'not made known to the owners expressly or by implication the particular purpose for which the goods are required' and that the goods were in fact fit for the purpose for which she required them. When the car was delivered it turned out to be quite unroadworthy and, as the county court judge put it, it was a danger both to its occupiers and to other road users. Mrs Lowe sued the finance company for damages on the ground that the car was not reasonably fit for driving on the roads. The argument of the finance company was, apparently, that there was no implied condition of fitness for purpose under this agreement: not because it had been excluded, but because it had never been implied in the first place, since the clause in the agreement specifically said that no purpose had been made known. The Court of Appeal, in a robust judgement, was not persuaded by this argument. Mrs Lowe wanted to acquire a second-hand car: by implication, therefore, she had made it known that she wanted it for the purpose of driving it. What other purpose could she have had? The clause relied on by Lombank Ltd was simply an attempt to evade the provisions of the Act. No one had pointed out this clause to Mrs Lowe, let alone made its effect clear to her. She was therefore awarded £160 damages.

The Bill which is likely to become the Supply of Goods (Implied Terms) Act 1973 will change hire-purchase law in a number of respects. The provisions about implied terms and exemption clauses will no longer depend on whether the hire-purchase price is £2,000 or less. Instead, the implied terms as to title will operate for all hire-purchase agreements, and the implied conditions as to merchantable quality, and (where the purpose for which the hirer requires the goods is known) fitness for purpose will operate for all hire-purchase agreements where the owner lets the goods in the course of a business (which for all practical purposes means all hire-purchase agreements).

The implied condition of merchantable quality will not apply as regards defects (a) if the defects were specifically drawn to the hirer's attention before the agreement was made or (b) if the hirer examined the goods before the agreement was made and the examination ought to have revealed the defects. The implied condition of fitness for purpose will not apply if it is shown that the hirer did not rely on the skill or judgement of the owner or the dealer, or that it was unreasonable for him to rely on them. If the hire-purchase agreement is a 'consumer agreement' (see p. 92, above), any exemption clause will be void. If it is not (e.g., if the hirer takes the goods in the course of a business), an exemption clause will be unenforceable if it would not be fair or reasonable for it to take effect.

DEALER'S LIABILITY

In *Lowe* v. *Lombank Ltd* (above, p. 176), Mrs Lowe was protected by the Hire-Purchase Act. Despite the impending change in the law it is worth looking at the common law position a little more closely. Suppose there had been no Hire-Purchase Act. Could the common law have helped Mrs Lowe?

First we may note that, quite apart from the Hire-Purchase Act and apart from anything in the agreement itself, the common law would imply into Mrs Lowe's agreement a term that the car was fit for the purpose of using on the road. Next, would the protective clause have been effective? It is likely that the courts would have treated it as an attempt to exclude the implied term, as in the case itself. And we have seen in Chapter 2 how the doctrine of fundamental breach of contract has enabled the courts to disregard exemption clauses – indeed several of the cases cited in that Chapter (*Karsales (Harrow) Ltd* v. *Wallis* (1956), *Yeoman Credit Ltd* v. *Apps* (1961), and *Farnworth Finance Holdings Ltd* v. *Attryde* (1970) were hire-purchase cases then outside the Hire-Purchase Act.

But even if the exemption clause had protected the finance company, there is another way in which the courts might have given Mrs Lowe a remedy – not against the finance company, but against the dealer. Where a finance company is putting up the money, the dealer is not a party to the agreement. In this situation it seemed at one time that he could never be made responsible by the hirer for any defects in the goods unless it could be proved that he was guilty of actual fraud. Now, because of court decisions in past years, there are two other ways in which the dealer might be made liable. If he has made any express statements about the goods which turn out to be false, he may be liable in damages to the hirer for breach of contract, even if he did not know that his statements were untrue. And even if he has not made any such statements, he may be liable for any personal injuries suffered by the hirer where it can be shown that the dealer has been negligent.

In a case decided in 1950, *Brown* v. *Sheen and Richmond Car Sales Ltd*, Brown was told by a dealer's sales manager that a certain car was in perfect condition and 'good for thousands of trouble-free miles'. The car was sold to a finance company which let it out to Brown on hire purchase. Brown found that the car was not in a satisfactory condition and he had to have a number of repairs carried out on the car at a cost of £60 to £70 so as to put it in a proper roadworthy condition. The court awarded Brown £66 damages against the dealer on the basis that the statements quoted amounted to a warranty as to the state of the car which induced Brown to make the hire-purchase agreement, and that this warranty had been broken.

In a 1940 case, *Herschtal* v. *Stewart and Arden Ltd*, a dealer had purchased a second-hand Morris car and had then repaired and reconditioned it. So that it could be taken by a customer on hire purchase, he arranged to sell it to a finance company which then made the hire-purchase agreement with the customer. The day after the car was delivered at the customer's flat, he drove it only a few miles when a wheel came off and he suffered nervous shock. The court held the dealer liable in damages for negligence. In the court's view, the dealer owed a duty to take reasonable care to see that the car, which he knew would be put on the road by the customer, was not in such condition that a wheel might suddenly fly off.

Both these cases were followed by Mr Justice McNair in 1956, in *Andrews* v. *Hopkinson*. A second-hand car dealer had a Standard car in his possession for a week or so before making arrangements for it to be taken by a customer on hire purchase. The dealer was confident of the car's qualities and told the customer: 'It's a good little bus. I would stake my life on it. You will have no trouble with it.' But the life at stake was not the dealer's. A week after the deal, owing to a failure in the drag-link joint in the steering, the customer was involved in a collision and suffered serious injuries including the fracture of three ribs and a fracture of the left wrist. The judge held the dealer liable in damages: first because his statement amounted to a warranty on the strength of which the hire-purchase agreement was made; secondly because the dealer had been negligent. The defect could have been discovered by any competent mechanic and the judge considered that a second-hand car dealer always owes a duty to carry out a reasonable examination so as to prevent possible injury from defects, or to get some other qualified person to make an examination, or at least to warn the customer that no such check has been made. The dealer had done none of these things.

These cases show that sometimes the hirer may have a remedy against the dealer even though the goods are taken

on hire purchase from a finance company. Such a remedy
has hitherto been based either on an express statement
made by the dealer, or on physical injury or damage
caused by the dealer's negligence. So far no dealer has
been sued in such a situation if he has not been negligent
and if he has made no statement about the goods. But in
Andrews v. *Hopkinson* the possibility of a contract between the dealer and the hirer, not based on an express
statement about the goods, was considered by Mr Justice
McNair. There is no contract of sale between the dealer
and the hirer (the sale by the dealer is, as we have seen, to
the finance company); but their relationship is so similar
to that of a sale that, provided a contractual relationship
can be established, the judge felt that there is much to be
said for an implied term that the goods are fit for use,
similar to that in section 14 of the Sale of Goods Act;
he was not, however, prepared to base his decision on this
ground, being content with throwing out the idea for
later judges to consider when necessary.

At common law it is not normally possible to make the
finance company liable for statements made by the dealer.
The dealer is not regarded as the agent of the finance
company so as to make them responsible for anything he
says, and in addition the hire-purchase agreement usually
contains an express denial of any such agency. But under
section 16 of the Hire-Purchase Act 1965 any statements
made by the dealer are deemed to have been made as
agent of the owner. Thus in *Andrews* v. *Hopkinson* it
would now be possible to sue the finance company for
breach of contract, relying on the statement made by the
dealer, if the Hire-Purchase Act applied. In the ordinary
way, however, if an agent acts on behalf of a principal so
as to make the principal liable for his statements, the
agent himself cannot be sued for breach of contract.
Under the Hire-Purchase Act the position is rather different: the dealer's statements are deemed to have been

made as agent of the owner, so as to make the owner liable as a principal, but 'Nothing in this section shall exonerate any person from any liability (whether criminal or civil) to which he would be subject apart from this section', so the agent himself remains liable under the principles in *Andrews* v. *Hopkinson*.

MORE PROTECTION

A number of other abuses are also dealt with by the Act. It had been possible before 1938 to persuade a hirer to take goods on hire purchase when, if he had appreciated how much more this would cost him in the end than if he had bought for cash, he would almost certainly have declined. Now, in any hire-purchase transaction governed by the Act, a prospective hirer has a right to be informed of the price at which the goods may be purchased for spot cash, that is, the 'cash price'. It is good enough if the hirer has inspected the goods or similar goods and tickets or labels attached show the cash price. Similarly, it is sufficient, where goods are selected by reference to a catalogue, that the catalogue states the cash price. Failure on the part of the owner or finance company to satisfy these statutory requirements results in the owner being unable to enforce the agreement in court or to claim the return of the goods. This is a potent sanction. The same sanction applies to certain other requirements of the Act – that the agreement must be in writing, be signed by the hirer personally (and not by anyone else acting for him, not even his wife), set out the details of the deposit and instalments to be paid, and show both the hire-purchase price and the cash price. This is so that the hirer can see for himself the extra he is paying, in the way of interest or charges, by taking the goods on hire purchase rather than buying them outright. To ensure that no blanks are left in the agreement when the hirer signs, to be filled in

later, the hirer must be given a copy of the agreement
when he signs it; if at that time it has not been signed
by or on behalf of all the other parties to the agreement,
he must be sent a further, complete, copy within seven
days after it takes effect. Regulations made under the
Hire-Purchase Act permit only black or dark grey print
on white paper, prohibit small print, and require that the
hirer signs in a red-printed box which warns him that he
is signing a hire-purchase agreement and that he must
not sell the goods.

A 'COOLING OFF' PERIOD

One of the important reforms introduced by the 1964
Act, based on a proposal of the Molony Committee, was
the 'cooling off' period for hire-purchase agreements
signed at home – or, indeed, anywhere other than at a
shop or finance company office. This gives the hirer a
right which is unique in the law of contract – a right to
cancel an agreement, after he has signed it and even after
it has been signed by the other parties and has been acted
upon.

For some years there had been concern over the high
pressure salesmanship displayed by door-to-door canvassers which can easily result in over-commitment on hire-
purchase transactions. One manifestation of slick sales
techniques is the practice of 'switch selling' (where an
expensive article is foisted on a customer who has expressed an interest in a cheap article) which depends on
a quick deal for its success. A time-lag during which
people can ponder the obligations they are being asked to
enter into should lead to fewer rash commitments.

Under section 11 of the 1965 Act the hirer who has
signed at home has three clear days to change his mind
and serve a notice of cancellation. Moreover, the three
days run, not from the day he signs, but from the day he

receives by post a copy of the hire-purchase agreement (his second copy, for he will already have received a copy at the time of signing). Both these copies must contain, in red print in a red-printed box, a notice telling the hirer of his right of cancellation.

There have already been suggestions that the Act's provisions are being evaded. Designed to protect the consumer against the forceful salesman who calls at the door and refuses to leave until he obtains a signature just to get rid of him, the right of cancellation operates only if the agreement is signed at a place other than premises at which the owner normally carries on a business, or at which goods of the contract description or a similar description are normally offered or exposed for sale in the course of a business there carried on. Sometimes a keen salesman, having persuaded the customer in his or her own home to take the goods, has offered to run the customer to his office or shop in his car to clear up the formalities. In this way the agreement is signed at business premises, and no right to cancel arises. But it is of course harder to get the customer out of the house to sign than to obtain a signature on the spot. No statistics are available to show the effect of the cooling-off provisions on the number of ill-considered agreements entered into. One result may have been to reduce the number of hirers going to gaol for failing to pay hire-purchase instalments until this means of coercion was abolished.

Imprisonment for civil debts, although familiar to readers of Charles Dickens, was abolished as long ago as 1869 when a new procedure was introduced. The creditor, after obtaining a judgement ordering the debtor to pay money, could apply to the county court and satisfy the judge that the debtor had sufficient means to pay off the debt, usually by instalments. The judge would make an order for payment and if the debtor failed to comply the judge might eventually be convinced that the debtor, although he had the money to pay, was deliberately refusing to carry out the order. At that stage the judge might commit the debtor to prison. In 1970 there were 2,252 people sent to prison by the county courts under this procedure.

Many people were concerned about the social problems caused by sending people – usually the poor or inadequate – to prison for not paying their debts, and the Payne Committee on the Enforcement of Judgement Debts, reporting in 1969, recommended that this last vestige of the debtors' prison should at last be abolished. This was done by the Administration of Justice Act 1970. Now, under the Attachment of Earnings Act 1971, a creditor is able to apply for an order requiring the debtor's employer to make regular deductions from the debtor's earnings and to remit them to court.

INTEREST RATES AND ADVERTISEMENTS

Very often a customer does not fully appreciate how much he is being required to pay by way of interest or charges, and this may be because the charges are expressed in a misleading way. If a man is told he will only have to pay 10p in the £ or 10 per cent per annum over a two-year period, that is generally calculated on the amount initially borrowed, that is, the amount outstanding after the deposit has been paid. But since he pays back the loan not in one lump sum but week by week or month by month, the real rate of interest is more like 18 per cent. Disclosure of the true rate of interest is not yet compulsory (see p. 195 below), but the quotation of interest rates in advertisements is controlled.

Misleading advertisements, which emphasize the deposit payable and either omit to say what instalments are payable as well, or relegate the instalments payable to small print, are already illegal under the Advertisements (Hire-Purchase) Act 1967, which consolidates earlier Acts of 1957 and 1964. By this Act, when a sum of money is mentioned in any kind of advertisement for goods offered on hire-purchase or credit-sale terms, the complete picture must be given by including in the advertisement the amount of the deposit, the number of instalments with the amount of each, whether they are payable weekly, monthly, or whatever the period is, and a statement of the cash price and total hire-purchase price. Moreover, the interest rate, if mentioned at all, must be the true rate of interest calculated as a percentage in accordance with a mathematical formula set out in the Act. (The result of this seems to be that advertisements now rarely quote the rate of interest at all.) The Act applies even if the price of the goods advertised is above £2,000, and breach of it makes the dealer liable to a fine. The Molony Committee recommended that the Board of Trade should accept the positive duty of enforcing the Act and should encourage the submission of reports about offences from all agencies conducting consumer protection work. A striking weakness of this Act is the fact that its only sanction is a criminal prosecution. It would be a valuable penalty for infringement if the hirer were enabled to defend a claim by proving that the advertisement which led him to enter the agreement was in breach of the Advertisements (Hire-Purchase) Act.

CREDIT SALES AND CONDITIONAL SALES

It has long been acknowledged that the legal form of the hire-purchase agreement – a hiring coupled with an option (which need not be exercised) to purchase the goods – is nothing but a legal fiction. It is a device to achieve a sale of the goods while affording to the seller (or 'owner') protection he could not receive under an outright sale. We saw earlier in this chapter how section 9 of the Factors Act 1889 (repeated in section 25(2) of the

Sale of Goods Act 1893), passed to protect innocent purchasers of goods, led to the vital distinction between contracts of sale, even if disguised as hiring agreements as in
Lee v. *Butler* (1893), and hire-purchase agreements
(*Helby* v. *Matthews*, 1895).

This distinction in turn led to the judicial development of the whole law of hire purchase as a body of law
separate and distinct from that of the law of sale.
Strangely enough, the law has now come full circle. The
1964 Act abolished the vital technical distinction between
hire purchase and sale, while leaving the body of hire-
purchase law in existence.

To understand this, it is necessary to distinguish between three types of transaction, all designed to enable
the customer to enjoy the possession and use of goods
before he has paid for them, as they exist under the Hire-
Purchase Act 1965.

A credit-sale agreement is a sale of goods whereby the
buyer becomes the owner of the goods immediately the
agreement is entered into, though the price is paid by
instalments; if there are five or more instalments and the
price is £2,000 or less, certain provisions of the 1965 Act
apply, mainly (where the price exceeds £30) relating to
the information given to the buyer in the agreement and
the right of cancellation where the agreement is signed
at home.

A conditional sale agreement is in form a sale of goods,
the price being paid by instalments, under which the
buyer does not become the owner until specified conditions – usually payment of the last instalment – are
fulfilled. *Lee* v. *Butler* (1893) was such an agreement, but
where the price is £2,000 or less the significance of that
case has been removed, since for most practical purposes
the 1965 Act equates conditional sale agreements with
hire-purchase agreements. Thus, under section 27 of the
Hire-Purchase Act 1965, the buyer now has the right to

terminate the agreement just as if it was a hire-purchase agreement and, by section 54 of the 1965 Act, section 9 of the Factors Act 1889 and section 25(2) of the Sale of Goods Act 1893 no longer apply to conditional sale agreements. Thus the whole of the original *raison d'être* of hire-purchase agreements has been done away with where the agreement is within the £2,000 limit.

A hire-purchase agreement is not a sale at all, but a hiring under which the hirer is given the right, if he wishes (as he almost invariably does), to buy the goods. The main object of this form of agreement, as opposed to a conditional sale agreement, was originally to permit the owner to get the goods back from any innocent person who unwittingly purchased them from the hirer. As a result of the 1964 changes, we find that (a) innocent purchasers can in general obtain no rights to the goods whether they bought them from a conditional buyer or from a hire-purchaser, but that (b) if the goods are motor vehicles – which are not only portable and valuable, but also commonly the subject of second-hand sales – an innocent purchaser, provided he is a private purchaser, will obtain ownership even if he bought it from a hire-purchaser. This protection for innocent buyers applies even if the hire-purchase agreement is outside the £2,000 limit and not otherwise caught by the Hire-Purchase Act; it is discussed in Chapter 3, above.

Now that conditional sale agreements which fall within the Act and hire-purchase agreements have much the same effect, we may regard them both as hire-purchase agreements. Conditional sale agreements have not been much used in this country, although they have been popular in parts of North America. Credit sale agreements, on the other hand, have been and will continue to be used here.

One reason for using credit sale in preference to hire purchase has been that when they were in force the

Government's economic controls, regulating the size of the deposit and the repayment period, have laid down different rules for the two types of transaction. But in this book we have not concerned ourselves with these particular hire-purchase regulations, which were of a transitory nature and were frequently changed as the Government decided to inflate or deflate the economy. In 1971 the Crowther Committee recommended the abolition of these economic controls, and they were in fact withdrawn (though whether temporarily or permanently is not known) soon after.

The main legal distinction between hire purchase and credit sales lies in the remedies available to the seller or owner if instalments are not paid. Under a credit-sale agreement there is no right to demand the return of the goods – the only right is to secure payment of the rest of the price. Conversely, the buyer has no right to return the goods (unless they are unsatisfactory and he has the right to reject them under the Sale of Goods Act 1893: see Chapter 3). If therefore the goods depreciate rapidly in value, the seller may well choose credit sale – he would rather get the money than have the goods back again.

Since the latest reforms to hire-purchase law came into operation at the beginning of 1965, some finance companies have displayed an interest in credit sale in preference to hire-purchase even for motor vehicles, where a substantial second-hand value is of course maintained. They regard the restrictions on recovery of the goods in case of default as expensive and time-consuming, cancelling-out the theoretical advantage of being able to get the goods back. From the buyer's point of view, it seems attractive that under a credit-sale agreement he becomes the immediate owner of the goods, whereas under a hire-purchase agreement he does not acquire ownership till the last instalment is paid and his 'option' exercised. In practice, however, he may be better off under a hire-purchase agreement, because of the wealth of protection afforded by the Hire-Purchase Act. He may not be the owner of the goods in legal theory, but once one-third has been paid they cannot be taken from him without the consent of the court, and the most likely court order if he is in real difficulties is to reduce the size of the instalments, thus giving him more time to pay.

Under a credit-sale agreement, on the other hand, the seller's remedies may be quite effective. The credit-sale agreement may well contain a term stating that if the buyer falls into arrears with any one payment at any time, or if he sells the goods (which he is admittedly entitled to do, being their owner), then the whole of the unpaid balance of the price is to become payable immediately. This gives rise to an immediate debt of all the unpaid instalments. It is unlikely that the buyer will be able to pay all this off at once, and the seller is entitled to sue for the money without further notice; there is almost certain to be no genuine defence to this claim in the majority of cases, and under a speedy procedure available for uncontestable debts in the High Court the seller may well obtain a judgement for the whole sum within three or four weeks. This can be enforced in a variety of ways, the details of which cannot be described here. Suffice it to say that one method is to instruct the sheriff of the county to seize the debtor's goods and sell them to raise money to pay off the judgement; and if the debtor is still in possession of, say, the car he bought under the credit-sale agreement, this may be seized and sold with no court having the power to intervene. It is clear that customers should consider the alternatives very carefully if given the choice of credit sale or hire purchase.

The main application of the Hire-Purchase Act to credit-sale agreements is in relation to the formation of the agreement. As in the case of hire purchase, the potential buyer must be informed of the cash price before he signs the agreement, and the agreement must contain clear information on certain essential matters such as the price and instalments. Having signed he must receive a copy immediately, with a second copy later if it does not take immediate effect. If the agreement is signed at home, the three-day 'cooling off period', already described in relation to hire purchase, is available for the buyer and the necessary information about this must be contained in red ink in the agreement.

But whereas all this applies to every hire-purchase agreement within the £2,000 limit, it applies to credit-sale agreements only if they are for £2,000 or less and *for more than* £30. When the original Hire-Purchase Act was passed in 1938 the agreement provisions applied to credit-sale agreements for more than £5, the intention being to exclude very small transactions, usually of a temporary nature. The 1964 Act increased this figure to £30. The result is that, although it may be that a number of common and everyday transactions are freed from tiresome regulation, the consumer is deprived of protection in transactions involving what is to many people a tidy sum of money. There is already some evidence that door-step salesmen are obtaining signatures to two credit-sale agreements, each for £30 or less, rather than to one agreement for all the goods, in order to evade the 'cooling off period', and some goods previously sold on the doorstep for more than £30 have now been reduced to just below £30 for the same reason. The statutory protection afforded to buyers under credit-sale agreements is limited enough in all conscience: even at the expense of impeding some honest transactions, we believe that the £30 limit should be lowered without delay, ideally back to the £5 in the 1938 Act.

ANOMALIES IN THE LAW

The present law of hire purchase is replete with anomalies. It must be admitted that, despite its complications, it is a sounder body of law now than it has been for many years. Yet it must be doubted whether its complications and technicalities are a necessary part of a system of providing credit to purchasers of goods and security to sellers.

It is for example regrettable that the present law is so difficult to understand that no customer can be blamed for signing an agreement without reading it. This lends itself to attempts to evade all the controls over hire purchase by preparing agreements which, although to the lay eye they look like hire-purchase agreements, are in reality nothing of the kind.

Thus an encyclopedia publisher has been supplying books by way of hire, rather than hire purchase. The customer agrees to hire the many volumes for ten years by paying regular monthly instalments for the first two or three years, and then paying 'an instalment of £1 for the next twenty years payable on or before the end of twenty years' from the date of the agreement. It is reasonably clear that the real price is to be paid by the instalments over the initial two or three years, and that no one is likely to worry if the succeeding twenty-year instalment is not paid. Yet in law this is probably not a hire-purchase agreement, for the document does not provide for the customer ever to become the owner of the goods: they will always belong to the encyclopedia company. This form of contract can evade, it seems, the right of cancellation given to hire-purchasers in respect of doorstep agreements. It could in addition impose harsh terms on the hirer.

Sitting in court in 1964, Lord Justice Sachs had this to say after trying a case for the hire of a £1,000 caravan:

'It is becoming increasingly apparent ... that there is a tendency on the part of some finance companies, at any rate, to try to use contracts of ... simple hire in order to ensure that the hirer does not have the protection of the Hire-Purchase Acts. These contracts of hire to which finance companies are inclined are simple only in the sense that technically they are not contracts of hire purchase. One has but to look at the contract in this particular case to see in its small print how far from simple it is, either from the layman's or indeed the lawyer's point of view. The sooner the legislature is apprised of this tendency and the sooner it takes in hand the problem, the fewer will be the occasions when finance companies are able to inflict on an unwary hirer hardships of the type which have become manifest in the present case.' He then gave judgement for the finance company.

THE CROWTHER REPORT

The Molony Committee considered evidence calling for a major recasting of the law of hire purchase but rejected it in their 1962 report: this would involve 'substantial alteration of long-established common law conceptions and statutory provisions,' they said, and 'we are not interested in law reform merely for the sake of reform.' But neither consumer bodies nor trade interests were satisfied with the law, and in 1968 the Government set up the Committee on Consumer Credit under the late Lord Crowther; its important and persuasive report was published in 1971.

The Crowther Report attacked the present law for its lack of any functional basis – 'distinctions between one type of transaction and another are drawn on the basis of legal abstractions rather than the basis of commercial reality' – and for its failure to provide just solutions to common problems. The Committee was therefore in favour of a sweeping re-formulation of this part of the law, based on the recognition that the whole point of hire purchase is purchase, not hire: the dealer is concerned with selling his goods, the consumer with buying them without paying the whole price at once. In reality, therefore, the extension of credit is a loan, and the retention of ownership until payment of the last instalment is a device intended to provide the owner or seller with security in case of non-payment – it fulfils the functions of a mortgage over the goods. As we have seen, the legal rules that apply at present to chattel mortgages are totally different from those applying to hire-purchase or conditional sale agreements: the Committee recommended that the Bills of Sale Acts and Moneylenders Acts should be repealed and replaced by a new legal structure applicable uniformly to all types of security interest in goods.

If these proposals are put into effect, the role of the finance company (see p. 161 above) will change. It will no longer need to buy goods in order to supply them to the consumer: it will be able freely to acknowledge that its real function is to lend money. There is nothing wrong, in our modern economic society, with money-lending: indeed, credit is the foundation of modern business. The finance company will therefore be seen to perform a function comparable to that of a bank or a building society.

This change would bring into prominence an area of contention. From the finance company's point of view, it seems illogical for the company to be liable for faulty goods. If a man raises the money for a motor cycle by means of a bank overdraft he cannot sue the bank if the machine breaks down; why then, it is said, should he be able to sue a finance company? Yet the present law, as we have seen, imposes such a liability on the finance company. Would this be changed if the finance company no longer bought the goods in order to supply them to the consumer? The Crowther Committee thought it should not: it is usual for a finance company to have a regular arrangement with the dealers with whom it does business, the finance company controls the contract documents used by the dealer, and it pays him a substantial commission for introducing business; moreover the finance company's financial support for the dealer often helps him to stay in business. 'To a considerable extent,' said the Committee, 'the finance house and the dealer are engaged in a joint venture.' They therefore recommended that a distinction should be drawn between a completely independent lender (like the consumer's own bank) and a 'connected lender' who has a relationship with the dealer of the kind described. The connected lender should be liable (as the finance company is under the Hire Purchase Act) for defects in the goods and for misrepresentations made by the dealer. In this they came to the same conclusion as the Molony Committee nine years earlier.

In a similar way the radical change in legal structure would not change any of the present protection given to the consumer by the Hire-Purchase Act, and legislation passed to implement the Report should, it was said, contain detailed provisions giving much the same protection as there is now. In some respects it would go further – for example, all advertisements of consumer credit facilities in which reference is made to the cost of borrowing should be compelled to state that cost in terms of a rate per cent, and so should all consumer loan agreements. This compulsory disclosure of the true rate of interest in agreements would, as we have seen (p. 185 above), be an innovation in the law. The Committee did not favour any rigid ceiling on interest rates even though the existing safeguards against the imposition of extortionate charges are inadequate; instead everyone who carries on the business of granting consumer loans should be licensed; this system of licensing would replace the present inadequately enforced control under the Moneylenders Acts, and the persistent charging of excessive interest would be a ground for revoking a licence.

CHAPTER 7

AT YOUR SERVICE

MOST of the transactions considered in earlier chapters
have related to the supply of goods, but the consumer is
also concerned with the supply of services: the cleaning,
washing, and repairing of clothes, furniture, cars and all
the many articles which help to make up the twentieth-
century household.

However informal, an arrangement for carrying out
services in return for payment is a contract. Like all contracts, the rights of the parties are governed by what has
been expressly agreed: 'leather soles', or 'tubeless tyres',
or 'clean and press'. But often nothing is said of many
important questions, such as the standard of workmanship and the care to be taken of the goods being handled,
and here the law steps in with 'implied terms' – terms,
so the theory goes, which the parties would have agreed if
they had thought about it.

The keynote to these implied terms is the word 'reasonable'. The work must be carried out to a reasonable
standard. The materials used must be reasonably fit for
use. Reasonable care must be taken of goods. What is
'reasonable' is not capable of precise definition; the word
is inherently vague, and all the circumstances must be
considered. The effect is that the courts have some discretion in determining what is fair and just.

Two problems have caused most litigation: the loss of,
or damage to, goods received for cleaning or repair, and
the use of faulty materials, or faulty workmanship, in
repairing them. Some examples will show how the law has
developed.

REASONABLE CARE FOR ANOTHER'S GOODS

English law is essentially empirical in its approach. The function of a judge trying a case is first and foremost to resolve the dispute between the parties in accordance with established principles of law. In doing so he may perhaps explain or extend or qualify the existing legal principles, and his judgement may establish a precedent for the future. But because his duty is to decide the particular case before him, only so much of his decision as is necessary to dispose of that case can be invested with the peculiar power of authority accorded to judicial decisions. Anything else he may say in the course of the judgement – his views on other problems, for example, or his attempts to rationalize or systematize the law – must be regarded merely as his own personal views, entitled to more or less respect according to his individual reputation and the court in which he sits, but not absolutely binding on any other judges.

In 1703 the case of *Coggs* v. *Bernard* came before the Court of King's Bench. Bernard had agreed to move several casks of brandy belonging to Coggs from one cellar to another. Bernard carelessly broke one of the casks and some brandy was lost. When Coggs sued him, Bernard argued that as he was not to receive payment he was under no liability: there was no consideration for his agreement, so he could not be sued for breach of contract. The court held that Bernard was liable. In modern terms we would say that Bernard, simply by taking possession of Coggs's property, was under a duty to take reasonable care of it, though the court at the time attempted to spell out the presence of consideration.

The chief interest of this case lies in the judgement of Sir John Holt, Chief Justice of the Court of King's Bench. Not content with deciding the case before him, Holt launched into a detailed analysis of the law of bailment. A bailment arises when one person (the bailee or possessor) comes into possession of goods belonging to another (the bailor or owner). Holt discovered six sorts of bailments: deposit, where the possessor looks after the owner's goods without charge; gratuitous loan, as where an umbrella is lent to a friend; hire, where the possessor pays for the use of the goods; pawn or pledge; a wide class, where goods are in the possessor's hands for carriage from one place to another, or for work to be done to them, in return for a payment to the possessor; and a similar class, where goods are to be carried or worked upon without payment.

The facts of *Coggs* v. *Bernard* fell into this last class, so that the Chief Justice's remarks on the other classes were not strictly necessary to his decision. Nevertheless, Holt proceeded to analyse the liability of the possessor if the goods were lost or damaged while in his possession. Where the bailment was that described as deposit, he said, the possessor will be chargeable only if he is guilty of 'gross negligence', but not for 'ordinary neglect'. Where there is a gratuitous loan, the possessor is answerable for the 'least neglect' and must use the 'utmost care', as must the possessor who is hiring the goods. A pawnbroker or pledgee must use 'ordinary care'. A possessor who is to carry the goods or do work on them for reward, apart from special cases like common innkeepers and common carriers, is 'only to do the best he can', that is, to take 'reasonable care'. Finally, a possessor who receives no reward for his pains must not act negligently, but must exercise 'diligent management'.

Much of this detailed analysis was not drawn from established decisions of the courts; nor was it the fruit of Sir John Holt's own creative reasoning. It was borrowed largely from the principles of Roman Law, expounded in writings completed in the sixth century. Roman Law depended largely on analytical statements of principle, and on classifications of a rigid nature, but English lawyers were not used to dealing with concepts of this kind. The judges loyally attempted to follow Holt's rules, but without specific cases to guide them soon found difficulty in distinguishing between the different degrees of negligence. In 1843, Lord Cranworth, unable to see the differenece between negligence and gross negligence, said that 'it was the same thing with the addition of a vituperative epithet.' This no doubt summed up the views of many common lawyers, and although some judges have continued to use such expressions – as recently as 1947 a decision was based on the possessor's 'gross negligence' – the tendency has been to discard them. The present law has, indeed, a deceptive simplicity. We can say that in bailments of every kind the possessor is under a duty to take reasonable care of the owner's goods. The particular circumstances will be taken into account in deciding what is reasonable: no doubt it is reasonable to take more care of another's property if you are being paid to look after it than if you are doing a friend a favour. But an attempt to define 'gross negligence' as opposed to 'ordinary negligence' – as if a certain amount of negligence is to be expected – can only confuse the meaning of 'negligence'.

Thus the views of Chief Justice Holt, unnecessary for deciding Bernard's liability and therefore *obiter dicta* – things 'said by the way' – have ceased to influence English law. But the discussion will have emphasized one vital principle: that a possessor, whether paid or not, is not automatically liable simply because the goods have been lost or damaged. He is not an 'insurer' of the goods. If he proves that he took reasonable care of the goods, and that the loss or damage occurred despite his reasonable care, the loss falls on the owner of the goods. For example, in *Searle* v. *Laverick* in 1874 the owner of a coach paid to leave it at the defendant's livery stable. In a gale the upper storeys of the building collapsed and damaged the coach. The disaster was a result of the negligence of the builder employed by the defendant; but the defendant himself had taken reasonable care in selecting an apparently competent builder, and was not called upon to compensate the owner of the coach.

If it were for the owner of goods to prove to the court that the person to whom he had given possession had been negligent, his task would be well nigh impossible and his chance of recovering compensation correspondingly slight. In most cases he knows little more than that he gave possession of the goods to the bailee and that they were returned damaged, or were never returned at all. Fortunately, by a valuable rule of evidence, that is all he need show in support of his claim. Faced with this situation the possessor must now show that he was not negligent, that the goods were lost or damaged in a way consistent with his having taken reasonable care. If a consumer's sheets are not returned by the laundry, the launderer must show that the sheets vanished without any negligence on his part. If, for example, the laundry caught fire, it may well be possible to show that all reasonable precautions were taken to prevent a fire, and to deal with it if it broke out: then there will be no negligence, and no liability. If your watch has been stolen from a repairer's shop, the repairer has to show that he took reasonable steps to prevent theft: if he can satisfy the court on this he is not liable – and nor, as we shall see in Chapter 9, is his insurance company.

In practice it is not easy for the possessor to show that neither he nor his employees have been negligent. Only in exceptional circumstances, such as fire or theft, are articles lost or damaged without a lack of reasonable care on someone's part. But sometimes it may be possible to deny that any bailment existed – in other words, to deny any obligation whatsoever to take care of the owner's goods. For example, in *Ashby* v. *Tolhurst*, decided by the Court of Appeal in 1937, the owner of a car left it at the 'Seaway Car Park' at Southend-on-Sea, paying an attendant one shilling. When he returned, the car was not to be found: the attendant had permitted a stranger to drive the car away. It was held that the owners of the car park were under no obligation to take care of parked vehicles. They were not bailees of the cars, for the transaction amounted to no more than this: for the fee of one shilling they permitted owners of cars to leave them, but they did not take possession of the cars. A bailment involves a delivery of possession, so that the bailee becomes the legal possessor of the article bailed, with legal rights as well as legal obligations. But as Lord Greene, then Master of the Rolls, said, 'Parking a car is leaving a car and nothing else.'

It is not always easy to distinguish between a bailment and a mere permission to leave an article somewhere. If something is to be done to the goods – if they are to be washed or repaired – then the transaction is sure to be a bailment. But what of mere temporary storage? In *Ultzen* v. *Nichols*, as long ago as 1894, an overcoat was stolen from a hook in a restaurant. The diner himself had not hung it up, but a waiter had taken it from him without being asked and hung the coat where the diner could not see it. The county court judge who tried the case found that there was a bailment, and the restaurant was liable for the loss. On appeal to the High Court the judges were uncertain but, on the footing that it was at least possible that there was a bailment, refused to disturb the lower court's finding of fact. More recently, in *Samuel* v. *Westminster Wine Co. Ltd*, in 1959, a mink coat was stolen from the Prince of Wales Hotel in Wimbledon. Its owner, arriving for dinner at the hotel, had found no attendant on duty in the room where there were already a number of coats, and where she had left her coat with an attendant on previous occasions. She left her mink lying on a chair, and never saw it again. Mr Justice Thesiger held that this constituted a bailment of the coat and held the defendants liable on the ground of negligence. On the other hand, when a motor-cycle was left at a pub in *Tinsley* v. *Dudley* (1951), in an unattended part of the premises advertised as 'Covered Yard and Garage', the Court of Appeal held that there was no bailment. The proprietor of the public house did not know the cycle was there, and there was no reason why he should have known. It is more than likely that a distinction must be drawn between cars, cycles, and vehicles, where convincing evidence of a bailment is necessary, and other articles, where a bailment will more readily be held to exist.

EXEMPTION CLAUSES

More frequent than disputes about the existence of a bailment are disputes about the terms on which a possessor has taken possession of the goods. The obligation to take reasonable care of the goods may, as we have seen in Chapter 2, be varied or excluded by express agreement, and many possessors take advantage of this principle. Several of the examples discussed in Chapter 2 were, indeed, bailments, and the general principles were there described. In this chapter some more illustrations will be given, all drawn from the field of bailment.

The first concern of the courts, when faced with a clause which must be treated as part of the contract between the two parties, is as to its meaning. The reluctance of the possessor to reveal too plainly that he is seeking to exclude his legal obligations leads to clauses which are obscure and ambiguous. The courts interpret such clauses narrowly, and the benefit of any doubt must go to the consumer on the principle that to exclude a liability imposed by the law there must be a clear agreement. Thus if a clause excludes liability for 'loss caused by negligence' or for 'loss, whether or not caused by negligence' it is sufficiently clear and explicit to be effective.

At one time the courts seemed to take the view that if a clause was clear to a lawyer that was enough. So it was said that if a bailee relied on an exemption clause it would be effective even if it did not mention negligence. This was because, as we have seen, a bailee is not liable for damage to or loss of the goods unless he has been negligent, so without negligence there would be no liability and hence no need for an exemption clause; presumably the clause was intended to have some effect, or it would not have formed part of the contract; therefore it must operate to exclude liability for negligence.

This reasoning was applied in *Alderslade* v. *Hendon Laundry Ltd* in 1945. Ten Irish linen handkerchiefs were not returned by the laundry. When sued they relied on a condition: 'The maximum amount allowed for lost or damaged articles is twenty times the charge made for laundering.' This did not mention negligence, so the plaintiff argued that it did not protect the laundry. But the Court of Appeal found in favour of the laundry, whose maximum liability was limited in accordance with the clause.

In a later case, in the Court of Appeal in 1972, it was however emphasized that a clause excluding liability for negligence should make its meaning plain 'to any ordinarily literate and sensible person'. The Court was bound by the decision in the *Hendon Laundry* case, and could not overrule it; but Lord Salmon explained the earlier decision by pointing out that the ordinary person would understand that almost always when goods were lost or damaged while at a laundry it was because of the laundry's negligence, and would therefore understand that the clause was intended to protect the laundry against that liability.

The facts of the 1972 case, *Hollier* v. *Rambler Motors (A.M.C.) Ltd*, were however rather different. The plaintiff's car was damaged by a fire at the company's garage where it was being repaired. The fire was caused by the company's negligence, but they relied on a clause saying 'The Company is not responsible for damage caused by fire to customers' cars on the premises.' Even assuming that the clause had been incorporated into the contract, the Court of Appeal held that it did not protect the company, for it was not sufficiently clear to exclude liability for negligence. The ordinary motorist reading the clause would take it, not as an exclusion of liability, but rather as a warning that if there was a fire not caused by the fault of the company then the company would not be liable – in other words, its function could be assumed to be to draw attention to the common law position.

Another illustration of the need to be explicit as to the nature of the protection given by an exemption clause can be found in *White* v. *John Warwick & Co. Ltd* in 1953. The bailment was one of hire, a shopkeeper hiring a tradesman's cycle from the defendants. Here, therefore, the exemption clause sought to protect the bailor, who supplied the cycle, from claims made by the bailee, his customer. In most hiring agreements the common law implies a promise on the part of the owner that the goods are reasonably fit for the purpose for which they are hired, and the owners had broken this implied promise. The saddle nut was so rusty that it could not be fully tightened; as a result the saddle slipped and the shopkeeper was thrown to the ground. The shopkeeper claimed damages, but the exemption clause read: 'Nothing in this agreement shall render the owners liable for any personal injuries.' It failed to protect the owners. If there had been no exemption clause they could have been made liable on two alternative grounds: they could have been sued for breach of contract for supplying a defective machine, or in tort for their negligence in failing to take reasonable care that the cycle would not cause injury. Since the exemption clause did not mention injuries caused by negligence, it was effective only to exclude liability for breach of contract – a liability which did not depend on negligence, and which would have been the same even if every possible care had been taken.

Even if the exemption clause does cover negligence it may not give protection for, as we saw in Chapter 2, if the person relying on an exemption clause has himself broken the contract in a fundamental respect there is a presumption that the exemption clause is not intended to protect him. *Davies* v. *Collins*, where the uniform of an American Army officer was lost (see p. 49), was decided in 1945, at the same time as *Alderslade* v. *Hendon Laundry Ltd.* The exemption clauses were remarkably similar in the two cases. But the cleaners failed to get the protection afforded to the laundry because there was a fundamental breach of contract caused by their sub-contracting the work to another cleaner.

Indeed, if a bailee is guilty of a fundamental breach of contract by acting in a manner inconsistent with the bailment he will become liable even if he is not negligent. In *Edwards* v. *Newland* (1950), furniture was stored during the war. The possessor's depository being full, the storing was sub-contracted to another storage-contractor's depository. The goods were damaged in an air raid, and normally this would not make the possessor liable because clearly the damage could not be said to be due to negligence. But the sub-contracting was done without the owner's knowledge or permission and, because the personal care of the possessor is of the essence of a contract for the storage of furniture, the possessor was held to have committed a fundamental breach of the contract by parting with the goods. He was therefore liable for their damage, his care or negligence being irrelevant. There was no exemption clause in this case, but if there had been it would have made no difference.

The Law Commission and the Scottish Law Commission published a Working Paper in 1971 suggesting that exemption clauses in contracts for services might become subject to a test of reasonableness, to be applied by the courts in the light of the particular circumstances.

DEFECTIVE REPAIRS

The other problem which has given rise to many serious disputes is whether there is liability for poor workmanship or for faulty materials used in repairing the goods. The problem of workmanship can be soon disposed of. If the repairer follows a trade or profession, he must exercise the skill of a reasonably competent member of that trade or profession. This principle, familiar in its application to doctors and solicitors, applies equally to jewellers, watchmakers, garages, electricians, shoe repairers, and so on. If the repairer does not follow a recognized trade or profession there is no comparable standard by which to judge him, but he must exercise such skill as he has or as he pretends to have.

These principles are all very well as a matter of law but, of course, their practical application is not so easy. The standard is comparative – that to be expected from a 'reasonably competent' member of the trade or profession. So, too, only a 'reasonable price' can be charged if no definite price is fixed. If an estimate is accepted, this is a firm contract to charge, and to pay, the estimated price, by which both parties are bound.

But how is the ordinary consumer to judge what a reasonably competent trader would do, or what is a reasonable price? *Shopper's Guide* has demonstrated how helpless he is when faced with electrical or mechanical equipment. In the first investigation (*Shopper's Guide*,

November 1961) two simple faults were deliberately introduced into an otherwise perfect television set, which
was then submitted to six different service agents in the
London area. Only two succeeded in remedying both
faults, and another two remedied one fault each. One
dealer replaced a perfect valve with a faulty valve, charging for the 'replacement'; another charged for replacing
a 'faulty valve' although none of the valves had been
changed. The bills ranged from £1 2s. 6d. to £4 11s. 3d.,
the best repairer charging £2 10s. 0d.

The second test (*Shopper's Guide*, July 1962) was on
car repairs. Two faults were introduced into a two-year-
old car in excellent condition, and ten garages in the
London area tackled the job in all innocence. Only three
garages were wholly satisfactory. Three did not complete
the repairs needed, two fitted unnecessary items which
increased the cost of the repairs and two were guilty of
both faults. The charges ranged from £1 9s. 2d. (for an
excellent job) to £4 13s. 4d. (for an unsatisfactory
repair).

More recently some of the local Consumer Groups have
been carrying out similar investigations in different parts
of the country. That they cannot help the consumer to
choose the best is convincingly demonstrated by the survey of the Oxford Consumers' Group, which asked its
members' opinions of different garages. Of the garages
which received more than one comment, over one-third
had at least one regular customer who was highly satisfied, and at least one customer who would not willingly
use it again. As the Group's News Sheet pointed out, a
large garage employs many mechanics, often with a rapid
turnover, and they are bound to vary in skill and care.
The virtue of unheralded investigations is, of course, that
they help to keep repairers on their toes.

Reporting in August 1967 the National Board for Prices
and Incomes revealed that motorists were charged more

than necessary for garage repairs and servicing: charges had risen by 19 per cent between 1964 and 1966, compared with a rise in the retail prices index in the same period of 9 per cent. The Board found that there was a 'wide variation' between garages in the prices charged for comparable jobs, and that there was evidence of consumer dissatisfaction with the service provided by garages in terms of price, quality, and time taken on jobs. But this dissatisfaction would not have much effect on garages, said the report, because of limitations in the customer's choice through location of garages, and the consumer's lack of knowledge about the right price or quality.

One attempt to meet this helplessness on the part of the consumer is the Investigation and Advisory Service introduced in October 1965 by the Motor Agents' Association. If a dispute between a customer and a member of the Association cannot be settled amicably, the Association will investigate and try to encourage the parties to reach agreement. If this fails, the Association recommends arbitration: each party deposits £5, and the dispute is referred to an independent arbitrator; the successful party gets his £5 back. Arbitration is not compulsory, but the Association is confident that most of its member garages will agree to the Association's advice. The big advantage of the Investigation and Advisory Service over ordinary legal remedies is, of course, its low cost to both parties, compared with court proceedings, and, it is hoped, its speed. In 1972 a national council, composed of an independent chairman and representatives of the motoring organizations, the motor trade and other interested parties, was set up to act as a 'watchdog' on garage work. It is intended to handle complaints and to establish a system whereby garages would guarantee that the work paid for had been done, and done to a proper standard. The Consumers' Association has expressed scepticism because the new council lacks power to ensure that its recommendations are implemented. It may be that a compulsory licensing system is needed.

Where faulty materials are used in repairs, the relevant legal principles resemble those discussed in relation to the sale of goods in Chapter 3. The materials supplied by the repairer are goods, and the purpose for which they are to be used is generally beyond argument, since it is the repairer himself who uses them for the specific job. Provided, therefore, that it is in the course of the repairer's business to supply such materials, there is an implied term of the contract of repair that the materials will be of good quality and reasonably fit for use. For example, in *Stewart* v. *Reavell's Garage* (1952), the brakes of a 1929 Bentley were to be repaired. Unsuitable linings were used and the following day, travelling at 60 m.p.h., the owner discovered that they were not reasonably fit for their purpose. He successfully sued the garage for £361, the cost of repairing the damage caused when the car overturned, although there was no suggestion of negligence. However, just as in the comparable provisions of section 14 of the Sale of Goods Act 1893 (p. 75), if the owner of the goods did not rely on the repairer's skill or judgement there may be no such term: this will depend on whether the circumstances show that the owner is taking the risk of the materials being unsuitable. Again, just as under the Sale of Goods Act, the implied terms may be excluded by a clause in the contract, a common feature of contracts for car repairs.

In strict law, the supply of spare parts in the course of repair is not a sale of the parts, even though the effect of the transaction is that the ownership of the parts is transferred from the repairer. In the same way, if a famous artist paints a portrait, this is not a sale of the painting even though the ownership of the frame and the canvas and the paint on the canvas passes from the artist to the person who has commissioned him. The real object of these transactions is the workmanship and skill – of the repairer, or of the painter. The consequence is that this sort of contract is not governed by the Sale of Goods Act. That Act, however, as we have seen, did not mark a radical change in the law, but rather represented an authoritative statement of the common law, with only a few amendments. The common law governing contracts for work and materials, or for skill and labour, to give them an alternative name, is, it seems, so similar to the old common law of sale (and, therefore, to the present statute law of sale) that for present purposes we need not bother about the differences. In *Samuels* v. *Davies*, for instance, a patient complained about the fit of a set of false teeth, basing his claim on section 14 of the Sale of Goods Act. The dentist argued that the Sale of Goods Act had no relevance – this, he claimed, was not a sale of false teeth, but a contract for his skill and labour. No matter, ruled the Court of Appeal: whichever it is, there is an implied term that the teeth must be reasonably fit for their purpose. Similar principles apply to hair dyes, a frequent cause of distress, if the law reports are to be believed.

RIGHTS OF THE POSSESSOR

The law is not a one-sided instrument. It would be wrong to give the impression that the law is concerned only with the possessor's duties, for it also gives him rights. His most important right is, of course, to secure payment in accordance with the terms agreed. What if the owner fails to pay?

The possessor can, of course, sue the owner for the money owing. But this is not very practical advice to give to a shoe repairer when his customer fails to pay him a pound or two, or to a cleaner claiming fifty pence. The law does, in fact, give a possessor an additional right of considerable value: he can refuse to return the goods on which he has worked, whether they are a pair of trousers or a motor car, until he has been paid for his work and materials. In legal language, he has a lien on the goods.

There are several limits on the operation of this lien. The right to retain goods comes to an end when the amount due in respect of those very goods has been paid, even though other money arising out of different transactions is still owing. Thus if a jeweller repairs for the same owner a ring (charge £5) and a watch (charge £1), he can refuse to part with them until he is paid. But if he is paid £1 for the watch, he must return it. If he returns the watch without being paid at all, he loses his lien on it – it is a right to retain possession, not to regain possession. Suppose he is then paid £5: if nothing is said by the customer about how the money is to be allocated, the jeweller can allocate £1 to the charge for the watch and £4 to the ring. His lien on the ring then remains until the final pound is paid. But if the customer specifically allocates the whole £5 to the ring at the time of payment, the jeweller has no option but to return it: he cannot retain it until the £1 for the watch has also been paid.

A more serious limitation on the lien is this. It is simply a right to retain possession, and nothing more. Suppose, for example, that the customer is unable to pay the £5 for the ring. The jeweller has no right to sell the ring at common law. All he can do is to retain it in the hope that, some day, the customer will be willing to pay the £5 in order to get his ring back. The jeweller's right is, therefore, an inconvenience to the customer, but it is not a very effective way of putting pressure on the customer to secure speedy payment. This common law limitation on the lien has, however, been modified by statute, the Disposal of Uncollected Goods Act 1952. The reason for the Act was said to be the dire plight of shoe repairers, whose premises were crowded with unclaimed shoes. Sale was impossible, since if the true owner turned up later, no matter how many years had passed, and demanded his shoes, the repairer would be liable to him for failing to return them. It may be doubted whether cobblers, or even dry cleaners, were under a real risk in practical terms, however. More serious, it may be, was the plight of jewellers, for the real danger arises not from sale itself (provided a reasonable price is obtained and the repairer is prepared to hand over the money received after deducting his charges) but – since the repairer's liability depends on the value when he is sued – from an increase in the value of the goods after they have been sold – a danger not likely to give shoe repairers sleepless nights.

No convincing evidence was produced to show that jewellers' repair rooms were cluttered up with unclaimed gems and precious metals, and it might have been predicted that the Act would prove to be a dead letter. The Act gives repairers and cleaners a right to sell goods if their charges are unpaid, but it only comes into operation if at the time the goods were received a notice was conspicuously exhibited referring to and explaining the Act. The repairer must notify the owner of the goods in writing when the goods are ready for delivery, he must then wait a year, and he must then send a further notice to the owner telling him that he intends to sell the goods. Hedged about with these formalities as it is, the Act does not seem to have been popular with repairers. Certainly notices under the Act are not a conspicuous feature of the décor of repairers' shops.

The main reason, no doubt, is because it is so easy to obtain a right to sell goods after a shorter period with no formalities. The common law gives no right to sell, but it enables one to be created by the parties by agreement: it is always possible for the owner of goods voluntarily to give the repairer the right to sell the goods. This reference to voluntary agreement will no doubt suggest how such a right can be obtained. The fiction of 'freedom of contract' enables the repairer to exhibit notices or print tickets or receipts which expressly grant him the right to sell goods. Thus, in *Watkins* v. *Rymill* (see p. 26) the proprietor of a repository was held entitled to sell a waggonette after one month when his charges were not paid. Reporting in 1971 the Law Reform Committee recommended that every bailee should have, by law, a positive right to sell the goods if he has failed, after making reasonable efforts, to obtain instructions from the owner. The Disposal of Uncollected Goods Act would no longer be necessary and would be repealed. This recommendation has not yet been implemented.

HIRE

Most of the transactions so far discussed have been bailments in which the owner of the goods is the consumer. The bailment of hire differs from these in that the owner of the goods is the trader, and the consumer is the bailee (or hirer). In this situation it is the consumer who must take reasonable care of the goods in his possession, and the owner who draws up the written contract, if there is one – and there usually is. Hire covers not only car hire but also so-called 'rental agreements', as of radio and television sets and, for business offices, internal telephone systems.

Since the written agreement is drawn up by the owner, a striking difference is found from those relating to other bailments. Instead of clauses designed to relieve the possessor of his responsibility, hiring and rental agreements may attempt to impose on the hirer duties greater than those imposed by the general law. For example, some car-hire agreements require the hirer to return the car in the same condition as when the hiring commenced and to bear the responsibility for all accidental damage or for loss by theft – though naturally the insurance terms (often obscure unless the hirer carefully reads the whole policy) are of great practical importance.

On the other hand, these agreements often attempt to relieve the owner of *his* liability. A good example is the case of *White* v. *John Warwick & Co. Ltd*, the hire of a tradesman's cycle, the facts of which were given earlier in this chapter (p. 205). This case also emphasizes that when goods are hired the owner is under a double duty at common law: he must take reasonable care to see that the goods will not cause injury or damage, a breach of this duty giving rise to the tort of negligence; and he is taken to promise that the goods are reasonably fit for the purpose for which they are hired, so that if they are not he becomes liable to an action for breach of contract. The contractual duty is stricter than the duty in tort, for it is no defence for the owner to prove that he did in fact take reasonable care; if the goods are defective, the only defence to an action for breach of contract is, it seems, to show that it was impossible to discover the defect.

A particularly important provision in a contract of hire is the length of time for which the hiring is to continue. From the consumer's point of view this should be related to his own needs, and in particular to the undesirability of committing himself for too long a period. The hiring may be terminable by notice; but if the agreement for the hire of a television set states that it is to continue for, say, five years, it cannot be ended within that period no matter how inconvenient it may be to the hirer to carry on. Or rather, the hirer can end the agreement, if he cannot obtain the owner's consent, only by breaking the contract and becoming liable to pay damages. The principles on which the amount of damages are assessed were reviewed by the Court of Appeal in 1958.

The hiring in *Interoffice Telephones Ltd* v. *Robert Freeman Co. Ltd* was of a large internal telephone system, with thirty-nine extensions, at a rent of about £260 a year; but although the hirers were a company occupying large offices, the law applies equally to the hire of a television set at 50p a week. This particular contract contained a clause saying that the hiring would continue for twelve years, and there was no provision in it permitting the hirers to end it earlier. The hirers had to leave their offices and no longer needed the telephone system. The Court of Appeal held that they must pay damages representing all the money which the owners would lose: the total of all the rent for the rest of the twelve years, less the estimated cost of maintaining the equipment which the owners would save.

It was argued that this large sum of money – as the agreement had six years to run, the total rent was almost £1,700 – was far too much, for the hirers had returned all the equipment and the owners could – and, indeed, ought to – let it to another customer. This argument failed, because the owners showed that there was no shortage of equipment and that they had sufficient in stock – or could obtain it elsewhere – to meet all predictable demands.

In all cases we have considered dealing with contracts for services and bailments, two things stand out. The first is that, in the absence of agreement, the common law supplies rules and 'implied terms' which both impose duties on and benefit both sides, and are inherently reasonable. The second is the vital importance of the provisions which have been expressly agreed, however unreal the 'agreement' is. This is yet another field where the standard-form agreement and the fiction of 'freedom of contract' usually govern the situation. We have discussed the ways in which the consumer might be protected from contracts in which there is little genuine 'freedom' in Chapter 2.

CHAPTER 8

THE BANK AND ITS CUSTOMER

In the seventeenth century, when few people used banks to look after their savings, merchants used to keep their surplus money in the Tower of London. To Charles I, always kept short of funds by an intransigent Parliament, the presence of this gold in the Tower was a big temptation. A 'loan' was arranged and the merchants, seeking a safer place for the deposit of their money, began to leave it in the hands of the goldsmiths. Dr Milnes Holden, in a study of the history of cheques, recounts that the goldsmiths would often lend these funds to other people who required capital, and they were willing to give merchants some assistance when they wished to make payments to their creditors. A merchant would simply ask the goldsmith to make a payment on the merchant's behalf to the latter's creditor, and the goldsmith would carry out the merchant's request. Sometimes the request was made in favour of the creditor 'or order', and sometimes in favour of the creditor 'or bearer'. One of the earliest of these documents, still in existence, is dated 14 August 1675. The Institute of Bankers have it in their collection in London. Drawn upon a goldsmith called Thomas ffowles, it reads:

Mr Thomas ffowles, I desire you to pay unto Mr Samuell Howard or order upon receipt hereof the sume of nine pounds thirteene shillings and sixe pence and place it to the account of Yr Servant, Edmond Warcupp.

This sort of document is, of course, the precursor of the modern cheque. The word 'check' was first used in the eighteenth century, and the modern spelling 'cheque' was adopted in the nineteenth century.

A CURRENT ACCOUNT

When anyone opens a current account at a bank, he is lending the bank money, repayment of which he may demand at any time, either in cash or by drawing a cheque in favour of another person. Primarily, the banker-customer relationship is that of debtor and creditor – who is which depending on whether the customer's account is in credit or is overdrawn. But, in addition to that basically simple concept, the bank and its customer owe a large number of obligations to one another. Many of these obligations can give rise to problems and complications but a bank customer, unlike, say, a buyer of goods cannot complain that the law is loaded against him.

The bank must obey its customer's instructions, and not those of anyone else. When, for example, a customer first opens an account, he instructs the bank to debit his account only in respect of cheques drawn by himself. He gives the bank specimens of his signature, and there is a very firm rule that the bank has no right or authority to pay out a customer's money on a cheque on which its customer's signature has been forged. It makes no difference that the forgery may have been a very skilful one: the bank must recognize its customer's signature. For this reason there is no risk to the customer in the modern practice, adopted by some banks, of printing the customer's name on his cheques. If this facilitates forgery it is the bank which will lose, not the customer.

However, corresponding to this obligation on the part of the bank is an obligation on the part of the customer to inform the bank if he learns that someone has been forging his signature on cheques. In *Greenwood* v. *Martins Bank Ltd*, 1933, Mrs. Greenwood confessed to her husband that she had forged his signature on a number of cheques in order to help her sister who was a party to legal proceedings. She begged her husband not to tell the bank. Eight months later, Greenwood discovered that his wife had deceived him because her sister was not, in fact, involved in any legal proceedings. He told his wife that he must now inform the bank, and as a result she committed suicide. It appeared that Mrs Greenwood had forged her husband's signature on a total of forty-four cheques and the bank had debited his account with the sum of £410 6s. 0d. The House of Lords held that the bank had a legal right to debit Greenwood's account with this amount because if he had gone to the bank when his wife had first confessed to forgery, the bank could have made a claim against her. Under the law then existing, the bank could not pursue a claim against her property after her death. Since Greenwood had failed in his duty to disclose what he knew, he could not now deny his signature to the prejudice of the bank.

Sometimes a forgery comes to light when a customer goes through his bank statement and returned cheques at, say, the end of the quarter. Somewhat curiously, however, there is no obligation on the customer to examine his statement or (if he still gets them) returned cheques. As a result, even though a series of forgeries would have been halted if a customer had taken reasonable care in this respect, the bank may not debit his account with the amounts of any forged cheques, irrespective of whether they were drawn before or after the customer could have discovered what had been going on.

THE CUSTOMER'S DIRECTIONS

Where the amount of a cheque has been wrongly altered or 'raised', without the customer's assent, the bank is only entitled to debit its customer's account for the original amount. However, the customer does owe an obligation to his bank to draw his cheques with sufficient care so that the amount cannot be readily altered. It seems eminently reasonable that this is so. The rule was established by the House of Lords in 1918 in the case of *London Joint Stock Bank Ltd* v. *Macmillan and Arthur*. Macmillan and Arthur, a firm of City merchants, employed a clerk, one of whose duties was to fill out cheques for signature by one of the partners. One day the clerk prepared for signature a cheque for £2 payable to 'Bearer'. The amount was not given in words and there was space both before and after the numeral 2. The clerk secured the signature of one of the partners just before he was hurrying out to lunch, inserted a 1 before the 2 and 0 after it and filled in 'One hundred and twenty pounds' in words. The bank paid him £120 in cash and debited Macmillan and Arthur's account with that amount, and the clerk disappeared. Macmillan and Arthur sued the bank for £118 on the basis that they had directed the bank to pay out £2 only and the bank had, in fact, paid out £120. However, the House of Lords held that the bank was entitled to debit the account for the whole of the £120 because Macmillan and Arthur had not taken sufficient care to anticipate possible alteration. The Lord Chancellor, Lord Finlay, said:

… the customer is bound to exercise reasonable care to prevent the banker being misled. If he draws a cheque in a manner which facilitates fraud, he is guilty of a breach of duty between himself and the banker, and he will be responsible to the banker for any loss sustained by the banker as a natural and direct consequence of this breach of duty.

The customer's obligation to take care in drawing his cheques does not, it seems, go very far. He may, for instance, fail to draw a line between the name of the payee and the printed words 'or order', and although many customers do take this precaution, it seems that they are under no legal duty to do so. In *Slingsby* v. *District Bank*

Ltd, 1922, executors employed a firm of solicitors, Messrs Cumberbirch and Potts, to advise on the investment of funds. The executors signed a cheque for £5,000 prepared by one of the solicitors, which was payable to a firm of stockbrokers, 'John Prust and Co. or order'. There was a space between the name of the payees and the words 'or order', and after it had been signed, the person who had prepared the cheque, for his own fraudulent purposes, inserted in this space 'per Cumberbirch and Potts'. He paid it into a bank to the credit of a company in which he was interested, and the bank on which the cheque was drawn paid out the amount of the cheque and debited the executors' account. The Court of Appeal held that the bank must reimburse the executors with the amount because it had failed to obey its customer's directions to pay 'John Prust and Co. or order', even though the alteration was in the same writing as the rest of the cheque and could not have been detected. The Court did not consider that the executors were under any obligation to help the bank by ensuring that the payees' name could not be altered.

Perhaps bank customers cannot safely assume that this decision would be followed by a court today. Drawing a line after the payee's name is probably more usual nowadays and banks always advise customers to take this precaution. Mr Maurice Megrah, a leading authority on banking law, has pointed out that 'with the education of the cheque-using public to which the banks devote no little time and money, another case on the lines of *Slingsby* v. *District Bank Ltd* might well be decided differently.'

STOLEN CHEQUES

What happens to the money if a cheque is stolen? Most cheques are drawn on a printed form supplied by the bank (since this bank holds the customer's money and eventually pays it out in exchange for the cheque, it is known as the paying bank), and the printed forms usually read

Pay   or Order

followed by a space for the sum of money to be inserted. When the cheque is drawn the customer fills in the payee's name so that it reads 'Pay John Jones or Order.' This means that the paying bank is instructed to pay the money to John Jones, or to anyone else to whom John has ordered the money to be paid. The way in which he can order payment is by endorsing the cheque – that is, by putting his instructions on the back of the cheque and signing his name.

In practice at least 97 per cent of all cheques are never endorsed at all. John Jones pays the cheque straight into his own bank account, and his bank (known as the collecting bank) collects the money from the paying bank on John's behalf. Before 1957 even such cheques as these had to be endorsed on the back with the payee's signature, and since the endorsement on every one of the 600 or 700 million order cheques issued each year had to be examined by bank employees a considerable amount of time and effort was involved. But since the Cheques Act of 1957 came into force a cheque paid into the payee's account does not need to be endorsed.

In a small percentage of transactions, usually when the payee of the cheque does not have a bank account of his own, the cheque is negotiated by the payee to someone else. He may, for example, take the cheque to a local shop and ask the shopkeeper to 'cash' the cheque for him. He will endorse it by signing his name on the back and hand the endorsed cheque to the shopkeeper in exchange for cash. The shopkeeper will then pay the cheque into his own bank account. In theory a cheque could be nego-tiated any number of times from one person on to another, but such dealings are so rare that we can ignore them.

If all cheques were always paid into the payee's own account there would be no risk of theft, except in the rare cases where the thief opens an account in the payee's name or the cheque has been made payable to the wrong person. Sometimes a cheque is paid over the counter by the paying bank, but if the bank does not know the payee it is taking the risk of paying the wrong person, so this is not very common. The fact that some cheques are not paid into the payee's own account but are negotiated to someone else, however, means that here is an opening for theft. If a cheque payable to John Jones is stolen from him, or is stolen before it reaches him, the thief might pretend to be John Jones and cash the cheque with a shopkeeper, or else he might pay it into his own bank account pretending that John Jones had negotiated it to him. It is clear that in these situations the thief never has any right to the cheque or to the money, and if he has received the money it can be reclaimed from him – if he still has it, or is worth suing. As he probably does not still have it or is not worth suing, the question is usually as to the liability of the paying bank, the collecting bank, the shopkeeper, and the drawer.

The shopkeeper's position depends on whether the cheque was endorsed by John Jones before it was stolen. If it was, the shopkeeper, provided he gave value for the cheque without knowledge of the theft or suspicious circumstances, will become the owner of the cheque, just as he would of a banknote even if it was stolen. In that case all the loss will fall on John Jones. It does not matter whether or not the cheque was crossed but if, in addition to a crossing, the cheque bore the words 'not negotiable' the position will be quite different: the shopkeeper will obtain no rights to the stolen cheque and will have to repay the money to John Jones.

If the cheque was not endorsed before it was stolen, it can never be endorsed thereafter. True, the thief will write on the back what looks like John Jones's endorsement, but this will be a forgery and therefore a legal nullity. Thus the shopkeeper, however innocent, can obtain no right to the cheque and, if he receives the money, will have to return it to John Jones.

What of the banks in this situation? On general principles they should be in much the same position as the shopkeeper. The collecting bank would have no more right to deal with the cheque than the shopkeeper or, indeed, the thief, and the paying bank would not have paid the money to John Jones or in accordance with his instructions and so would be liable to its own customer. But these rules placed banks in a difficult and risky situation, and influential bodies such as these have often found it possible to change the law in their own favour. The result has been that, by Act of Parliament, special protection is now given to banks.

This protection is based on the practice of paying a cheque into a bank account, the paying bank paying the money to the collecting bank rather than to an individual. In this way it is possible to trace the money from the drawer's bank account through to the recipient's bank account, so that if the recipient was not entitled to the money he can be identified. Moreover this procedure normally takes two or three days, allowing a little time for discovery of the theft before the money is paid out. Most bank customers are familiar with the practice of 'crossing' cheques, the practical effect of which is to compel the paying bank to pay only to another bank unless it is quite sure it is paying to the right person: thus the cheque will not normally be paid over the counter, but must be paid into a bank account. The essence of a crossing is two parallel lines across the face of the cheque (the words '& Co.' are optional); sometimes the name of the bank is added, in which case the cheque must be paid into the named bank.

The collecting bank is protected, whether or not the cheque is crossed, by section 4 of the Cheques Act 1957, provided it has acted in good faith and without negligence. One can generally assume that banks act honestly, but they have not always acted without negligence. This requirement puts the collecting bank on its guard. If a cheque is paid in for the credit of the payee's account then, provided it made proper inquiries when it opened the account, it will not be liable – unless there are suspicious circumstances, as in *Bute* v. *Barclays Bank Ltd* in 1954. In this case the bank was held to have acted negligently when it permitted a customer to pay in Government warrants (documents similar to cheques) made payable to himself. The customer had been a farm manager for the Marquis of Bute and, acting on behalf of the Marquis, had applied to the Department of Agriculture in Scotland for sheep farming subsidies. By the time the warrants were issued he had left his job and was living in Yorkshire, but the warrants were addressed to him personally and forwarded unopened. Each warrant was payable to the customer by name, but had a note in the margin 'for the Marquis of Bute'. He paid them in to the credit of his own account, and the bank cashier made no inquiry as to his right to the money. Mr Justice McNair held that the bank could not claim its statutory protection, for no reasonable cashier could have thought that these documents were meant for the customer personally without at least asking questions.

More often the question of negligence is raised when the customer pays in a cheque not payable to him but endorsed over to him. Unless the bank makes inquiries to establish that the named payee has no bank account of his own, and to find out the relationship between the payee and its customer, it is almost certain to be held negligent, and most banks are very loath to accept 'third-party' cheques at all. Thus in *Ross* v. *London County and West-minster Bank Ltd*, in 1919, a sergeant in the Canadian army paid into his own private account cheques made payable to the Estates Office of the Canadian Overseas Military Forces. The court found the bank to be negligent; indeed, it is difficult to think of any convincing explanation why such cheques should be paid other than to an official bank account. In *Lloyds Bank Ltd* v. *Savory* cheques payable to a firm of City stockbrokers were paid in to the credit of a housewife's account at Redhill. The bank was held negligent in that it had failed to inquire of its customer, when she opened the account, the name of her husband's employers. If it had done so it would have discovered that he was a clerk employed by the stockbrokers to whom the cheques were payable.

Sometimes cheques are crossed 'Account Payee'. These words have no statutory recognition, and their only effect is to make it more difficult than ever to convince the collecting bank that the payee has no bank account into which he can pay the cheque.

The paying bank has similar protection under section 80 of the Bills of Exchange Act 1882, provided it too has acted in good faith and without negligence. It is, of course, harder to charge the paying bank with negligence since it will have no idea into whose account the cheque was paid. This section applies only to crossed cheques (this causes no difficulty, for the collecting bank itself will cross all open cheques before passing them on to the paying bank by way of the Bankers' Clearing House), and only if the paying bank has paid them to another bank. If the bank is protected by this section in respect of a cheque stolen from the payee, then, even though the payee has never received the money, he cannot claim payment from the drawer of the cheque who is thus also protected. Paying banks have further protection under section 60 of the

Bills of Exchange Act 1882 and section 1 of the Cheques Act 1957 in respect of both crossed and open cheques where the endorsement is forged, unauthorized, irregular, or non-existent, but only if they have acted in good faith and in the ordinary course of business.

Much of this special protection for banks is needed because of the rule that a forged endorsement has no legal effect. In most continental countries a forged endorsement is effective so far as innocent parties are concerned, and it is worth considering whether such a rule would not be an improvement on our own law. Even better, no doubt, would be some power given to the court to apportion the loss between the innocent victim of the theft and the equally innocent purchaser.

HONOURING CHEQUES

There is no doubt at all that a bank is under an obligation to honour any cheque drawn by a customer if there are sufficient funds in his account to meet the cheque or if a sufficient overdraft has been arranged. But if the customer draws a cheque for more than he has in his account, or for more than the agreed overdraft – even if the excess is only one penny – the bank is under no legal obligation to pay. As a matter of practice banks often do pay if the excess is small, but the responsibility is the customer's to ensure that he does not overdraw.

What if a customer draws a cheque, and there are sufficient funds to his credit in the bank to meet it, but the bank (no doubt because of a mistake) declines to pay it? If the customer is a business or professional man, the courts presume that the bank's failure to honour his cheque will injure his financial standing, and will award him substantial damages. This is so no matter how small the amount for which the cheque was drawn – indeed, it is often said that the smaller the cheque, the greater the injury. The private customer, on the other hand, will only obtain nominal damages – often two pounds or less – unless he can positively prove that the unjustified dishonour of a cheque has caused him real harm. In a case heard by Lord Reading, then Lord Chief Justice, in 1917, *Evans* v. *London and Provincial Bank Ltd*, the wife of a naval officer sued her bank for dishonouring a cheque when she had funds in her account to meet it. The jury awarded one shilling damages only, the jury foreman pointing out that they did not consider Mrs Evans had suffered anything more than annoyance.

Because of this rule, it is sometimes thought that, for a private customer, an action for libel based on the bank's answer when refusing to pay the cheque may be more profitable. The law, however, is uncertain. Banks are usually cautious in giving their answers and the phrase 'refer to drawer' or R/D is common. This is probably because Lord Justice Scrutton, in the 1915 case of *Flach* v. *London and South Western Bank Ltd*, said that these words were not reasonably capable of a defamatory meaning since they merely mean 'we are not paying; go back to the drawer and ask why'. It has, however, been suggested that to most people the words 'refer to drawer' are not so innocuous as Lord Justice Scrutton suggested, and that the innuendo is plain. But there is even doubt as to whether other, more explicit, answers sometimes made by banks can be libellous – 'not sufficient' or 'no assets', for example. Different judges have voiced different opinions. In New Zealand, words instructing the payee to 'present again' have been held to be capable of a defamatory meaning, on the ground that they indicate that the drawer has failed to provide funds so that the cheque can be paid at once by the bank when it is presented and, therefore, the words tend to lower the drawer 'in the estimation of right-thinking members of society generally'.

When a customer has drawn a cheque and handed it to the payee, he may change his mind and want to stop payment on it. He has the right to countermand payment by telling his bank not to pay and the bank must obey this instruction. The bank is entitled to require written confirmation of a telephone call or telegram countermanding payment of a cheque, but if the cheque is presented for payment before the confirmation is received, the bank will in practice postpone payment.

POST-DATED CHEQUES

Post-dated cheques are much disliked by the banks because banks justifiably assume that customers will date their cheques with today's date. Suppose that on 1 March 1973 a man draws a cheque and dates it 1 May 1973. The bank should not pay it before 1 May 1973, but if, perhaps because the bank does not notice it is post-dated, it pays the cheque some time in March, and then in April the customer instructs the bank not to pay it, the bank has no right to debit the customer's account with the amount. Small wonder that the banks disapprove of post-dated cheques. Paget's *Law of Banking* is particularly scathing:

> Post-dated cheques are habitually in use in certain business circles, facilitating transactions of dubious financial soundness; while to the banker they are a perpetual source of annoyance and possible loss.

SECRECY OF A BANK ACCOUNT

The bank-customer relationship is a confidential one, and the customer is entitled to assume that the bank will never divulge the state of his account to anyone. Even after his account is closed, the bank's duty of secrecy in respect of the customer's financial affairs continues. There are, however, some limits on the bank's obligation of secrecy. If, for example, the customer has given the name of his bank as a reference he is taken to have authorized the bank to disclose information as to his financial standing and the way in which he conducts his bank account. (In practice a bank will answer inquiries received from another bank without checking that this results from a bank reference given by its customer – a practice which may one day prove to be dangerous if the customer objects.) Again, if the customer fails to repay an overdraft the bank may sue him: for this purpose it may reveal the state of the customer's account to its solicitors and, of course, to the court. In time of war a bank would be under a public duty to disclose details of an account to the proper authorities if it showed that he was trading with the enemy.

A more controversial qualification is where the bank is under some legal compulsion to disclose information about a customer's account. There are, for example, a number of instances in which the Inland Revenue authorities can compel a bank to give information about a customer's account. It would be alarming if inroads into the bank's obligation of secrecy were extended further.

A BANK GIVING ADVICE

If a customer seeks a bank's advice before investing his money the bank may decline to give such advice and simply refer the customer to a stockbroker. If this is the case, the bank would owe a duty to take reasonable care in the selection of a suitable stockbroker, but would be under no responsibility for the latter's advice. On the other hand, if a bank manager himself gives advice as to a particular investment, and the manager appears to be acting with the bank's authority, the customer can hold the bank liable if the advice is shown to have been careless and he loses his money. In *Woods* v. *Martins Bank Ltd*, in 1958, the manager of a local branch of the bank told Mr Woods that the bank would be only too pleased to take care of his financial affairs. In consequence of advice received from the manager, Woods, a man of little or no business experience, invested over £14,500 in one company and signed a guarantee of another company's overdraft for £990. All this money was lost and Woods sued the bank for damages. Lord Salmon described Woods as 'a pleasant and honest young man but rather stupid and extremely gullible . . . he was, in fact, the very prototype of the lamb waiting to be shorn.' The judge found that the bank manager had no reasonable grounds for advising that either company in which Woods had invested his money was financially sound. Apparently, the bank had issued a booklet which said 'you may consult your bank manager freely and seek his advice on all matters affecting your financial affairs'. On this basis, there was no doubt that the manager had authority from the bank to give advice, and Lord Salmon held there was a duty on the bank to advise him with reasonable care. That duty had been broken and the bank had to compensate Woods for his loss.

Although the decision in *Woods* v. *Martins Bank Ltd* was obviously reasonable, there was some controversy as to whether it was rightly decided, because it was not clear that Woods was a customer when the advice was given. For many years it had been thought that there was no liability for financial loss caused by false statements which were made negligently unless there was a contract between the maker and the recipient of the statement, or unless fraud could be proved. Thus in *Hedley Byrne & Co. Ltd* v. *Heller & Partners Ltd* the defendant bankers were asked by the National Provincial Bank to give a reference for their customers, Easipower Ltd. A favourable reference was given which the National Provincial Bank passed on to the plaintiffs who were advertising agents. As a result, the plaintiffs lost over £17,000 when Easipower Ltd was wound up. Accepting that the reference was given negligently (though this was denied) the Court of Appeal applied what they thought was the law and held that as there was no contract between plaintiffs and defendants there could be no liability. In 1963 the case came to the House of Lords, which held that in such circumstances the speaker or writer may become liable for a negligent misstatement. As Lord Devlin put it, there must be a relationship between the parties either of contract, or of special trust, or one 'equivalent to contract, that is, where there is an assumption of responsibility in circumstances in which, but for the absence of consideration, there would be a contract'. On the facts of the case, however, the bankers were not liable, for they had headed their letter 'Without responsibility on the part of the bank or its officials' and therefore made it plain that they had not assumed any responsibility to take care.

The general principle laid down in this case is of importance in many fields of law, but the ease with which the duty can be avoided can hardly be considered satisfactory. When a man seeks a bank's reference, he naturally and reasonably expects that it will not only be an honest reference but that the bank will have taken proper care before giving it. The law falls short of a man's reasonable expectations and it is significant that an article in *The Banker*, aptly titled 'Careless Talk Costs – Nothing', refers to the present state of the law as being 'ludicrously out of touch with life as it is lived today'. When even banking circles are critical of a law which favours banks, it is evident that the law is in need of reform.

Moreover, a bank is not even liable if it gives a false reference dishonestly. This astonishing rule is established by an Act of Parliament known as the Statute of Frauds Amendment Act 1828, ostensibly passed to prevent fraud but in practice apt to protect dishonest persons from the consequences of their fraud. Section 6 of this Act provides that no action can be brought to make a defendant liable by reason of any representation relating to the 'character, conduct, credit, ability, trade or dealings' of any other person made to assist that other person to obtain credit, money, or goods, unless the representation 'be made in writing signed by the party to be charged therewith'. Bank references are usually given in writing, but the 1828 Act specifies that the writing must be signed, and does not permit signature by an agent. Even if the bank reference was signed by the manager, therefore – and normally they are not – this would not suffice to make the bank liable. If the bank is a limited company, it has been held that before it can be sued for fraud the dishonest reference must have been impressed with the embossed 'common seal' of the company, a procedure reserved for the most formal of legal documents. If the bank is not a limited company but a partnership the reference must be signed by all the partners. It is remarkable that this section, the sole purpose of which is to protect persons giving fraudulent references, should have remained unrepealed for over a hundred and forty years.

THE LAW LOOKS AFTER THE CUSTOMER

From the foregoing description of the mutual obligations of a bank and its customer, it would seem that the customer's interests are fairly protected by the law. The law seems to lean over backwards in looking after his interests. Indeed, a man is far better protected by the law in his dealing with a bank than he is, for example, in his dealings with retailers, hire-purchase finance companies, or insurance companies. The reason perhaps is that the first customers of the bank were merchants and traders, and they had sufficient strength and influence to ensure that their unwritten contract with the bank provided adequate safeguards for their interests. But whatever the reason, it is not only the trader but the ordinary private customer who today enjoys the benefit of rules of law built up by the courts in the last and present centuries. The one unsatisfactory feature of the present law is the bank's ability to evade liability in respect of financial loss suffered as a result of negligent (or, in exceptional cases, dishonest) statements or references.

ARE BANKS MOVING WITH THE TIMES?

However, while the law governing the bank–customer relationship may be fair and satisfactory, it is open to question whether the banks are providing an adequate service for the needs of today. Are they moving with the times, opening their doors to larger numbers of people, developing up-to-date techniques?

The banks are proud of the fact that they have introduced electronic equipment, personalized cheques, and streamlined their bank statements. Presumably, these measures have led to administrative savings for the banks, but the customer is not always clear how he has benefited. Indeed, many customers have been vocal in protesting against the introduction of mechanized bank statements, which in some banks are much less communicative than the old type because the names of the payees of cheques drawn are no longer shown. The service the customer receives from his bank has been reduced in this respect – and he may not take advantage of other services – while bank charges have certainly not fallen. The limitations of the computer are seen from the case of *Burnett* v. *Westminster Bank Ltd* in June 1965. Mr Burnett had current accounts with the A and B branches of the bank. As the bank had introduced a computer which could read the magnetic characters of a cheque but not ordinary ink, the cheque book issued by the A branch bore on its cover (for the first time) a statement that cheques must not be used to draw on any other account. Mr Burnett did not read this prohibition and made out a cheque for £2,300, altering the cheque in ink so that it was addressed to the B branch. Shortly afterwards, he told the B Branch not to pay it but as the computer was blind to the alteration the cheque was collected from the A branch and Mr Burnett's account there was debited with the £2,300. Mr Justice Mocatta held that Mr Burnett was entitled to have his account with the A branch credited with the £2,300 because he had never instructed the bank to debit his account at the A branch with that sum. The judge did not consider that Mr Burnett had *agreed* to the provision on the cheque book cover.

Are the banks doing anything to introduce the 'banking habit' to the many people who do not now have a bank account? Commenting in 1958, Sir Oscar Hobson said that the banking habit penetrates about to the middle of the middle class. That is still broadly true today. In 1958 the Midland Bank started a 'personal cheque' scheme which some observers saw as one of the major innovations of post-war banking. Under this scheme current account facilities, strictly limited to the receipt of funds and the payment of cheques drawn against them, were offered at a standardized cut-rate. Designed for 'people living on modest incomes, young married couples, technicians, artisans, and factory workers', only a small charge was made for each cheque and, of course, no overdrafts were permitted. But the scheme was evidently not a great success and it was withdrawn in 1970.

It has often been thought that one inhibiting factor that prevented a rapid increase in the number of bank customers was the law that manual workers might not be paid their wages by cheque. The Truck Act 1831 provided that all manual workers must be paid their wages in full in cash, and in no other way. There was an exception if the bank on which the employer's cheque was drawn was licensed to issue banknotes. Since today the only bank licensed to issue banknotes is the Bank of England, which does not open accounts for ordinary employers, the exception is of no practical importance. However in 1960, because of the serious increase in wage robberies, the Payment of Wages Act was passed, which permits the payment of wages to a manual worker by money order, postal order, or by a direct credit to his bank account – but only if the worker so requests. Since March 1963, a manual worker may also be paid by cheque, but again only if he requests. Has this meant a big increase in the number of 'wage-earning' bank accounts? It seems doubtful. Clearly, if the worker is accustomed to spending his wages as he receives them, there is no point in his asking to be paid by a credit transfer into a banking account or by cheque. Even if he wants to save part of his wages, it will still be inconvenient for him to be paid by credit transfer or cheque because his bank may not be very near his place of work and its opening hours almost certainly will not suit him. Moreover, if a man is 'persuaded' by his employer to take his wages in the form of a cheque, he might prefer to cash it with a shopkeeper rather than go to the trouble of opening a bank account. Finally, many wage earners are in any case still distrustful of banks.

Perhaps a radical change in banking practice with the opening of branches on factory premises, a growing flexibility in opening hours, and an all-out advertising campaign to combat distrust of banks could have made a difference. The National Board for Prices and Incomes, in a report published in 1967, said that banks should experiment with longer and more flexible opening hours, varying the times for city centres and suburbs. The Board did not consider that bank charges were too high but thought that the present secretive method of assessing charges is erratic and probably discriminates against small and uncomplaining depositors. It suggested that a set system of charges should be published by each bank so that customers should be able to work out the current balance required to have their accounts worked free. More doubtful, from the consumer's point of view, was the Board's opinion that many small branch banks should be closed as uneconomical. Unfortunately, since the Board's report, the banks have become less accessible by closing on Saturdays. The inconvenience thus caused to customers has only been mitigated to a slight extent by longer opening hours during the rest of the week and, at some branches, by the introduction of automatic cash dispensers available day and night.

There is a further limiting factor in the banks' attempt to increase the numbers of their customers. Unless traders are far more willing than now to take a cheque from a wage-earning customer, what is the point in him having a cheque-book?

CHEQUE CARDS AND CREDIT CARDS

It was in order to secure greater willingness on the part of traders to take cheques that the Midland Bank introduced its 'cheque card' scheme in 1966. The trader will very readily take a cheque for up to £30 from anyone able to produce such a card because the Midland Bank guarantees that the cheque (which must be crossed) will be met. The cardholder is also able to obtain £30 in cash from *any* branch of the Bank and the Bank makes no charge for this service either to the trader or to its customer. All the commercial banks agreed in 1969 to issue a standardized form of cheque card, except for Barclays Bank which issues a credit card known as 'Barclaycard'.

Credit cards have been popular in the United States

for many years and the schemes run by American Express and the Diners Club have been operating on a small scale in Britain. The 'Barclaycard' arrived on the scene in 1966. As long as you can give satisfactory references you do not need to be a customer of Barclays to obtain a Barclaycard and there is no subscription. With it, you can order goods up to the credit limit allowed by the Bank from any trader who has joined the scheme merely by producing the card – you do not have to write out a cheque. Up to £25 can be drawn in cash from any branch of Barclays, though a non-customer of the Bank has to pay a charge of $2\frac{1}{2}$ per cent on the amount withdrawn (50p on £20) for this particular service. Apart from this service, interest is charged (at $1\frac{1}{2}$ per cent per month, or over 19 per cent per annum) only if 25 days have elapsed from the date when the monthly statement was sent out. Something that must worry the cardholder is that if he loses his card, someone else may use it and run up credit. By his contract with Barclays the cardholder is responsible for all losses incurred until such time as the Barclaycard Centre in Northampton or any branch of Barclays Bank is informed of the loss. Although it may be thought unlikely that Barclays would seek to enforce their rights against an innocent victim, it is unfortunate that their contract entitles them to do so. A cardholder might not notice his loss for several days, and in that time thousands of pounds could have been debited to his account by a thief. Seven other leading banks launched a similar scheme with their 'Access' card in October 1972. Unfortunately the conditions impose a similar liability if the card is lost or stolen. In the United States a law was passed by Congress in 1970 to limit the liability of a cardholder for unauthorized use of a credit card to a maximum amount of $50 (about £20), and in practice many banks issuing credit cards do not even take steps to claim this amount.

No doubt credit cards are here to stay but it is too soon

to tell whether their use will mean any considerable decline in the use of cheques. Traders are charged to join the scheme and in the end no doubt consumers generally will have to pay through higher prices – those who do not make use of credit cards may be subsidizing those who do.

Some concern is also felt that we shall all be forced to try and obtain cheque cards or credit cards if we do not wish to use cash. The schemes might therefore make it harder to find shops willing to take cheques: they may feel that a person without a card from his bank could not get one and is therefore a poor credit risk. If this happens, the banks may find cheque-books becoming less popular not more popular unless they are prepared to issue cards more freely.

CREDIT TRANSFERS

Another development that may be of benefit both to bank customers and to people who do not have a banking account is the credit transfer system or Bank giro, which enables funds to be transferred to the bank account of a customer of any branch of any bank in the United Kingdom, as an alternative to paying debts by cheque or postal or money order. Even before the introduction of the scheme in 1961, customers were able, by signing standing orders, to arrange transfers to settle recurring debts like rent and insurance premiums. The scheme is an extension of this sort of arrangement and provides certain facilities for non-customers. For the business customer, credit transfer provides a helpful and economical method of making a number of payments at once. The only drawback is that he must know the name and address of the bank of each of his creditors. Assuming he does, he will send to his bank a completed form for each creditor he wishes to pay, together with *one* cheque to cover the total of all the payments. His use of credit transfers will be taken into account when bank charges are assessed, but his saving in stationery and postage may be considerable.

For the private customer, however, the scheme is not likely to be so widely used because he does not normally have many debts to pay at any particular time, so the saving involved would be trivial. In any case, it is bound to take time for customers to give up the habit of paying each debt by a separate cheque. If someone without a bank account wishes to use the scheme, he will complete a form for each of his creditors and pay cash to cover the total amount, together with a charge of two or three pence for each transfer. Any bank will then arrange the transfer to the bank account of each creditor. The charge imposed on the non-customer is a modest one and he is saved the expense of postage and of purchasing postal or money orders. Habit again will no doubt inhibit any substantial use of the scheme and it cannot be used where the creditor insists on payment by cash. If the scheme thrives, it would represent a real breakthrough. After all, the traditional payment of each debt by an individual cheque is a cumbersome business for all concerned. The drawer posts the cheque to his creditor, the creditor takes it to his bank, and this bank has to collect payment on it from the drawer's bank. The credit transfer system is much simpler than that.

So far, the banks' credit transfer scheme seems to be working smoothly and no legal problems have arisen. If a bank were to mislay a transfer form, or credit the wrong account, the resulting dispute would no doubt be settled on principles similar to those governing bank accounts. Even if the person paying in the money does not have an account, it seems that his payment of the charge would establish a valid contract between him and the bank so that he would be treated as if he were a customer.

THE NATIONAL GIRO

On the Continent the post offices have for some time been used to make credit transfers in what is termed the 'giro' system. The possibility of such a system here was, no doubt, a factor behind the banks' own credit transfer scheme. But large sections of the community do not use banks and in 1958 the Radcliffe Report on the working of the monetary system favoured an investigation of the possibility of a post office 'giro' system. In 1965, the Postmaster-General announced that such a system was, indeed, to be introduced. He stressed that mail-order business had doubled over the previous seven years, as had payments of hire-purchase instalments over the previous four years. For this kind of business, an inexpensive and speedy money transfer service would be useful.

As a result, the Government decided that a giro would be a useful addition to the existing methods of transmitting money and the National Giro was set up in 1968. Three basic facilities are offered: (i) the free transfer of money from account holder to account holder; (ii) the deposit of money into one's own account free of charge by passing it over a post office counter; non-account holders can pay bills by depositing money into anyone's account at a charge of 10p per transaction; (iii) the withdrawal of money at post offices by account holders; non-account holders can cash postal 'cheques' sent to them through the giro office. Under certain conditions, account holders are able to withdraw up to £20 on demand at one chosen post office at the cost of 8p each time. Withdrawals of over £50 need advice beforehand to a nominated office of payment and the cost is 10p each time. The charge for cashing a Girocheque at a post office is 10p, and bills can be paid by Girocheque at a fee of 6p each cheque. Many of the above charges are subject to an additional fee of 5p if the account holder does not have at least £30 in his account. Account holders are charged for their supply of 'cheques' and envelopes, but postage to the giro office is free. The National Savings Bank remains: it is a deposit bank, paying interest but without cheque facilities, while a giro account is rather more like a bank current account.

The giro service has been in operation for several years but, although post offices are open on more days and for longer hours than banks, it has not had a conspicuously successful start. It was originally hoped that by 1973-4 Giro would have over a million account holders; so far there are no more than half a million. The target was at least £120 millions in deposits by 1973-4; by 1971 this had not got past an average of £55 million. Certainly the banks are no longer anxious about the competition.

CHAPTER 9

INSURANCE

THE contract creating an insurance policy is essentially unfair, in that the parties are not negotiating on equal terms. The consumer might be surprised to know, however, that from the practical point of view the scales are weighted in his favour. The reason is simple: knowledge. When the consumer takes out an insurance policy he is covering a risk: he is arranging for financial compensation if the event insured against – fire or storm or theft, or whatever it may be – occurs. Inevitably he knows more about many factors affecting the risk than the insurance company or the underwriter, or would know more if there was anything to know. The insurance company, for instance, would not know that three of the insured's previous houses were destroyed by fire, unless he told them. They would not know that he was accident prone. They would not know that he has a serious heart disease.

In the light of this it is not surprising that insurance companies (we will use this expression to include underwriters) have done all they can to redress the balance: they have been so successful that, as we shall see, any unfairness now usually operates against the insured (a term we shall use in this chapter instead of the less apt 'consumer'). What is less expected is that the law too takes an active hand to redress the balance in favour of the insurance companies, a striking contrast to its avowed neutralist attitude in most other branches of the law. *Caveat emptor* plays no part in the law of insurance.

THE UTMOST GOOD FAITH

The law intervenes by a doctrine, firmly established by the eighteenth century, that holds contracts of insurance to be 'of the utmost good faith'. The practical effect of this doctrine is that the insured is required to disclose to the insurance company, before the contract of insurance is entered into, all material facts, whether he has been asked about them or not. If he fails to do so, the insurance company can refuse to pay out a claim, though if the insured was not dishonest they must return all premiums paid.

It will be seen that this duty to disclose is limited to 'material facts'. When is a fact material? The answer to this question is judged by the standards and experience of insurance companies: is the fact one which would influence a prudent insurance company in making up its mind whether to take on the insurance, or in deciding what premium to charge? If so, it is material. Suppose only an insurance company would realize that a particular fact was material, and that a reasonable man, that hypothetical paragon whose standards govern so much of our law, would not have thought it necessary to reveal it? No matter: the fact is still material, for it is the judgement of insurance companies which settles the question. Reporting in 1957, the Law Reform Committee pointed out that this was not a satisfactory principle and that no legal difficulties would arise if the standard was changed from that of insurance companies to that of the reasonable man.

It should be emphasized that, where the insurance company is seeking to avoid paying after a claim has been submitted, the actual cause of the loss is not relevant in deciding whether a fact undisclosed is material. For example, if a house is insured against fire and flood, the fact that it is situated on low-lying land by the bank of a river and has often been flooded before is clearly material. If the insured fails to disclose this, the insurance company can avoid the contract. And it makes no difference that they discover the true facts only after the house has been destroyed by fire and a claim has been submitted completely unrelated to the risk of flooding.

This principle of good faith, therefore, effectively protects the insurance company against their lack of knowledge of the insured's circumstances. It is in striking contrast with the doctrine of 'misrepresentation' which prevails in other branches of the law, such as the sale of goods: there, silence can never be misrepresentation, unless what is not said makes what is actually said misleading. As Lord Atkin once put it, 'The failure to disclose a material fact which might influence the mind of a prudent contracting party, does not give the right to avoid the contract'; and Lord Campbell expressed the same idea more pithily a hundred years ago when he said 'Simple reticence does not amount to legal fraud, however it may be viewed by moralists.' But these statements have no application to insurance law.

There are a few other kinds of contract, in addition to insurance, where the doctrine of the utmost good faith applies. A leading example is the sale of shares in a company by the promoters of the company. 'Persons who desire to foist an undertaking upon the public,' say Dr Cheshire and Mr Fifoot in a leading students' textbook on the law of contract, 'are not usually remarkable either for the accuracy of their representations or for the industry with which they search for facts that might usefully be disclosed.' The courts therefore imposed on company promoters an obligation to disclose all material facts of which they knew, and Parliament later imposed a positive obligation to find out and publish facts in a 'prospectus', the Companies Act of 1948 listing a large number of matters which must be dealt with in a prospectus.

Why is there no comparable duty to disclose material facts in a contract for the sale of goods? There is ample evidence in the cases that the seller might know facts about the goods of which the buyer would remain ignorant until after he had purchased. One reason, no doubt, is that the law relating to selling and buying goods developed much earlier, in a primitive, agricultural society, while the law relating to insurance and, even more, company promotion, did not evolve until our civilization and its law were more sophisticated. It may be, too, that the later developments owed much to the importance and influence of insurance companies and underwriters, and of company shareholders. It should also be noted that the implied terms in contracts of sale of goods, particularly those of merchantable quality and fitness for purpose which developed in the nineteenth century, perform a similar function to the doctrine of disclosure.

WARRANTIES

By this duty to disclose facts imposed on the insured, the law redresses the balance in favour of the insurance company. But insurance companies have not been content to accept this legal protection. They have themselves gone further and created fresh obligations for the insured.

One limitation on the duty of the utmost good faith which troubled insurance companies was that it was limited to facts of which the insured was aware. 'The duty is a duty to disclose,' said Lord Moulton, 'and you cannot disclose what you do not know.' No doubt the insured could not deny knowledge of what he must obviously know, and a rule in the Marine Insurance Act of 1906, although limited as an Act of Parliament to insurance on ships and cargoes, almost certainly sums up the general law: the insured 'is deemed to know every circumstance which, in the ordinary course of business, ought to be known by him.' Nevertheless, there was room for argument as to whether the insured knew or ought to have known certain facts, and insurance companies did not relish arguments.

They avoided arguments by asking the insured questions before granting him insurance cover. For many kinds of insurance the insured has to fill in a proposal form which is in effect an application form (sometimes no proposal form is required for straightforward fire insurance, and the insurance contract – or 'cover' – is entered into by correspondence or even over the telephone). This proposal form contains a list of questions, and at the end of the form the insured has to sign a declaration, of which the following is typical.

I declare that the particulars and statements made by me above are true, and I agree that they shall be the basis of the contract between me and the — Company.

This has the effect of incorporating the answers into the insurance contract – in effect they form part of the insurance policy, although they are not set out in the policy – and if any answer is untrue the insurance company can refuse to pay out on a claim on the ground of 'breach of warranty'.

In this way two of the rules we have seen in relation to the doctrine of the utmost good faith are of no effect: the need for the insured's knowledge, and the principle of materiality. Take first the question of the knowledge of the insured: 'you cannot disclose what you do not know.' This has no application to the insured's warranties. For example, a common question in a proposal for a life assurance policy is: 'Are you now in good health and free from any physical defect or disease?' If the answer given is 'yes' but a post mortem after the insured's death reveals that he was suffering from, say, cancer at the date of the proposal, there is a breach of warranty, and the insurance company need not pay. It makes no difference that the insured did not know of his disease, nor even that in the absence of any symptoms, he could not have known. His answer was untrue, and that is enough. Nor does it make any difference that the disease was not the cause of his death: even if he was knocked down by a bus, the company can refuse to pay on the ground of breach of warranty.

Then there is the principle that, under the general law, the insured must disclose only *material* facts. Since, as we have seen, the criterion of materiality is the practice of insurance companies, the law is not over-generous to the insured. But no question of whether the fact misstated is material can arise under the doctrine of warranties. Even though the wrong answer could not and would not have affected the insurance company in any way, the mere fact that it was untrue enables the insurance company to avoid the contract. Thus in *Dawsons Ltd* v. *Bonnin*, which came before the House of Lords in 1922, a policy was taken out in respect of a motor lorry. The proposal form was filled in by an insurance agent and read:

1. Proposer's name: Dawsons Ltd
2. Proposer's address: 46 Cadogan Street, Glasgow
4. State full address at which the
   vehicles will usually be garaged: Above address

The answer to question 4 was inaccurate: there was no garage at Cadogan Street, and the lorry was in fact garaged at a farm on the outskirts of Glasgow. But Dawsons' secretary did not notice the mistake and signed the proposal form. Eleven months later there was a fire at the garage and the lorry was totally destroyed. The Lloyd's underwriters who had issued the policy refused to pay the £500 for which the lorry was insured, for the answers to the proposal form were incorporated into the policy by a 'basis of the contract' clause. The House of Lords pointed out that the place where the lorry was garaged was immaterial – the premium would have been exactly the same had the true address been stated, and the policy would have been issued in exactly the same terms. Nevertheless the majority of the judges felt compelled to hold that there was no liability under the policy. 'The result may be technical and harsh,' said Lord Haldane, 'but if the parties have so stipulated we have no alternative, sitting as a court of justice, but to give effect to the words agreed on.'

In an earlier case, *Joel* v. *Law Union and Crown Insurance Co.*, in 1908, Lord Moulton expressed himself more forcibly. 'I wish I could adequately warn the public against such practices on the part of insurance offices,' he cried. 'I am satisfied that few of those who insure have any idea how completely they leave themselves in the hands of the insurers should the latter wish to dispute the policy when it falls in.' He was considering a life insurance policy, and referred to a judgement of Lord St Leonards who had, in 1849, spoken of provisions which, 'unless they are fully explained to the parties, will lead a vast number of persons to suppose that they have made a provision for their families by an insurance on their lives, and by payment of perhaps a very considerable proportion of their income, when in point of fact, from the very commencement, the policy was not worth the paper upon which it was written.'

Not every policy can be avoided by the insurance company on these grounds. Some policies contain an express provision that 'This policy will be indisputable on any ground other than fraud.' It may be that every insured ought to insist on such a clause in every policy: it can certainly be regarded as desirable, if not essential, in every life insurance policy.

But such a clause itself takes effect, because it has been

agreed by both parties, under the doctrine of 'sanctity of contract'. Without such a clause, the law is powerless. There was therefore great interest when the question was referred to the Law Reform Committee. Its report, in 1957, was non-committal. Abuses had occurred, it admitted – the Law Reports bear sufficient witness to this. But the possibility of abuse was the result of express provisions in a contract rather than rules of law in the ordinary sense, and 'any proposal to alleviate such situations in the interest of the insured would involve interference with the liberty of contract of the insurer.' This, the Committee felt, went beyond the province of mere 'law reform' and involved a broad question of social policy. All the Committee would say was that an amendment to the law would cause no legal difficulties. It is striking that most countries in Europe, and most parts of the United States, do not concede to insurance companies such a generous power to mould the law to their own purposes: England is one of the few countries where the doctrine of freedom of contract applies even to insurance policies.

It is a matter for regret that the Law Reform Committee should have sought to create this artificial distinction between 'law reform' and 'social policy'. The proper function of the law, and the justice of its rules, are inevitably questions of social policy, and law reform without regard to such considerations is an arid and pointless technical exercise. Fortunately the Committee has not felt itself limited in this way in most of its other valuable reports.

There is now an urgent need to amend the law relating to disclosure and warranty so that it holds a fair balance between the insured and the insurance company. No false statement, or failure to disclose, should ever affect the policy unless it is material, and what is material should be judged by the standards of the ordinary man.

INSURANCE AGENTS

Many insurance policies are taken out as a result of a salesman calling on the insured and persuading him to take out insurance. Even when there is no element of persuasion an agent of the insurance company often calls on the insured to bring the forms, explain the purpose and effect of the policy, and help him to fill in the proposal. Suppose the true facts are told to the agent, but are not inserted on the proposal form: can the insurance company avoid the policy for breach of warranty? The answer is that they can.

A clear illustration is to be found in *Newsholme Brothers* v. *Road Transport and General Insurance Co. Ltd*, which came before the Court of Appeal in 1929. The owners of a motor bus took out an accident policy. The insurance company's agent called on the owners and filled in the proposal form at their dictation. The owners then signed the form, which had the usual clause warranting the truth of the answers and making them the basis of the contract. Some months later the bus was involved in an accident, and then the insurance company denied liability.

It appeared that the answers given on the form were inaccurate: a misleading answer was given to the question asking for details of previous accidents. But the form was completed in the agent's handwriting, and the court accepted that the owners gave truthful answers to the agent. No one knew why the agent wrote down the answers wrongly: it may be that he wished the insurance to go through without any hitch so that he could earn his commission. The owners of the bus therefore argued that although the written answers were wrong, the insurance company's agent knew the true facts, and the agent's knowledge was thus, in accordance with the ordinary principles of law, to be treated as that of the insurance company.

The court rejected this argument and held that the insurance company was entitled to repudiate liability. Although the agent had authority to find potential customers and to receive completed forms and premiums from them, it was not his job to fill in the proposal forms. When he did this, therefore, he was doing the insured a favour, and acting as the insured's agent. Thus the court divided the agent's functions: at some times he was the insurance company's agent, at other time he was the insured's agent. When he learned the true answers, therefore, he was the agent of the insured, not of his employers.

Lord Justice Scrutton explained the position in a different way:

If the answers are untrue and the agent knows it, he is committing a fraud which prevents his knowledge being the knowledge of the insurance company. If the answers are untrue, but he does not know it, I do not understand how he has any knowledge which can be imputed to the insurance company.

But the decisive consideration was undoubtedly the idea of sanctity of contract, which influenced the same judge so strongly a few years later in *L'Estrange* v. *Graucob* (p. 39) for he went on:

In any case, I have great difficulty in understanding how a man who has signed, without reading it, a document which he knows to be a proposal for insurance, and which contains statements in fact untrue, and a promise that they are true, and the basis of the contract, can escape from the consequences of his negligence by saying that the person he asked to fill it up for him is the agent of the person to whom the proposal is addressed.

No doubt the ordinary man would have even greater difficulty in understanding how the agent of an insurance company, whom he takes to be the representative of the company ('the man from the Pru', or whatever company it is) is mysteriously transformed into his own agent as soon as mistake or, sometimes, fraud, enters the scene. There have, for example, been cases where the agent has advised the insured how to fill up the form – 'Don't bother to put that down,' he said, 'they won't want to know' – and yet the insurance company has thereby been enabled to evade liability. It would clearly be a necessary and just reform if it were clearly established by Act of Parliament that information received by an insurance agent was to be treated as information received by his employers, and if his statements were taken to be those of the company.

INDEMNITY

If a claim is made under a valid insurance policy, how much money will the insured receive? In a life policy, the amount is specified in the policy itself: if a woman insures her husband's life for £5,000, she will receive that amount on his death. So, too, in a personal accident policy, the amount payable is specified, such as '£1,000 for the loss of both hands or both feet; £500 for the loss of one hand or one foot', and a similar scale for other injuries.

But as a general rule, other kinds of policy do not specify the amount payable. True, you may insure your house for £5,000, or your car for £500. But these do not necessarily represent the amounts payable if the house is destroyed or the car a total loss. They are, rather, maximum amounts. If your house is worth only £4,000 when it burns down, that is all you can receive from the insurance company. If your car has fallen in value to £400, that is your total claim.

The legal principle leading to this result is known as

the principle of indemnity. The purpose of insurance, it recognizes, is to protect the insured against loss, not to enable him to profit from the disaster. Thus in an indemnity policy the insured can never recover more than the value of the property at the time of the loss.

The practical effect of this is that there is nothing to be gained by over-valuing the property insured. Premiums will be paid on the value stated by the insured, but this will not preclude the insurance company from challenging the value when a claim is made. In theory, the insurance company might even evade liability completely, for it is possible that the value stated by the insured in a proposal form is a 'warranty'.

Perhaps it is more likely that the insured will undervalue his property so as to save on premiums; or he may under-insure by inadvertance, failing to note that the value of his house has increased. Here the conditions of the policy will be relevant, for if the insurance is said to be 'subject to average' the insured will never recover a full indemnity. Suppose, to take an unusual example, that the insured owns two adjoining detached houses, each worth £5,000. He takes out a single policy on both houses, but fixes the total cover at £5,000 rather than £10,000. He reasons that the chance of both houses being totally destroyed by fire is so slight that it can be ignored; if either house is destroyed his total loss will not exceed £5,000, and therefore that is sufficient cover. It is clear that this is unfair to the insurer: he is insuring both houses, but is receiving only the premium appropriate to one house. If the policy includes a clause 'subject to average', the result will be that the insured will recover only a proportion of his loss, in the ratio that the value stated (£5,000) bears to the true value of the property insured (£10,000). In other words, he will (in this example) receive half his loss: destruction of both houses would bring him the maximum of £5,000; destruction of one

house would bring him half its value, £2,500. Exactly the
same principle would apply to the insurance of one house,
worth £10,000, for £5,000 cover, if it was 'subject to
average'.

GAMBLING POLICIES

A word must be said about the relation between insurance
and gambling. There is clearly something of a gamble in
insurance: the insurance company gambles (normally
quite successfully) on the claims being smaller than the
premiums collected. In a sense, too, the insured gambles
on the happening of the event insured against. In return
for his stake or premium, he will receive his 'winnings' if
his house burns down. Why not, then, an insurance policy
against the risk that 'Holy Deadlock' will win the 2.30?
If the horse wins, the 'insurer' must pay up. The answer,
of course, lies in part in the principle of indemnity. The
'insured' loses nothing (other than his 'premium') if the
horse fails to win. This can be expressed differently in the
idea that the insured has no interest of an insurable
nature in the subject matter of the 'insurance'.

At common law the absence of an 'insurable interest'
was not fatal to an insurance policy. The result was that
there was no legal objection to gambling by way of insurance policies to which the principle of indemnity did
not apply – life policies. In the eighteenth century it was
common to bet on the number of years left to prominent
persons: the insurer would pay out if the Prime Minister,
say, survived beyond his seventieth year. If the 'insurer'
had enough money at stake, the temptation to ensure that
the life assured did not survive must have been strong,
and in 1774 Parliament stepped in with what has become
known as the Life Assurance Act. 'Whereas,' recited the
Preamble, 'it hath been found by experience that the
making insurances on lives, or other events, wherein the

assured shall have no interest, hath introduced a mis-
chievous kind of gaming . . .,' and the Act made policies
void unless there was an insurable interest in the life or
other event. There is, too, a more general provision in the
Gaming Act of 1845 which makes gambling contracts
unenforceable at law.

The result of this insistence on 'insurable interest' has
not always been obviously just. If Mr Smith takes out a
policy on 'his' house, but overlooks the fact that the house
belongs, at law and in equity, to his wife, he has no insurable interest in the house. He cannot therefore claim if
the house burns down; and nor can his wife, for she is not
a party to the contract of insurance – she has not insured
the house.

Again, the combination of the ideas of insurable interest, indemnity and privity of contract may produce
results unexpected to the layman. A window-cleaner
claims that he is 'fully insured'. He may be, in the sense
that he will be paid compensation by an insurance company if he is injured. But if he has an accident as a result
of a householder's failure to take reasonable care to see
that the premises are reasonably safe, the window-cleaner's
insurance policy will not protect the householder from a
claim brought by the cleaner. Another example can be
found from a contract with a dry-cleaner (the principles
of which were considered in Chapter 7). Suppose clothes
are damaged in a fire at a cleaner's premises, and the fire
was not caused by negligence. The cleaner may be fully
insured against fire, but the owner of the clothes may get
no payment from the cleaner's insurance company for the
insurance company's contract is with the cleaner, not with
the owner of the clothes. There are two possibilities. One
is that the cleaner has merely insured to cover his own
loss and personal liability to the owners of clothes in his
possession; as the fire was not caused by his negligence,
the insurance company will only be liable to meet the

cleaner's own loss by the fire, if any. On the other hand, if the cleaner insured to cover the loss by fire of clothes in his possession and not just his personal liability for such loss, the insurance company will be liable to the owner of the clothes damaged by fire. The trouble is that it is not always easy for the courts to tell whether the policy is of one kind or the other – a very careful look at the wording of the policy is called for.

THE CONTENTS OF THE POLICY

There is no room in this book for a full study of the different types of insurance policy. But no survey of the law of insurance from the point of view of the insured would be complete without a mention of the importance of the wording of the individual insurance policy.

An insurance policy is a contract, and the words used in the policy represent the precise terms of the agreement between the insured and the insurance company. There are no standard forms of insurance policy laid down by law so far as the ordinary person is concerned (though the Marine Insurance Act 1906 sets out the usual form of policy on ships and ships' cargoes). Thus the rights of the insured depend solely on the terms of the policy. Moreover, there are frequently slips of paper (or 'endorsements') stuck on to the printed policy: these also form part of the contract, and may vary the original printed form.

For example, what sort of loss does a 'comprehensive' insurance policy cover? The answer is not to be found by giving some meaning or other to the word 'comprehensive', but by reading the policy itself. In respect of valuable articles, there are policies which comprehend more than 'comprehensive', known as 'all risks'. Again these policies do not necessarily cover all risks: the exact scope of the policy can only be discovered by reading it.

Inevitably, therefore, there are sometimes disputes as to the meaning of an insurance policy, and these disputes are essentially as to the meaning to be placed on particular words. These questions are always questions of law. Thus in *Eisenger* v. *General Accident Insurance Corp. Ltd*, in 1955, the insured had taken out a policy which covered him, among other things, for the 'loss' of his car. He sold his car and, in return for a cheque of £745, permitted the buyer to drive the car away. The cheque was rejected by the bank, and the insured never saw his car again. He claimed under his policy, but failed on the ground that the policy did not cover the loss in these circumstances, for he had voluntarily parted with the car to the buyer, intending the buyer to become the owner. He had, it was held, lost not the car but the money he was to receive.

Perhaps the one shred of comfort to the insured lies in the principle that, where the policy is capable of two or more meanings – and it is surprising how ambiguous even carefully drafted legal documents can be – the meaning most favourable to the insured is taken. For example, in 1963 the High Court had to consider, in *Mills* v. *Smith*, the meaning of the words 'damage caused by accident'. The roots of an oak tree in the insured's garden had dried the land underneath the house next door and caused the foundations to subside. The insured had to pay nearly £1,000 to his neighbour as compensation. Was the damage 'caused by accident'? In one sense this was not an accident, but a natural phenomenon caused by the growth of the tree. On the other hand the damage was accidental, in the sense that it was not intended or expected. Mr Justice Paull held, in favour of the insured, that the damage was covered by the policy.

However, this principle of giving the benefit of the doubt to the insured comes into play only when there really is a doubt as to what the words mean. If they are clear, they must be given their ordinary meaning. For instance, many car insurance policies provide for a 'no-claim bonus', a reduction in the premium in successive years if no claim under the policy has been made. This means what it says – the bonus is to be given only if no *claim* is made. This often leads to misunderstanding, because many motorists think that it ought to be a 'no-blame' bonus; they feel entitled to the bonus if they made a claim but were able to show that another driver was at fault. If the other driver's insurance company has in fact paid up, they find it difficult to understand why they should lose their no-claim bonus. But although some insurance companies do still credit the bonus in these circumstances, the fact remains that the insured could not insist on it: by making a claim he loses the right to his bonus, whether he was at fault or not. And that is what the policy clearly says.

STRICTER RULES
FOR INSURANCE COMPANIES

By the Insurance Companies Act 1958 any company could engage in insurance business if it had a paid-up capital of £50,000. This was not a very substantial sum, especially when a court might require £20,000 or more to be paid on a single personal injuries claim. The failure of an insurance company is particularly serious in the field of motor vehicle insurance because the winding-up of a company may mean that thousands of motorists are put in the position of having immediately to obtain insurance cover elsewhere or of driving on the roads illegally. For example, this is what happened to over a quarter of a million motorists in 1966 when the Fire, Auto and Marine Insurance Company went into liquidation, and this event prompted the Board of Trade to seek greater control over insurance companies. Under the Companies Act 1967, the required minimum paid-up capital was raised to £100,000, but probably of more importance is the provision for greater regulation of the activities of insurance companies. But none of this avoided the Vehicle and General collapse in 1970. Perhaps more powers still are needed – or more vigorous use of existing powers may be enough.

CHAPTER 10

TRAVEL

TRAVELLERS have enjoyed the benefit of legal protection, at any rate with regard to the safety of their luggage, for a long while. From early times, the courts ruled that innkeepers and carriers of goods were under special liabilities. We saw in Chapter 1 how innkeepers, as far back as the fourteenth century, were strictly liable for their guests' goods, irrespective of whether or not the loss or damage could be attributed to any fault or negligence on the part of the innkeeper. We also saw how common carriers – carriers of goods who were willing to carry for anyone, and who did not pick and choose their customers – were under a similar strict liability. Neither the innkeeper nor the common carrier could avoid liability unless it could be shown that the loss was caused by a natural disaster, by an act of the Queen's enemies, or by the customer's own fault.

Yet, although innkeepers and common carriers were already, in the early Middle Ages, under this heavy liability in respect of goods, they owed no duty in respect of their customers' personal safety until some two centuries later. Even then, if a passenger on a stage coach was injured, the passenger had no legal remedy unless he could show that there had been lack of care on the part of the carrier. In other words, negligence had to be proved. It was easier for the traveller to establish liability for damage to his luggage than for injury to himself. By and large, that is still the position today.

Innkeepers were never allowed to contract out of their strict liability for the safety of their guests' goods. It is true that a common carrier could avoid his strict liability by the terms of a written contract, by terms referred to in a ticket handed to the customer, or by notices displayed on his premises. But, even in the nineteenth century, the hey-day of the principles of freedom and sanctity of contract, legislation was passed to limit the common carrier's freedom to avoid liability for damage to goods. The main point of the Carriers Act 1830 was that a common carrier should not be liable for loss of or damage to certain types of valuables, unless their nature and value had been disclosed and an extra charge paid. By another provision of the Act, however, the posting of a notice at the carrier's premises was no longer effective to exclude the carrier's liability.

THE RAILWAYS

The first public railway in the world carried passengers between Stockton and Darlington in 1825, and from their earliest days the railways were deemed by law to be common carriers, obliged to provide reasonable facilities for the carriage of goods. However, because of their monopolistic position, the railway companies were able to insist on conditions of carriage, printed or referred to on the ticket, which gave them wide protection from liability for loss of or damage to goods or for injury to passengers. This complete freedom of contract did not last long. Freedom to contract out of liability for injuries to passengers remained until the railways were nationalized in 1947, but contracting out of liability for the safety of goods carried was soon restricted. Under the Railway and Canal Traffic Act 1854 a railway company could only avoid liability for goods lost or damaged by their negligence (or the negligence of their employees) by a written contract signed by the customer, and even then only if the contract was 'just and reasonable'.

The courts did not like being left with the problem of

determining when a contract satisfied this vague criterion of being 'just and reasonable', but in 1863, in the case of *Peek* v. *North Staffordshire Railway Co.*, the House of Lords adopted a rough-and-ready formula to meet the difficulty. No contract by a railway company to carry goods was to be considered 'just and reasonable' unless the customer was offered a fair alternative between having the goods carried at his own risk ('owner's risk') and having them carried at carrier's risk at a rate not excessively higher than the rate for carriage at owner's risk. After 1928, until the Transport Act 1962, most merchandise carried by rail was carried on Standard Terms and Conditions, approved by an independent Tribunal. As a general rule, this meant that a customer had the option of having his goods carried at carrier's risk, in which case the company was under a strict liability, or (for a smaller charge) at owner's risk, which meant that the company was liable only for wilful default. Now, under the Transport Act 1962, the railways, or rather the British Railways Board, are no longer common carriers so they are free to reject goods at will; both the 1854 Act and the Standard Terms and Conditions are gone. But although in theory free to insist on any contractual terms it thinks fit, the new Board, with a due sense of its responsibilities as a public corporation, has adopted 'General Conditions of Carriage' under which merchandise is still carried at carrier's risk or at owner's risk.

PASSENGERS' LUGGAGE

There are special conditions for luggage which a passenger takes with him on a journey for his own use. If it is put in the guard's van, and there is any loss or damage, the Board is liable unless it can show that there was no negligence on the part of its employees. On the other hand, if the luggage is put in a compartment, the Board is only liable for any loss or damage if the passenger can positively prove negligence and even then only up to £50 per passenger. It is a matter of regret that these conditions, drawn up by the railways themselves and not approved by any independent body on behalf of the public, are less favourable to the passenger than the conditions operating before nationalization. The case of *Vosper* v. *Great Western Railway Co.*, heard in 1928, shows that at that time the railways were under a strict liability for passengers' luggage, even when put in a compartment, and could only escape liability for loss by showing that it was caused by a natural disaster, enemy action, or the passenger's own negligence. Vosper, having left his suitcase in a compartment, spent most of the journey either in the restaurant car or in another compartment, where he had found some friends. On returning to his compartment, his suitcase could not be found. The Court of Appeal held that the company was liable for the loss. The Court thought there was no negligence on the part of Vosper. He was under no duty, it said, to remain in the compartment all the time, and the court particularly took into account the fact that the company itself invited passengers to leave their compartments in order to have a meal in the restaurant car. Nor was there negligence on the part of the railway company; but their liability as carriers did not depend on negligence. From the point of view of the individual passenger, it is no doubt a pity that this decision is no longer law. The conditions of carriage adopted by the railways since 1947 make it virtually impossible for a passenger to claim for loss of luggage left in a compartment, for it is up to him to try to prove negligence on the part of the railways' employees. His only safety lies in taking out insurance.

A passenger on the railway is entitled to take with him free of charge 'passengers' luggage' up to 100 lb. (or up to 150 lb. if he is travelling first class). The basic meaning of 'passengers' luggage' is what he takes with him for his own personal use and convenience provided it is something in the nature of a package, but includes hand luggage used by a passenger for his trade or profession, such as a commercial traveller's samples. However, there are many subtle distinctions and British Rail's Conditions have to be combed through to learn, for example, that by way of concession children's cots, push-chairs (folded) and deck-chairs may be carried free of charge, but bicycles and hand carts have to be paid for. Unfortunately the 'concession' is two-edged because British Rail accepts no liability whatever for such luggage as is carried free by way of concession, and for such things as bicycles carried at extra charge there is liability only in the unlikely event of the passenger being able to prove wilful default. Most people know that a dog needs a ticket, but so does any other 'small or inoffensive' animal or bird that the Regulations permit to be taken on a train. While there is limited liability in respect of animals carried in the guard's or luggage van, the Board can never be made liable for any loss or injury to an animal in the passenger's own custody. It is all very complicated.

A bus or coach, running as part of a regular public transport service, and known in law as a public service vehicle, is still a common carrier for any passenger's luggage it carries, and the operator is, therefore, strictly liable for loss or damage unless the terms of the contract exclude or limit this liability. There is no legal restriction on any such contractual term.

While there has for some time been legislative control over the terms on which the railways may carry goods, it is only relatively recently that the same sort of control has been extended to the terms on which passengers are carried. Passengers on buses and coaches benefited first from legislative intervention when the Road Traffic Act 1930 enacted that any contract to carry a passenger on a public service vehicle purporting to negative or restrict liability for death or injury was void. The same provision is now to be found in the Road Traffic Act 1960. When the railways were nationalized, railway passengers were given similar protection by the Transport Act of 1947, and this is now embodied in the Act of 1962. So although the judicial reasoning in *Thompson* v. *London, Midland and Scottish Railway Co.*, the 1930 case of the excursion ticket (p. 37) is as valid today as it ever was, a clause of that type, excluding rights in respect of injury, is no longer possible.

Thus, today, whether a passenger is travelling by road or rail on public transport, if he suffers any injury during the journey, he has a claim for damages if he can establish negligence on the part of the carrier or his employees, any contractual provision to the contrary notwithstanding. One example will suffice. In *Barkway* v. *South Wales Transport Co. Ltd*, heard in 1950, a number of passengers travelling on a bus were killed when a tyre burst, and the bus veered across the road and fell over an embankment. The cause was an 'impact fracture' due to heavy blows on the outside of the tyre. Such a fracture might occur without leaving any visible external mark, but a competent driver would be able to recognize the difference between a blow heavy enough to endanger the strength of the tyre and a lesser concussion. The House of Lords held that the company had failed to observe a reasonable system of tyre inspection and was, therefore, liable for the deaths. As Professor Kahn-Freund has put it, a carrier warrants 'that all is as safe as *anyone's* reasonable care can make it' (our italics). It follows, therefore, that even if the passenger's injury is caused by the negligence of a repairer to whom the vehicle or carriage has been sent for repairs, the carrier is directly liable to the passenger. No provision on a notice, ticket or elsewhere can exclude these heavy liabilities to a passenger and this may even be so if he is travelling on a free pass.

We saw in Chapter 2 that the outlawing of exemption clauses by these provisions in the Road Traffic Act and the Transport Act might usefully be followed in other fields where there is a similar inequality of bargaining power in the contracting parties. In particular, it seems indefensible that a passenger on a sea trip is at the mercy of wide exemption clauses exempting the shipping company from liability. The relevant clause of one shipping company's form of contract reads as follows: 'The company shall not be liable for any loss of life, personal injury, illness, loss of or damage to property, loss, expense, inconvenience or delay whatsoever and wheresoever arising, and whether due to unseaworthiness of the vessel at the commencement or at any stage of the voyage . . .' In no other form of travel has the law allowed the principle of freedom of contract to remain inviolate. Since all shipping companies insist on similar conditions, a passenger has no option but to accept them if he is to travel at all.

AIR TRAVEL

It is appropriate that the conditions on which airways carry passengers and their luggage are largely determined by international agreement. The principal international Convention, the Warsaw Convention of 1929, which laid the foundation of the present law, was given statutory force in this country by the Carriage by Air Act 1932. The Convention was amended at The Hague in 1955 and the Carriage by Air Act 1961 enabled the Government to ratify the Hague Protocol which it eventually did in 1967. The intention of these international Conventions was that whether a man travelled by BEA or, say, Sabena or Air France, on an international flight, uniform conditions should apply. Unfortunately, the position is confused because not all countries have ratified the Hague Protocol or even the Warsaw Convention. Consider one important matter dealt with by the Convention rules: liability for a passenger's death or injury. There is unlimited liability under both the Convention and the Protocol if the casualty arises from acts or omissions done with intent to cause injury, or recklessly and with knowledge that injury would probably result. Apart from this sort of case, rare enough to be ignored, the airline's liability was limited to about £3,450 by the Warsaw Convention and to about £6,900 by the Hague Protocol, but these limits have been thought by many countries (including the United States and this country), though not by all countries, to be too low in relation to modern needs. In 1965 the United States went so far as to lodge notice of denunciation of the Warsaw Convention to take effect from 1966. The United States' action was followed by inter-governmental discussions and meanwhile a number of the world's leading airlines have made voluntary interim arrangements which have enabled the United States to withdraw its denunciation of the Warsaw Convention to which therefore it remains a party. In the United Kingdom special rules were laid down in 1967 to govern flights not covered by the Warsaw Convention or the Hague Protocol.

The present position is broadly as follows:

(a) Unless you are carried by one of the airlines that have agreed to the special arrangements applicable to journeys terminating in, originating from, or having an agreed stopping place in the United States (referred to in (d) below), you are subject to the £6,900 limit for all journeys to which the Hague Protocol applies, e.g. London–Paris, since both this country and France are parties to the Protocol.

(b) Again subject to the special arrangements referred to in (d) below, you are subject to the £3,450 limit for all journeys to which the unamended Warsaw Convention still applies, e.g. London–Vienna until Austria ratifies the Protocol, but London–Vienna–London round trip will count as carriage from London to London with an agreed stopping place in another State and will, therefore, be subject to the £6,900 limit.

(c) On domestic flights, e.g. London–Glasgow or London–Gibraltar, you are governed by a limit of about £24,000 and this limit also applies on journeys governed by neither the Warsaw Convention nor by the Hague Protocol, e.g. London–Ankara single as Turkey is a party to neither the Convention nor the Protocol.

(d) £24,000 is also the limit on journeys by most of the world's airlines which terminate in, or originate from, or have an agreed stopping place in the United States.

In (a), (b) and (c) above, the airline is exonerated entirely if it can show that the line or its employees have taken all necessary measures to avoid the injury or that it was impossible to take such measures. In other words, it is not necessary for the injured passenger (or his next of kin if the accident was fatal) to prove negligence: it is for the airline to prove that they were not at fault – that the pilot and crew, and airport staff, and everyone else did all that was necessary or reasonable to prevent an accident. And that is their only defence: conditions in timetables or on the ticket cannot affect the passenger's rights. However, a passenger cannot obtain more than the appropriate limited amount by bringing his action against the airline employee whose negligence has caused the accident instead of against the airline itself.

The Convention rules also cover all cases where an air passenger's baggage is lost or damaged during the period when it is in the charge of the carrier, either at the airport or on board the aircraft. There is full liability for wilful misconduct, but otherwise the liability of the airline is limited to 250 gold francs per kilogram of registered luggage (about £6.90 per kilo), unless the consignor has made a special declaration of value and paid a higher charge. The carrier is completely free from liability if it can show that all necessary measures were taken to avoid loss or that it was impossible to take such measures. In the case of 'hand luggage', that is, luggage kept by the passenger in his own charge, there is a limit to the airline's liability of 5,000 francs (about £138) per passenger.

Further changes, which would increase the liability of airlines to about £40,000 for each passenger, and take away their defence of proving absence of negligence, were agreed in Guatemala in 1971, but have not yet been ratified.

TRAVEL AGENTS

Many people book their holiday through a travel agent, especially when they are going abroad. The contract with the agent may be to provide a room at a certain hotel, to make rail or air reservations, or to provide a fully inclusive tour. It all depends on what has been agreed. If the customer is dissatisfied for some reason, it is the terms of the contract that determine whether he can claim a remedy against the agency.

Two decisions of the Court of Appeal in 1959 and 1960 show to what extent the traveller is protected by the present law. In *Trackman* v. *New Vistas Ltd*, Mr Trackman, a solicitor, arranged with the defendant travel agents to go with his wife and three small sons to Spain. When the family arrived at the Hotel Mañana, Lloret del Mar (the hotel named in the agreed itinerary), they were told that their rooms were not in the hotel itself but in an annexe, some 200 yards away. Dissatisfied with this, Mr Trackman and his family went to stay at a more expensive hotel, costing an additional £36. He sued the travel agents for breach of contract, seeking to recover not only the £36 but also further damages, alleging that he had been given inadequate notice to start his journey earlier

than arranged, that proper steps were not taken to find
his places on the train at Victoria, and failure to notify
him that they would not have couchettes. The Court upheld the plaintiff's claim, awarding him both the £36 and
£10 in respect of the other items of damage. In justification of Mr Trackman's rejection of the annexe accommodation, and his taking suitable substitute accommodation
where he could find it, Lord Evershed said this:

Anybody reading the itinerary would assume that by 'Hotel
Mañana' was meant what would be, in ordinary common
sense, described as an 'hotel', as distinct from outbuildings,
annexes, or private houses with accommodation available to
the hotel management but separated by appreciable distances
from the hotel itself. An hotel includes not only the sleeping
accommodation but other amenities – meals, sitting rooms
and so forth, and the services of the concierge and persons of
that kind.

A few months later, the Court of Appeal had a similar
case before it: *Cook* v. *Spanish Holiday Tours (London)
Ltd*. A honeymoon couple were suing the defendant
agents for failing to provide a room at the Voramar Hotel
in Tossa, Spain. The agency had agreed to provide them
with a holiday at the hotel for £104 and had made a block
booking for rooms there. However, when the couple
arrived at the hotel, it was full and they were offered a
filthy room in an annexe where there were beetles in one
corner. The couple returned to Barcelona, spent the
night on a bench at the airport, and flew back to England
the next day after bribing an official £4 to get them
seats on a plane. The Court held that the defendants had
totally failed to carry out their contract and ordered the
return of the £104 paid to them. In addition, Mr Cook
was held entitled as damages to £62 for expenses incurred
in returning to London, £25 for the disappointment
suffered, and the £4 paid as a bribe since, as Lord God-

dard put it, bribing an airways official was 'in accordance with the custom of the country'. The decision is significant because the Court of Appeal rejected the county court judge's view that the duty of the agency was merely to *book* a room. However, if the agency clearly specifies that it is merely agreeing to *book* a room, it is under no liability if the hotel fails to keep the booking – the disappointed traveller would be left, in that event, with the more difficult task of suing the foreign hotel. In the *Trackman* case too, the agency would not have been liable if the contract had qualified the agency's obligation. Perhaps the real significance of that case is that Mr Trackman booked by letter, not on a booking form provided by the agency. If a booking form is used the traveller has to read the small print if he is to discover his legal rights.

While there is no doubt that a travel agency may in law restrict its liability by the terms shown on a booking form, the principle of fundamental breach, analysed in Chapter 2, applies here as to other kinds of contracts. Thus it is almost certain that a condition imposed by a well-known London firm of travel agents, stating that they 'incur no liability whatsoever under this contract', is totally ineffective. Moreover, the terms of the contract will be construed so as to give effect to the substance of what has been agreed. For example, in *Anglo-Continental Holidays Ltd* v. *Typaldos Lines (London) Ltd* (1967) a firm of travel agents booked their clients on a large liner with two swimming pools and other amenities, for a cruise which would spend several days in the Holy Land. Shortly before the sailing date the shipping line found they had overbooked and attempted to transfer the bookings to a much older and smaller ship, lacking the amenities of the original liner, which would spend only a matter of hours in the Holy Land. When the travel agents sued for damages the shipping line relied on this clause: 'Steamers, sailing dates, rates and itineraries are subject to change without notice.' The Court of Appeal held that this gave no protection: it did not enable the shipping line to alter the substance of the contract.

Further protection for travellers has been given by two Acts of Parliament referred to in earlier chapters. In so far as the details to be found in travel brochures are statements of fact (such as descriptions of hotels or resorts) rather than promises as to the future they will be representations, and by section 3 of the Misrepresentation Act 1967 (see p. 58 above) any clause excluding liability for their falsity will be ineffective unless the court thinks that it is fair and reasonable. Such statements will also fall within section 14 of the Trade Descriptions Act 1968 (see p. 144 above) which makes it a criminal offence to make a false statement, known to be false or made recklessly, about the nature of any services, accommodation or facilities provided in the course of a trade or business.

A reckless promise that such facilities will be provided in the future would not constitute a trade description, so that a description of a hotel 'to be completed next Spring' could not be the subject of a prosecution under the Trade Descriptions Act. But it might give rise to a claim for damages for breach of contract, and might enable the Director General of Fair Trading (see p. 152 above) to take action under the Fair Trading Act 1973, either by making proposals for an order regulating the practice in question, or alternatively by seeking an order from the Restrictive Practices Court against an agent who persistently broke his contracts.

In the last few years, there has been increasing public anxiety over the precarious financial standing of many of the travel agencies and tour operators that have blossomed forth in the rapid development of the foreign holiday trade. The only legislative control over travel agents is under the Civil Aviation Act 1971: as from April 1973 some agents will need an air travel organiser's licence, and to get one they will have to show that they have the necessary resources and have made adequate financial arrangements. Apart from this, travel agents are not controlled by statute, though Mr Edward Milne M.P. made several unsuccessful attempts to bring in compulsory registration.

The Association of British Travel Agents (A.B.T.A.), which includes about 90 per cent of the country's travel agents, has sought to protect holidaymakers who lose money or are stranded abroad as the result of an agent's bankruptcy. Under the revised 'Operation Stabilizer' introduced in 1972 tour operators who are members of A.B.T.A. must provide security, such as a bond or guarantee, to protect customers on an inclusive holiday abroad against loss of deposit or money as well as being stranded in a foreign country. Retailer members of A.B.T.A. contribute to a fund to cover travellers against losses due to the default or bankruptcy of a member retailer.

Whilst the Consumer Council was still functioning, it pressed strongly for guarantees of this kind to cover all agents; it also sought the removal of contractual clauses restricting a travel firm's liability, and the establishment of an independent arbitration scheme for holiday complaints. As we have seen, the Misrepresentation Act and the Trade Descriptions Act have made travel brochures a bit more reliable; now the Law Commissions have put forward for discussion suggestions that exemption clauses should be invalid unless found to be reasonable in the circumstances.

HOTEL RESERVATIONS

Where a room is booked at a hotel and the reservation is accepted, there is of course a contract, the terms of which will be contained in any letters passing between the hotel and its customer and in any brochure sent by the hotel. It is a breach of contract if the customer cancels the reservation, though illness might be a valid defence. Where the customer is in breach of contract, the hotel proprietor is entitled to keep any deposit paid, and, in addition, to claim damages for any further loss resulting from the cancellation, taking into account the fact that bed linen has been unused and food not eaten. Of course, if the room is let to someone else and the hotel is full, it has suffered no real loss and any damage would be purely nominal. However, since the hotel is not bound to accept a cancellation – it can, if it wishes, continue to keep the room for the customer in case he does after all arrive – the hotel is then under no duty to make any efforts to try and re-let the room, such as by writing to people formerly refused accommodation.

It will be apparent from the travel agency cases that if a room is booked with a hotel and the hotel breaks the contract by not providing the room or services agreed, the customer may sue the hotel for damages. These would cover the financial loss from having to take substitute accommodation at a higher charge, and compensation for inconvenience and, possibly, for disappointment.

COMMON INNS

Innkeepers have been under a strict liability for the safety of their guests' goods for centuries. The historical explanation, already mentioned in Chapter 1, is that they were thought of as associates of thieves and cutpurses, with special opportunities for dishonesty. From the four-teenth century onwards, it was a 'custom of the realm' that if a guest's goods were lost, the innkeeper was liable unless he could prove it was caused by natural disaster, the action of enemies of the Queen, or the guest's own negligence. Since this rule preceded the idea of contract, it is not surprising that no contractual terms or warning to guests to take special precautions could alter or dimi-nish the innkeeper's obligations. This is one field of law where exemption clauses have always been void, and of no effect.

What factors determined whether a place was a 'com-mon inn'? It was defined as an establishment willing to provide refreshment and lodging accommodation to any traveller who was prepared to pay a reasonable price and who was in a fit state to be received. It was never a matter of social status and, possibly to their surprise, both the Dorchester and the Ritz Hotels in London have been held to be 'common inns'. There has, however, always been a distinction between inns and 'private hotels', that is, establishments which reserved the right to pick and choose their guests and did not hold themselves out as willing to take in any traveller who came their way. 'Pri-vate hotels' were never, and are not today, under a strict liability for their guests' luggage.

The first amelioration of the innkeeper's position of strict liability for his guests' luggage came in 1863. Under the Innkeepers' Liability Act of that year, by exhibiting a copy of section 1 of the Act in a conspicuous part of the hall or entrance to the inn the innkeeper could limit his liability to £30 unless the goods were lost or damaged through the wilful act or neglect of the innkeeper or his employees, or unless the goods were left with the inn-keeper for safe custody. However, the Act did not permit the innkeeper to limit his liability in respect of horses and carriages. Motor-cars had not then been invented, but when they were, they too were classed as 'carriages', so there was no way in which the innkeeper could avoid or limit his strict liability for any car left by a traveller within the precincts of the inn or its car park. The advent of the motor car, and the outcome of a number of court cases in which innkeepers were held fully liable for the loss of cars left by their guests in hotel car parks, led to a move for further changes in the law. The Law Reform Committee was asked by the Lord Chancellor to consider the position. It presented a report in 1954 and legislation embodying its proposals followed in the Hotel Proprietors Act 1956.

In evidence to the Committee, the Law Society (representing the solicitors' branch of the legal profession) suggested that the strict liability of innkeepers should be abolished, so that in future they would be liable only for negligence. In the Law Society's view, the historical reasons for the innkeeper's strict liability had largely disappeared – travellers were no longer exposed to danger from highwaymen in league with innkeepers. The Committee, however, rejected the Law Society's views. It agreed that innkeepers ought not to be strictly liable for the loss of cars, but thought that their strict liability in respect of other goods should remain, subject to a right to limit the amount of the liability by exhibiting a statutory notice. The Committee was influenced, in particular, by two practical considerations. One was that an innkeeper can insure against liability for loss of travellers' goods on their premises much more easily and cheaply than the ordinary traveller could insure if the law were altered. The other consideration was that it is often, in the nature of things, difficult if not impossible for a guest whose luggage has been lost or damaged to prove negligence on the part of the innkeeper or his staff.

The present law is contained in the Hotel Proprietors Act 1956. As a recognition of their higher social status (or social pretension), 'common inns' are now referred to as 'hotels', defined as establishments held out by their proprietors as offering food, drink (not necessarily alcoholic), and sleeping accommodation to any traveller who appears able and willing to pay a reasonable sum for the services provided and who is in a fit state to be received. Any hotel complying with this definition (that it calls itself a 'hotel' or 'inn' is irrelevant) must receive all travellers unless there is a reasonable ground for refusal. Thus in 1944, the late Learie Constantine, then a professional cricketer (and later diplomatic representative of Trinidad in this country and a peer), obtained damages against a hotel which operated a colour bar and had refused him admission. By the Race Relations Act 1968 it is unlawful to operate a colour bar in the provision of such facilities as hotel or boarding house accommodation or facilities for refreshment, transport and travel, but enforcement proceedings may be brought only by the Attorney-General and not by an ordinary member of the public.

The question of who is 'in a fit state to be received' has come before the courts many times. Older cases, like the one in 1899 where a lady cyclist wearing bloomers was held to be properly excluded from a hotel because she was not 'in a fit state to be received', may not be reliable guides in the changed social conditions of today. There is also a duty on hotel proprietors to provide food, but since the guest cannot insist on any particular form of meal and the proprietor has a good excuse if he has no food or if the food he has is being kept for travellers who have booked in advance, the duty seems to have little meaning.

As the Law Reform Committee suggested, the innkeeper's strict liability for loss or damage to a guests's goods (other than his motor-car or animals) remains, but only if the guest has reserved sleeping accommodation. Even then, the proprietor can limit his liability by exhibiting a notice near the reception desk or office. The notice is set out in the Act, and the older form of notice – a copy of the 1863 Act – although still seen, has no legal significance at all today. If he exhibits the new notice, the proprietor's liability to any one guest will not exceed £50 in respect of any one article nor £100 in the aggregate, unless the property was lost through wilful default or neglect on the part of the proprietor or his staff (like leaving room keys at an unattended reception desk), or the property was left with the proprietor for safe custody. It will be seen that the monetary limits of liability were raised in 1956, but inevitably, with the fall in the value of money, they seem rather low now. There is no liability on the innkeeper for any amount if the loss is caused by natural disaster, enemy action, or the guest's own negligence.

With regard to the traveller's car, an innkeeper is under no liability for loss unless the traveller can show a 'bailment', that is, a handing over of possession to the innkeeper or his employees, by putting it with the innkeeper's consent into a closed garage or by handing over the car keys. There is then a liability for loss unless the innkeeper can disprove negligence, but he is free to contract out of this liability, for example, by a notice to the effect that cars are left in the garage at the owner's risk. It is a pity that when the Hotel Proprietors Act was being debated by Parliament, it did not accept Lord Silkin's amendment whereby any contractual exclusion of liability for negligence would be void.

As a counterpart to the innkeeper's strict liability for his guest's goods, the innkeeper has been allowed by the common law a lien over his guest's luggage – a right to retain possession of it if the guest has left without paying his bill. Moreover, by the Innkeepers Act 1878, if the bill remains unpaid after six weeks, the innkeeper may, after putting a notice in certain newspapers, sell the guest's luggage so as to try and reimburse himself out of the proceeds.

PRIVATE HOTELS AND BOARDING HOUSES

We have seen that the law has always made a distinction between the liability of innkeepers and that of boarding-house keepers or the owners of private hotels. The distinction still exists. The proprietors of private hotels and boarding houses are only liable for loss of or damage to a guest's goods if the guest can prove negligence. This is not easy, but it is sometimes possible. In *Scarborough* v. *Cosgrove*, 1905, a man and his wife took a room in a boarding-house. Although they had told the owner that they had some property which they wished to keep under lock and key, they were told that the key to their room must be left in the door so that servants could clean the room. Some jewellery belonging to the guests was stolen by a fellow guest who had been admitted as a boarder without references, introduction, or inquiry. The Court of Appeal held that the owner of the boarding house was liable in damages for failing to take reasonable care of the guests' property.

A private hotel owner, unlike an innkeeper, is entirely free to contract out of liability for the safety of his guests' goods, but the terms of a notice in the hotel bedroom would be of no effect. It cannot form part of a guest's contract because the contract will have been made before the guest goes up to the room and sees the notice. The contract is made either when an advance booking is accepted, or when the guest, not having made any advance reservation, is allocated a room at the reception desk.

CHAPTER 11

MONOPOLIES AND THE CONSUMER

Adam Smith once said: 'People of the same trade seldom meet together, even for merriment and diversion, but the conversation ends in a conspiracy against the public or some contrivance to raise prices.'

Monopolies, trade combinations to keep up prices, and other kinds of restrictive trading practices are by no means exclusively modern phenomena. As far back as the Middle Ages both the legislature and the courts, anxious to preserve freedom of trade and free competition, were concerned at their growth. In Edward VI's reign, legislation was passed against price-fixing combinations and against such practices as 'engrossing' by which traders bought up large quantities of wares in order to sell them at inflated prices. Monopolies had been considered contrary to the law from the time of Magna Carta. It is true that monopolistic trading rights were often conferred by the Crown, but the powers of the Crown were curbed in this respect as in many others during the seventeenth century. In the *Case of Monopolies*, 1602, the court held that the grant by Elizabeth I to an officer of her Household of the sole right to import and make playing cards was illegal as a monopoly. The Statute of Monopolies 1624 confined the Crown's prerogative of granting monopolies to first inventions, a principle still applied in the law relating to patents.

A CONFLICT OF PRINCIPLES

Accepting a positive responsibility for preserving conditions in which free competition would thrive, the courts of Queen Elizabeth I ruled that all agreements restricting a person's right to carry on his trade were completely void. Such agreements, it was seen, might tend to privately-created monopolies. So in 1578 an agreement by an apprentice with his master not to exercise his trade in Nottingham for four years was held to be void.

During the seventeenth century, however, this rigid approach was relaxed and the courts expressly recognized that in some circumstances a contract which restricted a man's trading activities – a contract in restraint of trade – might be valid. It could be in the interests of both parties to enforce these contracts. How could the seller of a business get a good price from the buyer if his promise not to compete by setting up in business next door was void? And a master might be unwilling to train an apprentice if he was training someone who might take away his customers. In 1772 the statutes of Edward VI were largely repealed. In the nineteenth century the courts repeatedly held that contracts in restraint of trade which went no further than was necessary for the reasonable protection of the other party were valid, though they still refused to uphold 'general restraints' which sought to impose restrictions effective throughout the country. By 1894 even that qualification had gone, and all restraints were upheld if they were proved to be 'reasonable'.

The explanation is that the principle of freedom of trade was beginning to come into conflict with another principle – freedom of contract. We have seen in other contexts that freedom of contract was the dominant tenet of the nineteenth century, and it included the freedom of some traders to combine against others and freedom to combine to keep up prices. The then Lord Parker of Waddington referred to this clash of ideas in the case of *Attorney-General of Australia* v. *Adelaide Steamship Co. Ltd*, 1913:

Though, speaking generally, it is the interest of every individual member of the community that he should be free to earn his livelihood in any lawful manner and the interest of the community that every individual should have this freedom, yet under certain circumstances it may be to the interest of the individual to contract in restraint of this freedom, and the community if interested to maintain freedom of trade is equally interested in maintaining freedom of contract within reasonable limits.

By the time this statement was made the development of restrictive practices was already well advanced, and by 1919 the Government's Committee on Trusts could report that in every important branch of industry there was 'an increasing tendency to the formation of trade associations and combinations, having for their purpose the restriction of competition and the control of prices.'

THE PUBLIC INTEREST

In the case of *Nordenfelt* v. *Maxim Nordenfelt Guns and Ammunition Co.*, in 1894 – in which a world-wide restraint against competition was upheld on the sale of a world-wide arms business – Lord Macnaghten had voiced the modern attitude of the courts towards agreements that were calculated to restrict trade or competition:

... the public have an interest in every person's carrying on his trade freely; so has the individual. All interference with the individual liberty of action in trading and all restraints in themselves, if there is nothing more, are contrary to public policy and void. That is the general rule. But there are exceptions; restraints of trade and interference with individual liberty may be justified by the special circumstances of a particular case. It is sufficient justification, and, indeed, it is the only justification, if the restraint is reasonable ... reasonable that is, in the interests of the parties concerned, and reasonable in the interest of the public, so framed and so guarded as to afford adequate protection for the party in whose favour it is imposed, while at the same time it is in no way injurious to the public.

From that judgement, it looks as though the interest of the contracting parties and the interests of the public were intended to have equal weight. But this was not really so. In the later House of Lords case of *Morris* v. *Saxelby*, in 1916, it was made clear that once a restrictive trading agreement was shown to be reasonable in the interests of the parties to it (and they are deemed to be the best judges of what is reasonable between themselves), it was for the party impugning the validity of the agreement to prove that it was injurious to the public. This meant in practice that the public interest, the interest of consumers, was barely recognized by the courts at all.

In the first place, it seemed doubtful whether an agreement reasonable so far as the parties were concerned could ever be invalidated on the basis of injury to the public. Lord Parker of Waddington, in the 1913 case already referred to, had said that the House of Lords was not aware of any case in which a restraint, though reasonable in the interests of the parties, had been held unenforceable because it involved injury to the public. In *Palmolive Co. Ltd* v. *Freedman*, 1927, for example, the Court of Appeal held that an agreement whereby a wholesaler, in return for a full discount, agreed not to sell Palmolive soap under sixpence a tablet, was not illegal as being injurious to the public. The court made the point that since the plaintiffs were not the only manufacturers of soap in this country, the public was not bound to buy Palmolive soap. No one asked whether other manufacturers permitted cut prices.

Secondly, unless one of the parties to the agreement positively alleged that it involved injury to the public, possible harm to the public was not even considered by the Court. The case of *North Western Salt Co. Ltd* v. *Electrolytic Alkali Co. Ltd*, 1914, is instructive in this respect. An agreement had been made between a combination of all the salt manufacturers in the north-west of England, who had virtual control of the inland salt market, to keep up prices and regulate supply. The defendant company broke the agreement and was sued for damages. The company did not itself raise in its defence the possibility of the agreement being illegal because it harmed the public and the House of Lords held that, as the agreement was not on the face of it unreasonable, it was valid and could be enforced. Because neither party raised the issue of the public interest, the court declined to consider the matter and maintained a strictly neutral position. Far from accepting any responsibility as a guardian of the public interest, the court was prepared to do no more than hold the ring for the actual parties to the agreement. As Lord Devlin has said, it was this judicial inertia that led in due course to legislative intervention. In any case, if a judge did venture an opinion on these matters, the preservation of competition was not regarded very highly. Lord Parker, in the *North Western Salt* case, for example, said: 'it cannot be to the public advantage that the trade of a large area should be ruined by cut-throat competition'.

There was a third reason why the public interest seemed barely to be recognized by the courts: the great majority of agreements restricting competition never came before the courts at all for the simple reason that, generally, parties pursued their own interests best by adhering to these agreements rather than breaking them. Only a party to the agreement could challenge its validity, so that an agreement which might perhaps be held void by the courts if it ever came before them was fully effective if it never came before the courts at all. There was no way in which a member of the public, someone not a party to the agreement, could bring an action in court to have it declared illegal on the ground that it was a contract which was unreasonably in restraint of trade, and even one of the parties could do no more than raise the defence that the agreement was void if he was sued; he could not stop other parties voluntarily observing the restrictions, for it is no crime to abide by an agreement in restraint of trade.

Even an individual trader, forced out of business by some price ring, or cartel, from which he was excluded, had no right to challenge the agreement on the basis that it involved an unreasonable restriction on trade. He had to go further and prove that it amounted to a conspiracy with an unlawful object. It was a daunting task for a trader to prove that a combination's actions were an unlawful conspiracy for he had to show that the combination's predominant purpose was deliberately to harm his interests rather than to further the legitimate interests of its own members. Lord Chancellor Cave put it this way in the 1925 case of *Sorrell* v. *Smith*:

(1) A combination of two or more persons wilfully to injure a man in his trade is unlawful, and if it results in damage to him, is actionable.

(2) If the real purpose of the combination is, not to injure another, but to forward or defend the trade of those who enter into it, then no wrong is committed and no action will lie although damage to another ensues.

In practice, it was virtually impossible to show that the prime object of a trade combination was something other than the furthering of its members' own 'legitimate' interests. In the 1920s and 1930s, the courts went so far as to permit trade associations to enforce their prices collectively by bringing recalcitrant dealers before private courts, and ruthlessly employing the sanctions of blacklists, fines, and boycott. The House of Lords in *Thorne* v. *Motor Trade Association*, 1937, held that the use of these methods amounted to neither blackmail nor unlawful conspiracy. They were actions taken in reasonable pursuit of 'legitimate' business interests. Professor W. Friedmann of Columbia University commented acidly on the decision in his book *Law in a Changing Society*:

From the judgements ... it can be surmised that only action dictated by personal or vindictive motives ... or the demand of an extortionate fine would make the action illegal ... The law authorized corporate action which eliminated freedom of trade for the individual and it refused to interfere, except in very rare cases. The attitude was still neutrality, with silent abandonment of the liberal economic ideals of previous generations.

The conclusion is inescapable. Where restrictive agreements were challenged before the courts, the courts were largely ineffectual; and many other agreements either never were or never could be challenged under the existing law. Something more was required than the ordinary processes of the law. As Lord Wilberforce has pointed out, we were among the last of the western trading nations to take State action against monopolies and restrictive trading practices. While the United States had outlawed monopolies in the nineteenth century there was no legislative intervention in this country until 1948.

MONOPOLIES

It had long been realized that the interests of the consumer are threatened when a substantial part of the output of an industry is under one control. Monopoly power can readily exploit the consumer by fixing prices so as to provide excessive profits, it can limit the consumer's choice, it can reduce efficiency, and it can hold up the development of new techniques because there may be little incentive for change.

If one company supplies the entire production of a particular article it has a monopoly, but only if there are no close substitutes for the product and only if it can prevent newcomers from entering the market can it exercise its power over the market to the full. Otherwise a price rise will send consumers to other products or will encourage other firms to compete. We can see a monopoly situation exemplified by the British Match Co. as revealed in a report published in 1953. The company made 95 per cent of the matches produced in Britain and also sold to the public 85 per cent of all imported matches. It had achieved this dominance largely through its trading agreement with the Swedish Match Co. The Swedish company had agreed not to sell matches in Britain except through the British Match Co. and as the main supplier of match-making machinery in Europe had agreed not to supply any machinery in Britain except to the British Match Co. Competitors found it difficult to enter the British market: they could not get machinery from Swedish Match and had to pay higher prices to other, smaller, producers; British Match controlled many companies making raw materials and saw that competitors were charged more; and if an independent manufacturer did, despite these obstacles, start to market matches in Britain at lower prices, British Match produced a new brand and sold it below the price of its normal matches – but only where and as long as the competing brands were sold.

COMPETITION OR COLLABORATION?

At the end of the second world war there was much concern at poor productivity in Britain, particularly when compared with the United States. It seemed that the greater competitiveness of the American economy under rigorous legal regulation might be a contributing factor.

The American Sherman Act of 1890 contains a sweeping condemnation of all monopolies:

Every person who shall monopolize, or attempt to monopolize ... any part of the trade or commerce among the several states, or with foreign nations, shall be deemed guilty of a misdemeanor ...

The Act also declared that all contracts in restraint of interstate or international trade or commerce were illegal. Thus the common law of restraint of trade was strengthened immeasurably: by making such contracts crimes the government could, and did, effectively enforce the prohibition. The result has been that governmental control over restrictive trading agreements – like the price-fixing agreement by electrical manufacturers which, in 1960, led to the imprisonment of senior company officials – has been a major force in twentieth century America, and the Sherman Act was strengthened in 1914 by the Clayton Act which extended the ban on monopolies to agreements which substantially lessened competition, whether by mergers or by price discrimination.

In 1945, although few people in Britain would have advocated the adoption of the strict American prohibition, there was a growing belief that practices restricting competition should be put under public scrutiny. At the beginning of the century the British economy was the most competitive in the world; by 1945 it was minutely regulated. Tariffs had been erected before and after the first world war. During the depression of the 1930s the government had encouraged manufacturers to make agreements in order to share the available work. During the second world war the economy was regulated by rationing and price control. The government found it convenient to discuss supplies with a single, large firm, or with a trade association representing the interests of many. All this led to an atmosphere of fair shares for all – the antithesis of competition. On the other hand, unrestrained competition may not always be desirable – it may, for example, lead to wasteful over-production or unused resources.

THE MONOPOLIES AND MERGERS COMMISSION

When monopoly legislation came at last in 1948 it did not follow the American pattern. On the basis that a monopoly is not necessarily against the public interest it was thought that before prohibiting any particular monopoly there must be an investigation. The Monopolies and Restrictive Practices (Inquiry and Control) Act 1948 set up a Commission to look into allegations of monopolies and restrictive practices that were referred to it by the government. Originally called the Monopolies and Restrictive Practices Commission, it became simply the Monopolies Commission in 1956 when its oversight of some restrictive practices was taken from it by the Restrictive Trade Practices Act and is now to be renamed the Monopolies and Mergers Commission.

The Department of Trade and Industry may, under the 1973 revisions (see p. 302 below), refer the supply of any class of goods or services to the Commission for investigation if the Department thinks that one quarter or more of the goods or services in the United Kingdom or in a specified part of it are supplied by, to or for a single firm or group of companies, or two or more firms which conduct their affairs so as to restrict competition. If the Commission concludes that the one quarter test is satisfied, it must go on to investigate whether that fact, or the behaviour of the firms, operates against the public interest.

The Commission has been left to work out its own concept of the public interest, since the 1948 Act gives little guidance. 'All matters which appear in the particular circumstances to be relevant shall be taken into account,' says section 14. It then refers in very general terms to the desirability of efficiency, full employment, and the development of technical improvements. The nearest it gets to an explicit recognition of the consumer interest is a reference to the type, quality, volume and prices of goods and services 'as will best meet the requirements of home and overseas markets.' By and large the Commission has accepted that the main criterion should be the protection of consumers through competition, but it has also taken into account such matters as the interests of traders who would like to enter a profitable market, independently of the benefits to consumers that such increased competition might bring. An immediate reduction in price may not necessarily be in the consumer interest – it might discourage investment in plant or research – but the long term interest of consumers is the most important objective sought by the Commisssion.

INQUIRIES INTO PRICE FIXING AGREEMENTS

Between 1948 and 1956, eighteen of the Commission's twenty-one investigations were into trade association rules or recommendations, most of them fixing minimum prices and many allocating shares of the available market to each firm. In general the Commission condemned these agreements on the ground that they restricted competition, although occasionally price fixing agreements were upheld. In its 1969 report on Estate Agents the Commission made it clear that its general condemnation of price fixing in relation to goods applies equally to services. Thus the recommendations of trade associations and professional bodies relating to scales of charges will normally be condemned unless there is some special justification. In relation to estate agents the Commission recommended that fee scales based on the prices of houses and flats should no longer be published or enforced, and the government implemented this by the Restriction on Agreements (Estate Agents) Order 1970.

DOMINANT FIRM INQUIRIES

During the period 1948 to 1956 the Commission investigated two monopoly situations. The facts revealed in the 1953 report on Matches have already been referred to (p. 288 above). The Commission's conclusion was that this situation caused prices to be too high and operated against the public interest. The report may perhaps have deterred firms with control over a large share of the market from using tactics to keep out new competitors. The threat of investigation by the Commission is a real one: even in 1953 the cost of effective representation before the Commission may have amounted to nearly a quarter of a million pounds, apart from the cost of distracting higher management from their main task of running the company.

RESTRICTIVE PRACTICES

In addition to the power to refer a particular industry to the Commission, the 1948 Act also enabled the government to ask the Commission to report on particular restrictive practices prevalent throughout industry. The first general reference of this kind resulted in what can fairly be described as the Commission's most influential report. Published in 1955, it dealt with the general effect of specific kinds of collective discrimination: agreements to give the benefit of trade terms only to members of a particular trade association, and other collective boycotts such as collective resale price maintenance – agreements not to supply retailers who cut prices. The Commission commented that in all its inquiries it had never come across a harmless instance of collective discrimination, though the point was made that it might have desirable effects in some circumstances. A minority report concluded that since agreements to discriminate might conceivably be desirable it would be wrong to forbid them, at least until a tribunal had investigated them individually and decided whether each was desirable.

The Restrictive Trade Practices Act 1956, passed a year after the report on Collective Discrimination, largely adopted the view of the minority. Certain types of agreement commonly adopted to restrict competition in the supply and production of goods were to be registered, and a new Restrictive Practices Court was to decide whether each was contrary to the public interest. The work of this court will be considered in the next chapter.

PROBLEMS OF INQUIRY

The Commission, now known simply as the Monopolies Commission, continued its activities having, as its chairman until 1956 commented sadly, been 'depleted of half its name, half its membership, half its staff, and half its powers.' The impact on the public interest of monopoly situations is more difficult to assess than the impact of restrictive practices. When traders agree to keep up prices, it is fairly clear that consumers are prejudiced unless there are compensating benefits. This is also the case when a dominant firm adopts the sort of exclusionary tactics practised by British Match. These, however, are no longer common. Recently the Commission has been more concerned with whether unduly high prices are being charged, in other words with the levels of profits and with efficiency. This has probably lengthened their inquiries. It is extremely difficult to tell whether a large firm is being well run from a cursory inquiry by outsiders. Indeed, it is doubtful whether a team of efficiency consultants could do much for a firm that had not called them in voluntarily. Even if the Commission thinks that a firm has been well run and that its investment in such things as plant, research and development is about right, it is hard to tell what profit it should be allowed to earn. If it is well run, it should expect to make more than the national average return on capital.

PETROL

A solus agreement is an agreement under which a garage agrees to sell only the petrol of the company with which it contracts, and not to handle any other brand. A comparison of the way in which these agreements have been dealt with by the Monopolies Commission and by the ordinary courts throws light on these different techniques of control.

The Monopolies Commission reported on solus agreements in 1965. These agreements had advantages for the existing petrol companies. They saved on distribution costs. Moreover, by assuring outlets for oil products, they encouraged investment in refineries at a time when much of the petrol consumed in the U.K. was refined abroad. Most of the savings on distribution could have been achieved in less restrictive ways, for instance by giving large discounts to garages prepared to take a full load from the largest tanker permitted to travel on the highway. The ability of the oil companies to plan their distribution and the siting of their depots could probably have been achieved by shorter term agreements.

The disadvantages of the agreements from the point of view of motorists – the appropriate test of the public interest in the opinion of the Commission – are that there will be no choice of brand at any particular garage – according to the Commission not a serious objection given the similarity of the different brands – and that competition will be restricted by the difficulty of entering the market. New outlets cannot be created easily since the erection of a new garage requires planning permission which is rarely obtainable unless there is a stretch of 12 miles of road without a garage. As a result it became difficult for an oil company to enter the market once most of the existing garages had become tied. When Esso first began to make solus agreements in 1950, there was little detriment to the public. When Shell followed, the other oil companies had to do the same to ensure their outlets. By the time the Commission reported, over 95% of the outlets were tied to a particular supplier. Shortly afterwards, the Italian company, Agip, tried to enter the British market, but had such difficulty in acquiring new garages, partly because of the restrictive policy of the planning authorities and partly because so many existing garages were already tied, that it gave up the attempt. To make investment in a refinery in the U.K. worth-while, Agip needed to sell a fairly large minimum quantity which it failed to do soon enough.

The Commission did not condemn outright these agreements not to handle competing petrol. It acknowledged that they had brought benefits to motorists by reducing costs, and to some extent prices. Nevertheless, it concluded that the agreements ran for unduly long periods – many of them for twenty years or more. It recommended that they should be limited to five years, after which either party could bring them to an end by giving one year's notice.

Within a few years of the report of the Monopolies Commission on Petrol, litigation concerning solus agreements came before the House of Lords. In *Esso Petroleum Co. Ltd* v. *Harper's Garage (Stourport) Ltd* in 1967 there were two solus agreements concerning garages in the Midlands, one for $4\frac{1}{2}$ years and the other for 21 years. When, in 1963, Esso permitted garages to cut prices, Harpers found that profits were threatened and turned over to V.I.P. petrol at both their garages. Esso went to court for an injunction to enforce the solus agreements – an order forbidding Harpers to sell any petrol other than Esso. Harpers argued that both agreements were invalid because they were in restraint of trade and were unreasonable.

The first concern of the House of Lords was whether they had any power to control the solus agreements at all: were they contracts in restraint of trade? If a man agrees to work full-time for his employer, that contract effectively prevents him from working full-time for anyone else – yet such contracts have never been held to be bad for restraint of trade. Why then should a contract to take all one's petrol from Esso, and none from any other company, be in restraint of trade? Moreover, it has long been common for a landlord to let a house or a shop to a tenant restricting the purposes for which the tenant can use the premises. These leases have not been held to be in restraint of trade. Nevertheless the House of Lords held that, on balance, the essence of the solus agreements was to restrict the garage proprietor's freedom of trading. As Lord Wilberforce put it, the categories of contracts in restraint of trade 'can never be closed'.

This finding brought into play the principle that contracts in restraint of trade are void unless they are reasonable. In deciding whether these solus agreements were reasonable most of the Law Lords stressed the importance of taking into account the public interest. The House of Lords unanimously held that the $4\frac{1}{2}$-year agreement was reasonable but that the 21-year agreement was unreasonable and therefore invalid.

It is here that the limitations of the ordinary courts become apparent. When the Monopolies Commission reported on solus agreements all the major petrol companies, and some of the small ones, supplied statistics. The Commission was able to investigate the whole industry for nearly five years and to evaluate the benefits and detriments of the solus system to motorists and the trade. Its recommendations were made in the context of the market as a whole. In contrast, the courts in the *Esso* case had little evidence relating to the reasonableness of the ties in the solus agreements. The interest of the public was stressed, but there was little material other than the Monopolies Commission report, referred to by several of the Law Lords, on which to assess it.

The overall picture is clear: the House of Lords' decision is significant and important in relation to contracts in restraint of trade generally; but as far as petrol distribution is concerned, the important factor is the government's acceptance of the Monopolies Commission recommendation that the normal solus agreement should be terminable after five years. Although the decision in the *Esso* case is consistent with this, Lord Reid emphasized that that decision 'ought not in my view to be regarded as laying down any general rule as to the length of tie permissible in a solus agreement.' That is exactly what the Monopolies Commission was in a position to do for future agreements.

It is not yet clear how far the House of Lords' decision in the *Esso* case marks a radical change in the attitude of the courts to the public interest. In *Texaco Ltd* v. *Mulberry Filling Station Ltd* (1972) Mr Justice Ungoed-Thomas declined to consider whether the abolition of the restraint in a solus agreement would lead to the economic or social advantage of the country and thought that much of the evidence brought before him, directed to general considerations of economic policy, was irrelevant. He believed that 'the interests of the public' did not refer to the interests of the public at large, but rather to the proposition that the public has an interest in men being able to trade freely 'subject to reasonable limitations which conform with the contemporary organization of trade'. This approach is capable of leading back to the notion that the public interest is of little importance where the restraint is reasonable from the point of view of the parties; indeed, the judge referred to 'the habitual inclination of the court not to interfere with business decisions made by businessmen authorized and qualified to make them.'

MERGERS

Under the 1948 Act the Monopolies Commission had power to investigate monopolies that already existed, but could not be asked to investigate the desirability of mergers that might lead to a monopoly. Merger talks (ultimately abortive) between I.C.I. and Courtaulds, two giant manufacturers of man-made fibres, inspired considerable public discussion of mergers in the early 1960s. Concern was expressed that there was no machinery whereby the public interest could be taken into account when a merger was proposed, and it was pointed out that in view of the real difficulty of unscrambling a monopoly once it existed it would be more sensible to consider its desirability before it came about. Moreover, 1962 saw the report of the Royal Commission on the Press, chaired by Lord Shawcross, which recognized a special danger in newspaper takeovers and recommended the creation of a new court to have the power to veto a press merger. The outcome of these and other public discussions was the Monopolies and Mergers Act of 1965.

Any merger or proposed merger or takeover may be referred to the Monopolies Commission (a) where the merger would lead to or strengthen a monopoly, or (b) where the value of the assets taken over exceeds £5 millions. There is no obligation on the parties to a merger to apply for consent: it is up to the Department of Trade and Industry to decide whether or not to refer a merger to the Commission. Over 600 mergers which could have been referred to the Commission have taken place since 1965, but only 13 have been referred – and three of these were between newspaper proprietors, which the Department of Trade and Industry is obliged to refer. A proposed merger can be held up while an investigation is made by the Commission, which must report within six months or, in exceptional circumstances, nine months. If the Commission reports that the merger will operate against the public interest the Department has power to prohibit it, and this has been done in some cases.

It is far from easy to generalize about the criteria applied by the Commission when investigating mergers. In all but two of these references it has first considered whether the merger is likely to reduce competition substantially. Then it has looked to see whether there are any safeguards against the abuse of a dominant position, such as the countervailing power of customers. If there are, the merger may be permitted, even if there are no substantial compensating factors, but if not the Commission must be convinced that the merger is likely to produce substantial savings.

One or two examples will show the problems involved. The first merger referred to the Commission, in 1965, involved the acquisition of the Pressed Steel Company, the last independent producer of motor vehicle bodies, by the British Motor Corporation (B.M.C.). Pressed Steel was selling some 80 per cent of its output in roughly equal shares to B.M.C. and to Rootes, while four smaller firms also depended on it for their car bodies. If B.M.C., a powerful competitor, were to own Pressed Steel, these other customers would be concerned about their future supplies, but B.M.C. gave an assurance that it would continue to supply them on fair terms. The Commission considered the potential effects on Pressed Steel's customers in the light of this assurance and also the allegedly precarious position of Pressed Steel if the merger did not go through. It came to the conclusion that the merger was not against the public interest.

The first merger to be condemned was that proposed between the Ross Group and Associated Fisheries. The Commission, by a majority of six to two, did not accept the estimates of savings that would be made in the trawling fleets and the processing and marketing of fish and thought that the merger would substantially reduce competition. Some years later the government, without any further reference to the Commission, gave its approval to a merger limited to the trawling interests of the two companies.

The first newspaper merger to be referred to the Commission was that between *The Times* and *The Sunday Times*. With one dissentient the Commission reported in 1966 that the merger might be expected not to operate against the public interest. *The Times* could not continue without outside assistance and, in view of assurances received from the Thomson Organization, the Commission thought that there was every prospect that *The Times* would survive and that, in matters of editorial opinion, it would continue to speak with an independent voice.

ENFORCEMENT

One of the weaknesses of the monopoly legislation is the remoteness of the sanctions. It is in no way illegal for firms to adopt practices that the Commission has condemned time and again. The only deterrent is that predatory conduct may lead the Department of Trade and Industry to refer the products affected to the Commission, thus bringing considerable trouble and expense to the firms involved. During the inquiry the need for a favourable report is likely to moderate the conduct of the firms concerned; but the Commission's recommendations after the inquiry have no binding force. Their condemnation merely enables the government to make a statutory order forbidding certain types of conduct.

Usually the industry spends as much as two years negotiating with civil servants about the terms of the order. The latter will have read the report without access to the confidential matters disclosed to the Commission. The terms of the order are a political decision and industry may put pressure on the Minister to modify them. Usually no order is made, but the firms concerned give undertakings to the Minister. This informal and flexible procedure has some advantages. If conditions change, an undertaking is far more easily re-negotiated than an order, since there is no need for any Parliamentary procedure. Often it is difficult to frame the prohibitions in sufficiently precise terms for incorporation in an order, while the general language of the undertaking may be readily applied, since the parties know that an infringement of the spirit of the undertaking may produce an order in more stringent terms. Sometimes firms have accepted restrictions which the Minister could not have compelled by order. The disadvantage of this administrative procedure is that the only means of enforcement is a more stringent order, or a new reference to the Commission. Another disadvantage of secret negotiations is that the public cannot be kept informed.

TRADING AND PROFESSIONAL PRACTICES

Reports of the Monopolies Commission in 1969 and 1970 considered practices not confined to a particular product or service. In 1969 the report on Recommended Resale Prices recognized that the practice whereby manufacturers published recommended prices could mislead the public, but that the effect was not necessarily the same in different trades. The Commission did not favour an outright ban on the practice, but instead thought that there should be power to investigate the effect in relation to particular classes of goods, with the possibility of prohibiting recommended prices if the investigation showed this to be necessary.

In 1970 the Commission reported on the practice adopted by some manufacturers and distributors of refusing to sell to particular wholesalers or retailers – for example, in order to avoid supplying a shop which cuts prices or in order to protect the business of existing customers. It felt that no serious mischief existed, but that the practice should be watched carefully with a view to a specific reference either to the Monopolies Commission or to the Registrar of Restrictive Trading Agreements.

A controversial report in 1970 dealt with the effect of restrictive practices in the professions, such as restrictions on entry, regulation of fees, and prohibitions on advertising or touting. These restrictive practices are often said to be imposed for the protection of the public, but the Commission did not think that they always operated in the public interest and recommended that each profession should be investigated individually, and that each should itself examine its own practices in the light of the Commission's conclusions.

None of these three reports has yet resulted in legislative or governmental action.

FAIR TRADING BILL

Under this Bill the Director General of Fair Trading (see p. 152 above) may make references to the Commission, subject to the Minister's veto. The proportion of the market by reference to which monopolies are defined (see p. 290 above), which was one third under the 1948 Act, is reduced to one quarter.

CHAPTER 12

RESTRICTIVE PRACTICES

THE elimination of monopoly does not automatically result in competition. If five manufacturers share the market equally between them none has a monopoly; but agreements between them may restrict competition, and the effect on the consumer may be much the same as if one manufacturer monopolized the market. This was recognized in 1948 when the Monopolies and Restrictive Practices Commission was set up, and we saw in the last chapter that its 1955 report on Collective Discrimination called for action to regulate certain restrictive trading agreements. The minority view, that not all such agreements were necessarily undesirable and that they should be subjected to individual scrutiny, was followed in the Restrictive Trade Practices Act 1956.

Under this Act certain agreements that restrict competition in the supply or production of goods must be notified to the Director General of Fair Trading. The agreements to be registered are those which involve certain specified restrictions – for example, as to the prices at which goods may be sold, or the quantities and kinds of goods to be produced or handled, or the persons to be supplied, or the areas in which goods may be sold. If a registrable agreement is not registered the restrictions contained in it are void and it is unlawful to give effect to the agreement. An order may be made to forbid the carrying out of the unregistered agreement, and disobedience is then punishable by fine or imprisonment as a contempt of court. Moreover, anyone adversely affected by the unregistered agreement may bring a civil action for damages if effect is given to it.

The Director must bring every registered agreement before the Restrictive Practices Court. This Court, created by the 1956 Act, generally consists of one High Court judge and three non-lawyers. Unlike the Monopolies Commission, whose reports are merely advisory and have no effect unless the Government decides to implement them, decisions of the Restrictive Practices Court are automatically effective, like the decisions of the ordinary courts.

THE PUBLIC INTEREST

When the agreement comes before the Court there is a presumption that it is contrary to the public interest and therefore void. The Court will then normally ask the parties to the agreement to undertake not to make any other registrable agreement having a similar effect, and if they will not do so an order will be made. The parties may however defend the agreement and argue that it is not contrary to the public interest. Section 21 of the 1956 Act sets out the principles on which the Court must act in much more detail than the legislation governing the Monopolies Commission. The Court may only find that the agreement is not against the public interest if it is satisfied that there is sufficient benefit in it to pass through at least one of eight named 'gateways', and even if the agreement passes one or more of these gateways it must further consider whether these benefits are outweighed by any detriment to the public. Three of the eight gateways are of particular interest in the context of this book. They involve trying to establish that the restrictive agreement is of positive benefit to the consuming public or that it does not restrict competition, and we will consider each of these three in turn.

The 'Protection of the Public' Gateway

To pass through this gateway the Court must be satisfied

(a) that the restriction is reasonably necessary, having regard to the character of the goods to which it applies, to protect the public against injury (whether to persons or to premises) in connection with the consumption, installation or use of those goods (1956 Act, section 21(1)(a)).

In its first case, in 1958, the Court had to consider whether the *Chemists' Federation Agreement* was contrary to the public interest. The Federation consisted of manufacturers of proprietary medicines, wholesale chemists, and retail chemists owned by or employing a qualified pharmacist. The agreement imposed restrictions on members designed to ensure that medicines manufactured by members would only be sold to the public by qualified chemists and not by retailers who employed no pharmacist. One of the grounds on which the Federation sought to uphold the agreement was that the restrictions were justified under gateway (a). It maintained that the restriction of these sales to chemists' shops where a qualified pharmacist was in attendance to advise and warn customers was reasonably necessary to protect the public. In fact, as the Court pointed out, the restriction did not really protect the public at all because most proprietary medicines are sold over the counter by untrained assistants without any advice being given, and even if he was served by a pharmacist the customer might not ask for advice. Moreover, there were many proprietary medicines manufactured by non-members of the Federation and sold through non-qualified retailers, yet no proof was given of a single case of injury resulting from this practice, while a number of potentially dangerous drugs were legally controlled and available only on a doctor's prescription. The Court concluded that the risk of injury was too slight to justify the restrictions, which were ineffective to protect the public anyway. It was clear that the real purpose of the agreement was simply to protect retail chemists from competition.

Gateway (a) has been relied on in only one other case, *Re Tyre Trade Register Agreement* (1963). It was argued that restrictions which prevented mail order firms, discount houses and others not on a list of dealers from handling tyres were necessary to protect the public from the danger of 'do-it-yourself' motorists fitting their own tyres incompetently, but the Court did not agree. There was no risk to the public if car-hire firms, for example, employed experienced mechanics to fit their own tyres, but the agreement prevented them from buying tyres at a discount. Moreover, tyre-fitting is not the easiest or most popular of home chores, and the Court thought that the 'tight-budget motorist' was much more likely to contribute to accidents caused by tyre failures by failing to replace worn tyres than by fitting his own new tyres.

The 'Substantial Benefit to the Public' Gateway

The second gateway has been heavily relied upon in almost every case that has been heard. To succeed the parties must show

(b) that the removal of the restriction would deny to the public as purchasers, consumers or users of any goods other specific or substantial benefits or advantages enjoyed or likely to be enjoyed by them as such, whether by virtue of the restriction itself or of any arrangements or operations resulting therefrom (1956 Act, section 21(1)(b)).

Attempts have been made to persuade the Court that the consequences of restrictive agreements were beneficial to the public in a number of ways. For example, in the *Chemists' Federation Agreement* case it was argued that if the restrictions were removed the public would lose the benefit it enjoyed of having the Federation's Standards Committee vet all the proprietary medicines on the Federation's list, and the publicity for them. The Court dismissed this argument because there were other bodies which attempted to control the advertisement of medicines without imposing restrictions on their sale: from the public point of view the work of the Standards Committee was unnecessary. On the other hand, a specification in *Re Blanket Manufacturers' Association's Agreement* (1959) which laid down a minimum quality standard for certain blankets was upheld: the Association convinced the Court that there were specific and substantial benefits to the public which outweighed the disadvantage that cheaper blankets of poorer quality were harder to find. (Agreements requiring compliance with standards of design or quality approved by the British Standards Institution or the Department of Trade and Industry do not have to be registered.)

Gateway (*b*) has been relied upon in a number of cases to support two particular types of restriction: restrictions on traders permitted to handle the goods in question, and price-fixing agreements. In 1959 the Court, in *Re Federation of British Carpet Manufacturers' Agreement*, considered a restriction which prevented the giving of a wholesalers' discount to firms not on an approved list of wholesalers. The object of the list was said to be to benefit the public by keeping out wholesalers who had inadequate stocks, and in theory the criteria for admission to the list required the applicant to have, among other things, adequate storage space and showrooms, adequate finance, and a minimum turnover. In practice most applications had been dealt with in an arbitrary manner entirely for the benefit of the manufacturers, and the Court found that this list was the most objectionable feature of a complex agreement relating to trade terms for carpets.

It prevented new and enterprising wholesalers from buying a proper range of carpets and protected those on the list from competition. So far from conferring benefits on the public, it is clear that the Court believed the list to be detrimental to the public. The Court's judgment was in fact entirely consistent with the Report on Collective Discrimination published by the Monopolies and Restrictive Practices Commission (as it was then known) in 1955 which said: 'We recognize that manufacturers have a legitimate interest in the service given by distributors and may therefore need to select carefully those who are to handle their goods; we think, however, a manufacturer should be able to safeguard his interests – as many in fact do – by his own arrangements with individual distributors without being required to limit his trade to those who have been collectively approved.'

An agreement between the Newspaper Proprietors' Association and the National Federation of Retail Newsagents, Booksellers and Stationers, which came before the Court in 1961, imposed restrictions on new entrants into the newsagency trade. An attempt to defend the agreement was made on the basis that if these restrictions were discontinued, the public would suffer because there would be such a vast influx of new entrants that existing newsagents would lose profits and be obliged to restrict their delivery services. The benefit to the public of an early morning delivery service at very modest charges was readily acknowledged by the Court. However, it felt unable to accept the Federation's 'gloomy prophecy' as to the result of exposing the retail newsagency trade to competitive conditions comparable to those which subsist without disaster either to the public or to the traders themselves in other branches of the retail trade. An exaggerated assumption had been made that if new entrants into the trade were not restricted, the total number of retail newsagents might increase thirty-three-and-a-third per cent. To the Court, such an increase seemed 'quite outside the realms of probability'. For a newsagency to pay its way, it has to build up a clientele and a delivery service and this is a slow and difficult task for a new entrant. Needless to say, the Court declared the agreement contrary to the public interest and void.

An agreement between car manufacturers, in addition to enforcing list prices, obliged manufacturers not to prevent their dealers from selling the vehicles of other manufacturers. In seeking to uphold this term the manufacturers pointed out that their networks of 'franchise dealers' did not extend to the Highlands of north-west Scotland. Lord Diplock (*Re Motor Vehicles Distribution Scheme Agreement*, 1961) allowed himself a moment's cynicism in dealing with this point:

It must give considerable satisfaction to the lonely crofters of the western Highlands to know how often concern for their unique conditions is relied upon in the Restrictive Practices Court to justify restrictions applicable to the whole of the United Kingdom.

The whole agreement was declared contrary to the public interest, and the manufacturers were ordered to pay £3,150 costs because they had not been very forthcoming in producing documents before the Court.

Price-fixing agreements have been supported by manufacturers before the Court on such grounds as that they stabilized prices: when business was poor the price could not fall below the minimum fixed by the agreement and so manufacturers were encouraged to continue production; thus stocks could be built up which would meet demand when business recovered and so prevent price rises. In *Re Yarn Spinners' Agreement* in 1959 the Court, in its second case, said this:

What we have to consider is whether price stabilization as

an alternative to a free market is a benefit to the purchasing public ... We cannot think that as a general rule it is a benefit; if we were to hold that, we would be going contrary to the general presumption embodied in the Act that price restrictions are contrary to the public interest.

Thus it was necessary for the parties seeking to uphold the agreement to show the Court that price stabilization benefited the public in the particular case. In the *Yarn Spinners'* case the minimum prices fixed under the agreement were fairly high: in six or seven years prices had risen above the minimum price for only two periods totalling less than 30 months, and the minimum price had ensured a reasonable return for most spinners. The Court thought that prices had been maintained at an average level higher than would have occurred without an agreement, and that removal of the restriction would not deny the public any specific benefit. In the next case, however, the *Blanket Manufacturers' Agreement* (1959), the minimum price was so low that the Court believed it could not have any real effect and so could not be a specific or substantial benefit to the public.

In the Court's early years it looked as if no price-fixing agreement could survive a reference to the Court. Either the prices would be set higher than they would be without the agreement, and there would be a detriment to the public, or the minimum price would be so low that there could be no substantial benefit or advantages to the public. But later arguments persuaded the Court that other consequences of pricing agreements might have significant effects.

In the *Scottish Bakers'* case (1959) the Court made the point that price stabilization might operate against the interests of the consumer by preventing or retarding the introduction of progressive methods in the industry. But manufacturers argued that the absence of price competition had encouraged collaboration in research and development, and in a 1960 case Lord Diplock agreed that the high degree of co-operation within the industry under consideration might well be reduced if the price restrictions were removed. This reasoning was applied to uphold restrictions in later cases, though it has been criticized on two grounds. One is the difficulty faced by the Registrar in presenting evidence that individual research might have been successful whereas the parties can often point to some notable discovery actually produced by their collaboration. The other is the failure of the Court to consider whether successful collaboration might well continue even if price competition is allowed. In another case, *Re Glazed and Floor Tile Home Trade Association's Agreement* (1963), the Court upheld a price-fixing agreement on the ground that by encouraging standardization of sizes it had led to a reduction in costs.

The 'Non-Interference with Competition' Gateway

During the 1960s industry alleged that the gateways were too narrow and that many harmless restrictions were impossible to justify under the Act even if they were thought valuable to the parties and may have conferred slight benefits on consumers. This criticism was to some extent accepted by the Government in 1968 and a new gateway was added: –

(*h*) that the restriction does not directly or indirectly restrict or discourage competition to any material degree in any relevant trade or industry and is not likely to do so (1956 Act, section 21(1)(*h*), added by Restrictive Trade Practices Act 1968, section 10).

This gateway has not yet been pleaded, for only one reference has been heard since it was introduced. It is hard to imagine any restriction worth defending before the Court that does not discourage competition to some extent, and presumably argument is likely to centre on the question whether it is discouraged to a 'material degree'.

THE COURT'S CHANGING ATTITUDE

Although in the early cases the Court condemned almost all the agreements referred to it, in later years agreements were more readily upheld. There are no doubt several reasons for this.

In the early days of the Court's life officials made a point of first bringing before the Court agreements on which a judgment would bring out matters of principle and give the parties to similar agreements an idea of the Court's attitude. Thus it is likely that the weaker cases were thereafter uncontested, so that the cases fought later were those most likely to succeed. Moreover, professional advisers learnt from experience and arguments of greater sophistication were used.

Some observers believe that changes in the membership of the Court were responsible for the developments in the Court's approach. When Lord Devlin held office as the first president of the Court, section 21 of the 1956 Act was interpreted as meaning that competition was preeminently desirable as more likely to ensure reasonable prices and efficiency. It was then exceedingly difficult for parties to a restrictive trading agreement to rebut the statutory presumption that restrictions were against the public interest. In the post-Devlin era from 1960, under the presidency of Lord Diplock and his successors, the Court appeared more willing to countenance restrictions on competition and no longer assumed that competition was invariably preferable to collaboration. In a public lecture given in 1967 Lord Diplock explained that, desirable though it might be that the Court's decisions should be predictable so that businessmen might order their affairs with confidence, 'the very nature of the issues involved . . . makes it difficult to say that any case is similar to another. Circumstances vary so greatly from industry to industry and from trade to trade. The Court has accordingly discouraged any tendency to treat its decisions in particular cases as binding precedents affecting its decisions in subsequent cases.'

IS THE LEGISLATION EFFECTIVE?

Hardly any operative restrictions remain on the register. By June 1969, of the 2660 agreements registered only 290 contained operative restrictions. The number must now be below a hundred. It is of course not possible to say how many agreements are being made which should be registered but are being kept secret. Some instances of collusive tendering have been discovered, but it is probable that deliberate failure to register is not frequent: since the 1968 Act the consequences of being found out are too serious.

Once an agreement is registered it can be referred to the Court even if it has been terminated by the parties. This was decided by the House of Lords in *Re Newspaper Proprietors' Agreement* in 1964, where it was said that the Court could properly exercise all its usual powers in relation to an agreement that had been terminated, including the very important power of restraining the making of any further agreement having a similar effect. If the parties to an agreement break undertakings to the Restrictive Practices Court that they will not, for example, enforce price-fixing restrictions, or make any agreement similar to that before the Court, this amounts to contempt of court. Thus in 1965 fines of £102,000 were imposed on eight members of the Galvanized Tank Manufacturers' Association for contempt in breaking undertakings given in 1959. Twelve months later eight leading tyre manufacturers were each fined £10,000 for contempt in breaking undertakings given in 1963 not to operate minimum price agreements in tyre contracts with owners of bus fleets. So far the Court has fined only companies for contempt, but it has warned that in future higher managers may be sent to prison if they do not exercise sufficient supervision to ensure that undertakings are honoured.

AGREEMENTS AND ARRANGEMENTS

Under the 1956 Act the word 'agreement' is defined in wide terms. It includes not only a contract but also an agreement which is not intended to be legally enforceable, as well as an 'arrangement'. It is clear that a nod or a wink, if it is correctly understood as an understanding not to enter a new market or not to reduce prices, is registrable. If specific recommendations are made by a trade association to its members, the Act operates as if the members of the association agreed to comply with the recommendations, so they must be registered. It has been held by the courts that where each of two parties intentionally arouses in the other an expectation on which he is expected to, and does, act as to prices, quantity of goods to be produced, or parties to be supplied, then a registrable agreement has been made.

Nevertheless the Registrar of Restrictive Trading Agreements reported in 1962:

Not infrequently on the ending of a price agreement the parties enter into an information agreement under which they send to their trade association or to a central agency their price lists or the prices at which they have entered into contracts ... The trade association or other central agency then circulates this information to the parties as promptly, at as frequent intervals, and in as much detail as may be desired.

These agreements had been familiar in the United States

for fifty years under the name of 'open price agreements'. It was a matter of controversy whether they had to be registered under the 1956 Act, yet in practice they could hinder competition almost as effectively as the price-fixing agreements they replaced, for while they did not *require* the parties to give up price competition they enabled parties who did not wish to compete to keep an eye on what competitors were doing. They might also enable a secret price-fixing agreement to be effective. Since 1969 certain information agreements have been registrable under the 1968 Act.

Few new agreements are now being registered. If businessmen wish to enter into fresh restrictive agreements, their lawyers and economists will devote their energies to devising schemes which do not have to be registered. The 1956 Act contains exemptions which have been widely used to avoid registration. Many bilateral agreements between a supplier and a purchaser are expressly exempt, so a manufacturer can set up a dealer network and protect each dealer from competition by other dealers in the same brand (subject to the Resale Prices Act 1964, discussed below). Another exemption applies to patented products where an agreement between the owner of the patent and the manufacturers who are licensed to exploit the invention is free of control. And whether or not there is an agreement or arrangement, neither the Act nor the Court can force a party to compete if he does not wish to do so.

EFFECT ON CONSUMERS

What difference has the Restrictive Practices Court made to the ordinary consumer? Has the demise of price-fixing agreements meant any real shake-up, any increase in price competition to the general advantage of the consuming public? These questions are not easy to answer, for we can only guess what would have happened if the 1956 Act had not been passed.

We do know that over a thousand registered agreements were abandoned soon after the first decisions of the Court were given. In the summer of 1960 members of trades affected by 146 of the restrictive agreements cancelled before the middle of 1959 were questioned about the effect cancellation had had on price levels. Mr John Heath, an economist, who conducted the inquiry, thinks it is significant that, at a time of generally high demand, in at least nineteen per cent of the agreements prices were reported as being lower than they were before the agreements were terminated. Yet, in two-thirds of the agreements ended, both prices and the degree of competition were probably much the same as if the agreements had continued. One explanation is that prices are hardly likely to fall much when demand exceeds supply. Another explanation is that distributors who prefer uniform prices, and the unenterprising shopper who is suspicious of the cut-price dealer, provide no stimulant to competition among manufacturers. Manufacturers themselves may be reluctant to reduce prices perhaps because of old fears of cut-throat competition. But there is a further point. The ending of a price-fixing or price information agreement between businessmen cannot prevent them meeting together and exchanging information about prices, or voluntarily following the prices charged by their acknowledged 'price leader'. This is why price changes made by different manufacturers of similar goods are so often identical and sometimes even announced on the same day.

The criteria for registration of agreements may be criticized: specific kinds of agreements and arrangements are listed, rather than their effect. In particular they do not refer to the effect on competition, so some schemes have been devised which seriously limit competition but which are not subject to registration. On the other hand some quite innocuous schemes may be inhibited by uncertainty about the Court's attitude and the sanctions for infringement of the Act. Once an agreement is made and registered it is likely to be referred to the Court speedily, but the cost, time and trouble of proceedings before the Court mean that only very important agreements are worth defending. Some hearings have lasted over 40 days and cost the industry concerned at least £100,000.

IS A COURT THE APPROPRIATE BODY?

In a stimulating study of the working of the Restrictive Practices Court, written jointly by a lawyer and an economist, the use of a *judicial* body to determine whether a restrictive trading agreement should be allowed to continue is brought into question. Professors Stevens and Yamey argue convincingly that section 21, which defines the public interest, does not lay down a clear policy for the Court to apply. The 1956 Act is described as a step towards the promotion of competition, but 'it is very far from accepting competition as invariably desirable'. In their view the absence of a clear policy and the insufficiently precise criteria provided in section 21 mean that the judicial process is being invoked to deal with issues which it is ill-equipped to handle. The function of a court is to *apply* rules and standards and the policy that Parliament lays down, not to *make* policy except within fairly narrow limits. Yet the Restrictive Practices Court has been forced into overt policy-making because it has had to predict how industry would perform if a restrictive agreement was abrogated, e.g., the effect of abrogation on efficiency, technical co-operation between firms, the level and fluctuation of prices, exports and unemployment. The judges have had to allow for prospective changes in technology and market demand, and even in government policy – without hearing any evidence as to future government plans.

It is true that a body consisting of a judge as president and of a number of lay members drawn, as the Act puts it, from 'industry, commerce, or public affairs' is not very different from the typical composition of a Royal Commission, and the Monopolies Commission itself is presided over by an experienced lawyer (one of its former chairmen, for example, is now a Lord Justice of Appeal). What is different is the judicial procedure of the hearing before the Court. Judges are clearly experienced in ascertaining facts, and the briefing of counsel and the calling of witnesses is a good way of getting at disputed facts and arguing out the merits, though it is undoubtedly slow and expensive. But economic prediction based on those facts is quite another matter.

There is no clear line between those issues that are justiciable and those that are not. Decisions under gateway (a) as to whether a restriction is reasonably necessary to protect the public against injury are clearly justiciable. Decisions under the new gateway (h) as to whether a restriction discourages competition require rather more familiarity with economic theory and practice than is usually enjoyed by English judges (and so far the Restrictive Practices Court sitting in England has not included any professional economist in its membership, though there have been several on the Monopolies Commission). The main subject of criticism is gateway (b), which requires the Court to decide whether the removal of the restriction is likely to deprive consumers of substantial benefits. The outcome must be determined in the light of the alternative assumptions (i) that the restriction is permitted to continue, and (ii) that it is not.

It is often said that the judicial process is more predictable than an administrative decision. One of the reasons for the creation of the Court was a hope that guidelines for business conduct would be developed by its decisions. In practice, however, it is not easy to foretell the outcome of a reference. Because the Court is a judicial body it is confined to the case before it and cannot pursue more general inquiries into the prevalence in industry of the practices it discovers. The Monopolies Commission, as we have seen, has a freer hand in conducting its investigations. Yet the Commission's reports are merely advisory, and it is for the Government to decide what action should be taken; the Court's decisions, on the other hand, are self-implementing. Nevertheless, handing political and economic questions over to a judicial body does not make them any the less political and economic questions.

RESALE PRICE MAINTENANCE

Until 1964 it was not uncommon for manufacturers to fix a price at which shops should sell their products. If the manufacturer sold direct to the shopkeeper he could include in the contract of sale a promise by the shopkeeper not to sell at a lower price, and he could enforce this promise not to cut prices by legal action if necessary. If the manufacturer sold to a wholesaler, who in turn supplied the shopkeeper, there was no direct contract between the manufacturer and the shopkeeper. As long ago as 1904 it was held, in *Taddy* v. *Sterious*, that a manufacturer could not impose minimum price conditions on a shopkeeper with whom there was no direct contract even if the shopkeeper had notice of the conditions, and in *Dunlop Pneumatic Tyre Co.* v. *Selfridge & Co.* (1915) it was held by the House of Lords that Selfridges' contract not to sell tyres at cut prices, made with a firm of wholesalers, could not be enforced by Dunlops even though they were named in the contract between Selfridges and the wholesalers: Dunlops were not a party to the contract and could not therefore enforce it.

The result was that manufacturers sought other ways to maintain minimum resale prices. One widespread method was for trade associations of manufacturers to set up machinery for collectively enforcing prices by black-listing and boycotting price cutters. Rather than see their supplies cut off, many dealers were willing to pay 'fines' to the trade associations, and private courts, sitting in secret, were set up to 'try' offenders. Collective enforcement by means of black-lists was condemned in 1955 by the Monopolies and Restrictive Practices Commission's report on Collective Discrimination, and section 24 of the Restrictive Trade Practices Act 1956 prohibited collective enforcement by withholding supplies or imposing fines.

But the 1956 Act did not ban resale price maintenance by individual manufacturers: indeed, section 25 made individual r.p.m. easier by providing that a manufacturer (or a trade association on his behalf) could sue any retailer who did not observe price conditions of which he had notice, even though there was no contract between them. While a recalcitrant dealer could no longer be hauled before a trade court, he could be brought before the ordinary courts. The manufacturer was given a more effective and more respectable remedy against cut-price dealers than he had had before 1956.

In the years following the 1956 Act, r.p.m. was widely abandoned in some trades, particularly grocery, but injunctions against cut-price retailers were sought and obtained in respect of such diverse goods as cars, tyres, hair dryers and stockings. Often it was not the manufacturers themselves who were so concerned to stamp out price-cutting, but they were prodded into action by traditional dealers who feared loss of trade to discount houses and self-service stores. It was estimated that about 40 per cent of all consumers' expenditure on goods was on price-maintained goods, an annual value of £5,000m.

One of the cases heard by the Restrictive Practices

Court under gateway (*b*) of section 21 (see p. 306 above) was an r.p.m. case. This was *Re Net Book Agreement*, heard in 1962. The Net Book Agreement is an agreement between publishers – virtually the whole of the publishing trade – not to permit the retailing of their 'net' books below their published price. About ninety per cent of all new titles are 'net' books. It is not a price-fixing agreement because price competition between publishers is not inhibited, but since each publisher is under an obligation to enforce his published prices against retailers, price competition between retailers is inhibited. Although enforcement by individual publishers was simplified by section 25 of the 1956 Act, the agreement to enforce as between the publishers was void under section 21 unless it could be justified.

The Court accepted that if the agreement were abolished, r.p.m. in books would cease. Relying on evidence that has since been severely criticized by economists the Court came to the conclusion that this would lead to price cutting by supermarkets and department stores, to fewer stockholding booksellers, to smaller stocks and to fewer new titles. It was, therefore, held that the agreement benefited the public and should be upheld.

But, even if the decision was correct, it was widely accepted that books were a special case. The Government and the public became more and more concerned about the inflationary effects of r.p.m. as far as the mass of consumer goods was concerned. Whatever the extent of price reductions that the abolition of r.p.m. might make possible, customers would undoubtedly be free to choose between stores offering low prices and no amenities, and ordinary shops where the prices might be higher but which offered personal service and perhaps delivery and credit facilities.

The Resale Prices Act 1964 therefore prohibited r.p.m. The introduction of the Bill was said to have divided the

Cabinet, but the Bill was successfully piloted through the Commons, in the face of heavy opposition from the Conservative Government's own backbenchers, by Edward Heath, then President of the Board of Trade. The Act prohibited resale price maintenance subject to the power of the Restrictive Practices Court to permit r.p.m. to continue for specific goods. Not until 1970 was the last reference to the Court for exemption heard: r.p.m. was eventually condemned for all products except books and medicaments (including proprietary medicines), only two other applications for exemption being taken up to a final hearing.

The Act not only prevents legal action to enforce r.p.m. It also makes it unlawful to withhold supplies from a dealer on the ground that he is likely to sell the goods at cut prices. Thus in 1971 the High Court granted an injunction which in effect ordered wholesale importers of hi-fi equipment to supply a cut-price retailer.

It seems clear that consumers have benefited from the prohibition of r.p.m. though the effect is to some extent masked in a time of rapid price inflation. Still, over the whole area of retail trade, substantial savings can no doubt be made by observant consumers who are prepared to shop around.

THE COMMON MARKET

The effect of joining the Common Market will be to increase competition in two main ways: by eliminating customs barriers and by prohibiting agreements which restrict competition between member states of the Common Market.

Customs barriers between the United Kingdom and the other member countries will be progressively extinguished between 1973 and 1978. Some British industries will lose the protection they have had from import duties imposed on goods coming from member countries – Renault and Fiat cars, for instance, will benefit. Consumers will, however, be required to pay value added tax on goods taken from one Common Market country to another: this tax is levied individually by member states and not by the Community as a whole. This involves the continuing nuisance of customs clearance, but the sums payable should not be large.

The Treaty of Rome, which established the European Economic Community, has its own competition rules in Articles 85 to 89. Unlike the British rules they are drafted in terms of competition and operate only on agreements or concerted practices which substantially affect trade between member states in a way inconsistent with the integration of the Common Market. Article 85 provides that any restrictive practices which have as their object or result the prevention, restriction or distortion of competition within the Common Market are prohibited. Thus an agreement whereby one company agrees to sell a product only in England and another company to sell only in France is forbidden, but an agreement affecting England alone would be subject only to the British rules.

The Commission in Brussels, which administers these rules, takes the view that agreements between firms with small market shares do not infringe the rules; nor, it seems, do agreements between producers in a single state which are limited to home sales or exports to countries that do not belong to the Community. Another important difference between the competition rules of the Community and of the United Kingdom is that the provisions for exemption from the Community rules are applied liberally to agreements encouraging collaboration and specialization between small and medium sized firms. For example, Clima Chappée, a French manufacturer of some kinds of air conditioning machinery, agreed with Buderus, who produced other kinds in Germany, that each would sell the other's products and restrict its own production to certain items. In 1969 the Commission approved this agreement on the grounds that the longer production runs facilitated would save costs and part of these would have to be passed on to consumers since the firms met substantial competition in the Common Market from similar products of other manufacturers. The Restrictive Practices Court and the Registrar may give effect to such exemptions under our own law.

Many business advisers prefer the Common Market competition rules to our own. They can ask the Commission at Brussels for its view as to whether particular agreements are prohibited and whether they are likely to be exempted; they can even negotiate with the Commission, deleting some restrictions in order to preserve others. Firms can postpone investment until the Commission has come to a conclusion. It has also been far more co-operative than is possible under British restrictive practices legislation in granting exemption for joint ventures and specialization or standardization agreements. Some economists and lawyers, however, criticize the Commission for taking too long to complete the procedural steps needed to take a formal decision, and for concentrating too much of its resources on the less important types of agreement. Moreover, the Commission's willingness to negotiate secretly, although convenient to the parties to the particular agreements discussed, does mean that those not employed by the Commission cannot assess the precedents. The final agreement is published, but details of the restrictions abandoned in the light of opposition from the Commission are seldom published.

Under the European Communities Act 1972 the E.E.C. competition rules applicable to trade between member countries have become part of English law, although they will largely be enforced by Community organs. As the United Kingdom economy becomes integrated with that of the other Common Market states the E.E.C. rules will become increasingly important, but the British rules will continue to apply to purely local trade. There will be no compulsion to amend the British rules to fit in with the Common Market, but the movement towards the harmonization of laws within the Nine may cause a major reconsideration of the law relating to trading practices. There would be obvious advantages in bringing the rules governing trade, whether within a single country or with other countries inside or outside the European Community, closer together.

FAIR TRADING BILL

The Bill which is expected to become the Fair Trading Act 1973 does away with the office originally known as the Registrar of Restrictive Trading Agreements, and transfers his functions to the Director General of Fair Trading. It also extends the Restrictive Trade Practices Act 1956 to agreements between suppliers of *services* (other than services of a professional nature).

CHAPTER 13

THE CONSUMER IN PERSPECTIVE

LAW is not divided into watertight compartments. For convenience related topics must be treated together, and similar concepts dealt with in conjunction with each other. But certain ideas run right through the law, however its subject-matter is arranged.

The questions discussed in this book may not seem to be obviously related. They all affect the ordinary citizen in his capacity of 'consumer' in one way or another, but what legal principles bind together the rules relating to the supply of goods, the use of services and travel facilities, banks and monopolies?

There are, in fact, two common threads running through the earlier chapters. They are the sanctity of contract and the duty to take care. Both are of supreme importance to the consumer. Together, they form the basis of most of the legal rules, and of all the controversies, which have been described.

The first concept, the sanctity of contract, developed slowly through the centuries and reached its zenith in the nineteenth century. It is the basis of the consumer's relationship with the seller of goods, the supplier of services, banks, insurance companies, and carriers, and it is the basis too of the relationship between manufacturers and distributors, and between the members of trade associations. We have seen how the movement in this century has been away from this idea, with the growing realization that what two parties have agreed may not be in the interests of the community as a whole and may not represent what they themselves desire, and that one party may not even have grasped that his legal rights were affected.

The duty to take care is essentially a concept of the twentieth century. It has of course existed for centuries in certain limited fields such as in the obligations of carriers and surgeons. Only in the nineteenth century was it first perceived that the idea had wider applications. As the late Sir Percy Winfield, a distinguished Cambridge professor of law, put it:

Perhaps one of the chief agencies in the growth of the idea [of negligence] is industrial machinery. Early railway trains, in particular, were notable neither for speed nor for safety. They killed any object from a Minister of State to a wandering cow, and this naturally reacted on the law.

But it was not until the climacteric decision in *Donoghue* v. *Stevenson* (the 'snail in the ginger-beer bottle' case), as recently as 1932, that the fundamental position of the duty to take reasonable care was established in this country. The striking words of Lord Atkin – 'The rule that you are to love your neighbour becomes in law, you must not injure your neighbour', cited in full on p. 117 – epitomizes the twentieth-century approach. Professor William L. Prosser of California, a leading American authority on this branch of the law, has pointed out that 'As a formula this is so vague as to have little meaning, and as a guide to decision it has had no value at all.' Nevertheless, it is as an expression of judicial policy that these words have set the course for the development of the law in our modern society.

FUTURE DEVELOPMENTS

In describing the law we have laid stress on the way it has evolved and on the considerations which have influenced its development. We have, too, pointed to the way in which the law may develop in the future. But it is evident that there are many major defects in the existing law and that any worthwhile change will have to come from a radical reappraisal of the policy the law is to achieve.

As between the seller and the buyer of goods, as between the supplier and the recipient of services, we have no doubt that the law should, in the economic interests of the community as a whole, take sides. It is no longer possible or desirable for the law to affirm its strict neutrality. It is not just a question of 'consumer protection' or 'value for money'. The production and sale of shoddy or useless articles – the shirt which shrinks and is unwearable, the gadget which breaks and is thrown away – represent a shocking waste of time, labour, and raw materials which this country can ill afford. The only way to prevent this waste, short of rigid governmental control and inspection, is for the law to enforce the highest of standards. In many respects the law already recognizes the need for high standards: as Chief Justice Best put it in 1829, 'It is the duty of the court in administering the law to lay down rules calculated . . . to make it the interest of manufacturers and those who sell to furnish the best article that can be supplied.' The Molony Committee, too, reporting in 1962, recognized the need for the law to help to improve the quality of consumer goods, and suggested that this could be done 'by increasing the liability, and thereby heightening the interest in quality, of those who sell them to the consumer'.

But although this may be accepted as the policy of the law, it is clear that the pursuit of this policy has never been more than half-hearted. The slow, almost painful way in which the law has developed, the complexity of the legal rules imposing duties, the exceptions and limitations which exist, the unsatisfactory remedies available in the courts, and the ease with which duties can be excluded, all demonstrate beyond argument that the common law can no longer keep pace with the needs of our modern society. The whole way of thinking of the com-

mon lawyer is burdened with concepts which are irrelevant to the simple question: what functions ought our
legal rules to fulfil? Patterns of thought such as 'privity of
contract', 'damages', and 'consideration' conceal from
lawyers the possible uses and function of law.

We must therefore look to legislation to achieve the
objectives which we desire to attain. It is too much to
hope that there will be unanimity as to these objectives,
but it should be possible to arrive at a broad agreement of
the ends to be achieved. Once this has been done, the
legal machinery to give effect to these agreed ideas need
not be based on the existing common law, but on new
principles which can cut straight through legal tangles.

THE FUTURE

In the law relating to the supply of goods, for example,
the ideas put forward in the earlier chapters would lead
to a fresh formulation of legal principles. The new legislation would spell out the duties of each party. In part
these would be based on the existing law, such as the Sale
of Goods Act, but considerable simplicity could be
achieved. Thus the general rule would be that all goods
sold must be of merchantable quality, whether or not
they were sold 'by description' or examined by the buyer.
While it would be appropriate to give remedies to the
buyer alone if the goods are faulty and thus worth less
than they should be, it might be generally agreed that if
the goods cause damage, anyone who is injured by them
should be entitled to claim, even though he is not a party
to the contract of sale. It should be emphasized that the
real purpose here is not to make it easier to secure compensation, though this would follow, but to increase the
feeling of responsibility of the supplier and to reduce the
risk of faulty goods or of accidents. The consumer is not
interested in getting damages but in getting the goods and

services that he wants and in avoiding the risk of injury.

The new law would no doubt contain a general prohibition on exemption clauses – clauses which attempt to
exclude the rights given to the consumer by the legislation. We have seen that 'freedom of contract' is a pretty
tenuous philosophy today, and Parliament need have no
qualms about providing rules which are to take effect
'notwithstanding any agreement to the contrary'. The
Supply of Goods (Implied Terms) Bill introduced late in
1972 is an important move in this direction.

Again, the new law would deal with remedies. Two
points are clear from the earlier chapters: one is that the
consumer should have a clear right to get his money back
in all cases except where he has consciously affirmed the
contract; the other is that the law should recognize the
consumer's right to get what he wants, with the correlative
right to exchange a faulty article for a good one. What is
even more clear at the present time is that even if the law
gives the consumer rights, all too often he is powerless to
enforce them. No lawyer would advise a consumer, however just his claim, to go to court to enforce disputed
rights if the amount at stake is small; and even a dispute
about, say, a £60 television set which was not totally useless might not justify court proceedings.

One of the last research projects of the ill-fated Consumer Council dealt with this problem. Its controversial
report *Justice Out of Reach* advocated the creation of
new 'small claims courts' to deal cheaply and expedi-
tiously with minor disputes. It reminded us that the network of County Courts, now too expensive for consumer
complaints and, to judge by the statistics, largely debt-
collecting courts, were originally set up in 1846 to handle
small claims for the ordinary person. Inspired by this report, solicitors and traders in Manchester have set up an
experimental arbitration scheme to deal with consumer
complaints at low cost. The first signs are encouraging,

and a similar scheme is being planned for the City of Westminster, covering London's main West End shopping areas.

In what is at present the law of hire purchase the new scheme laid down by the Crowther Report (p. 193 above) would mean that it would no longer be necessary for the law to be framed on the admittedly artificial concept of 'hiring', coupled with an option to purchase. Instead, we could recognize what the rules of law are to achieve, and see that they do so. Basically the point of hire purchase is purchase, not hire: the dealer is concerned with selling his goods, the consumer with buying them without paying the whole price at once. Even if each party does what he has agreed, the law is still concerned with the financial aspects of the transaction. Any additional amount payable for the benefit of the credit facilities ('hire-purchase charges') is essentially interest for a loan, and we should not let the point that out of this interest the owner has to provide for his clerical and collection expenses obscure this fact. The interest charges should therefore be clearly expressed as a true interest rate.

The reason why 'hire' is introduced into what is really a sale of goods is to provide a legal basis for the owner's desire to retain a security interest in the goods – the power to get them back (or to threaten to take them back) if the consumer defaults in payment or wrongly sells them. We would recognize this security interest, and provide in detail when and how the owner is entitled to the return of the goods, without relying on the fiction of 'hiring'. So, too, the financial reckoning if the goods are returned or re-taken need not depend on the way in which payments made by the consumer – a 'deposit', or 'rental for hire' – are described, but on an overall appraisal of the loss suffered by the owner, the general principle being that the risk of depreciation in the value of the goods should fall on the consumer.

A similar spirit of realism, of penetrating through legal habits of thought to reach the hard facts of the situation and the desirable rules, would pervade the whole of the new approach. We could draw some assistance in developing a fresh and unfettered attitude to the law by studying the American Uniform Commercial Code. This is a valuable and intelligent reappraisal of most of the branches of law of importance in commercial transactions, which has been produced, after many years of hard work, by an impressive and distinguished team of American lawyers to replace existing legislation such as the Sales Act (based on and, in many ways, similar to the English Sale of Goods Act). It ranges over several of the branches of law which we have discussed in this book. Its whole approach is refreshing and concrete.

For example, in the Sale of Goods Act of 1893 the buyer's rights if the goods are accidentally damaged or destroyed depend on the question of whether he had become the owner of the goods, for under section 20 if the ownership of the goods has passed to the buyer 'the goods are at the buyer's risk whether delivery has been made or not'. The Uniform Commercial Code uncompromisingly rejects this approach to legal rights, and has sought

to avoid making practical issues between practical men turn upon the location of an intangible something [that is, the ownership of the goods], the passing of which no man can prove by evidence.

Under the Code, the buyer does not take the risk of accidental loss until the goods are delivered to him.

This Code is not specifically designed to protect the consumer, but by general agreement arrived at many conclusions which, in furtherance of the policies we have discussed, operate to the benefit of consumers. It was first published in 1952, has since been revised, and has already been passed into law in forty-nine of the fifty United States. There is as yet no movement afoot to introduce it into English law, but its lessons are of value to all lawyers.

This direct and realistic approach to the function of legal rules could with advantage be coupled with a relaxation of restrictions which do not benefit the consumer. Notably the archaic provisions of the Shops Act 1950, needlessly controlling shop opening hours and prohibiting Sunday trading (the penalties for which were inexplicably increased tenfold by the Criminal Justice Act 1972), could be swept away to provide more freedom for shopkeepers and customers.

In the result, therefore, we must look to Parliament to send the law forward in the right direction. This is the task of legislators, not of judges. The Fair Trading Act 1973 will be an important step on this road. The exact form and content of the legislation may be a matter of controversy. We hope that no reader of this book will be able to deny the need.

FOR FURTHER READING

THERE are plenty of books on the topics covered by this book. A useful guide to the law is *The Law for Consumers* by David Tench (Consumers' Association), which aims to inform without too much explanation. A very useful survey of the law of contract is *Introduction to the Law of Contract* by P. S. Atiyah (O.U.P., 2nd ed., 1971), and the leading textbooks for students are *The Law of Contract* by G. H. Treitel (Stevens, 3rd ed., 1970), *The Law of Contract* by G. C. Cheshire and C. H. S. Fifoot (Butterworth, 8th ed., 1972), *Anson's Law of Contract* (O.U.P., 23rd ed., 1969, by A. G. Guest) and *Sutton and Shannon on Contracts* (Butterworth, 7th ed., 1970, by A. L. Diamond and others). A general survey of commercial law will be found in *Commercial Law* by Gordon Borrie (Butterworth, 3rd ed., 1970). Everyone particularly interested in the law of consumer protection should, of course, study the report of the Molony Committee – *Final Report of the Committee on Consumer Protection* (H.M.S.O., Cmnd 1781, 1962). Some of the chapters in *Law Reform Now*, edited by Lord Gardiner and Andrew Martin (Gollancz, 1963), contain suggestions relevant to our subject-matter, and it also includes authoritative critiques of 'The Machinery of Law Reform' and 'The Administration of Justice'. An entertaining account of the work of an active consumer protection agency is Philip Schrag's article, 'On Her Majesty's Secret Service: Protecting the Consumer in New York City' (1971; 80 Yale Law Journal, p. 1529).

A large number of books and articles could be listed on the subjects dealt with in the different chapters. Here is a selection:

CHAPTER 1. The standard comprehensive work on English legal history is Sir William Holdsworth's *History of English Law*. Volumes 3, 7, and 8 are of more particular relevance to the subject-matter of this book. The leading one-volume works on the historical background to English law are *A Concise History of the Common Law* by T. F. T. Plucknett (5th ed., 1956) and *Historical Foundations of the Common Law* by S. F. C. Milsom (1969).

More detailed studies of the origins of our modern law on the sale of goods are contained in articles by S. J. Stoljar: 'Growth of Implied Warranties in Sale of Goods' (1952; 15 Modern Law Review, p. 425) and by S. F. C. Milsom: 'Sale of Goods in the Fifteenth Century' (1961; 77 Law Quarterly Review, p. 257). The original introduction to Sir Mackenzie Chalmers' book *The Sale of Goods Act 1893* (16th ed., 1970, by M. Mark) outlines the drafting and legislative history of the Sale of Goods Act.

CHAPTER 2. Judges, practising lawyers, and academic lawyers have all published books or articles touching on the theme of this chapter. Books by judges are Lord Denning's *The Road to Justice* (1955) and his article 'The Way of an Iconoclast' (1959; Journal of the Society of Public Teachers of Law, p. 77); Lord Radcliffe's *The Law and its Compass* (1961); and Lord Devlin's *Samples of Lawmaking* (1962). The growth of exemption clauses and standard form contracts are examined by H. B. Sales in an article, 'Standard Form Contracts' (1953; 16 Modern Law Review, p. 318). Among other critical studies of the existing law is Brian Coote's book *Exception Clauses* (1964). The shortcomings of the law in relation to the needs of modern society are strongly expressed in W. Friedmann's book *Law in a Changing Society* (2nd ed., Penguin Books, 1972). The Law Commissions' First Report on Exemption Clauses was published in 1969 (Law Com. No. 24).

CHAPTER 3. A very readable narrative study of the law of sale of goods is *The Sale of Goods* by P. S. Atiyah (4th ed., 1971), and a textbook which includes a reprint of the Sale of Goods Act is *The Sale of Goods* by C. M. Schmitthoff (2nd ed., 1966). Proposals for changes in the present law are contained in Cyril Grunfeld's article 'Reform in the Law of Contract' (1961; 24 Modern Law Review, p. 62). Other proposals for reform are to be found in the Law Revision Committee's Sixth Interim Report *Consideration* (H.M.S.O., Cmd 5449, 1939), and the Law Reform Committee's Twelfth Report *Transfer of Title to Chattels* (H.M.S.O., Cmnd 2958, 1966). Its Tenth Report *Innocent Misrepresentation* (H.M.S.O., Cmnd 1782, 1962) led to the Misrepresentation Act 1967, critically analysed by P. S. Atiyah and G. H. Treitel in 1967 (30 Modern Law Review, p. 369).

CHAPTER 4. Parts IV and VI of the Final Report of the Molony Committee contain matter relevant to this chapter, for example, on advertising and manufacturers' 'guarantees'. There are several textbooks on the law of tort which deal with negligence, such as *The Law of Tort* by Harry Street (5th ed., 1972), Winfield and Jolowicz on *Tort* (9th ed., 1971) and Salmond's *Law of Torts* (15th ed., 1969, by R. F. V. Heuston). M. A. Millner's *Negligence in Modern Law* (1967) is a stimulating and perceptive essay.

CHAPTER 5. Weights and measures legislation was the subject of the Report of the Hodgson Committee (H.M.S.O., Cmd 8219, 1951), and Part V of the Final Report of the Molony Committee dealt with the Merchandise Marks Acts in some detail. The Food and Drugs Act 1955, the Trade Descriptions Act 1968 and similar legislation are to be found in Bell's *Sale of Food and Drugs* (14th ed., 1968, by J. A. O'Keefe). There are several works on the Trade Descriptions Act alone, including *Trade Descriptions – The New Law* (1968) and *Trade Descriptions – Prosecutions, Enforcement and Complaints* (1970), both by Bowes Egan, and *The Trade Descriptions Act 1968* by J. A. O'Keefe (1968).

CHAPTER 6. Leading works on the subject of this chapter are R. M. Goode's book *Hire-Purchase Law and Practice* (2nd ed., 1970) and A. G. Guest's *The Law of Hire-Purchase* (1966). A rather shorter study is *Introduction to Hire-Purchase Law* by Aubrey L. Diamond (2nd ed., 1971). For a comparative survey, see *Instalment Credit* (ed. A. L. Diamond, 1970). The Report of the Crowther Committee on Consumer Credit was published in 1971 (Cmnd 4596).

CHAPTER 7. The leading academic work is *Bailment in the Common Law* by Sir George Paton (1952). The Eighteenth Report of the Law Reform Committee, *Conversion and Detinue*, was published in 1971 (H.M.S.O., Cmnd 4774).

CHAPTER 8. The background to the present law of cheques is examined in Dr J. Milnes Holden's book *The History of Negotiable Instruments* (1955). The same author has also written *The Law and Practice of Banking*, volume 1 of which deals with *Banker and Customer* (1970). General works on banking law include *Law and Practice Relating to Banking* by F. E. Perry (2 volumes, Penguin Foundations of Law series, 1968), *Law of Banking* by Lord Chorley (5th ed., 1967) and the standard work on the subject, Sir John Paget's *The Law of Banking* (8th ed., 1972, by M. Megrah and F. R. Ryder). The monthly publication *The Banker* often refers to recent developments in the law and practice affecting the banker-customer relationship.

CHAPTER 9. A useful and readable textbook is *The Law of Insurance* by R. Colinvaux (3rd ed., 1970). Criticism of certain aspects of the present law are contained in the Law Reform Committee's Fifth Report, *Conditions and Exceptions in Insurance Policies* (H.M.S.O., Cmnd 62, 1957).

CHAPTER 10. A fourth edition of Otto Kahn-Freund's book *The Law of Carriage by Inland Transport* was published in 1965. Changes made by statute in 1956 in the law relating to the liability of hotel proprietors were advocated in the Law Reform Committee's Second Report *Innkeepers' Liability for Property of Travellers, Guests and Residents* (H.M.S.O., Cmd 9161, 1954).

CHAPTER 11. A recent study of the history and meaning of restraint of trade at common law is J. D. Heydon's *The Restraint of Trade Doctrine* (1972). A comprehensive study of the present law, relevant for this chapter and the next, is *The Law of Restrictive Trade Practices and Monopolies*, by Lord Wilberforce, Alan Campbell and Neil P. M. Elles (2nd ed., 1966 with 1969 supplement). Dr Valentine Korah has written a shorter work for the Penguin Foundations of Law series: *Monopolies and Restrictive Practices* (1968), and reference may also be made to *Monopoly and Competition* edited by A. Hunter (Penguin Modern Economics Readings, 1969). The Department of Trade and Industry (and formerly the Board of Trade) publish annual reports of developments under the monopolies legislation, available from Her Majesty's Stationery Office, from whom the individual reports of the Monopolies Commission may also be obtained.

CHAPTER 12. A major study of the working of the Court is *The Restrictive Practices Court* by R. B. Stevens and B. S. Yamey (1965). J. B. Heath has written a short study of the legislation, 'Still Not Enough Competition' (Hobart Paper No. 11, 2nd ed., 1963). The periodic reports of the Registrar of Restrictive Trading Agreements contain résumés of the decisions of the Court and an account of the work of the Registrar's department. Full reports of the Court's decisions are to be found in the Law Reports and the All England Law Reports. Lord Diplock, a former President of the Restrictive Practices Court, has published a lecture entitled *The Role of the Judicial Process in the Regulation of Competition* (O.U.P., 1967). Works on resale price maintenance include J. F. Pickering's *Resale Price Maintenance in Practice* (1966) and *Resale Price Maintenance*, studies edited by B. S. Yamey (1966).

CHAPTER 13. The Consumer Council's report *Justice out of Reach* was published by H.M.S.O. in 1970.

TABLE OF CASES

TABLE OF STATUTES

INDEX